HARVARD UNIVERSITY
GRADUATE SCHOOL OF EDUCATION
MONROE C. GUTMAN LIBRARY

The CENTER for INTELLECTUAL PROPERTY HANDBOOK

Edited by **Kimberly M. Bonner**

and the **Staff of the Center for Intellectual Property**

Neal-Schuman Publishers, Inc.

New York   London

KF
2994
.C45
2006

#X77410

HARVARD UNIVERSITY
GRADUATE SCHOOL OF EDUCATION
MONROE C. GUTMAN LIBRARY

Published by Neal-Schuman Publishers, Inc.
100 William St., Suite 2004
New York, NY 10038

Copyright © 2006 University of Maryland University College

Cover Image by Andy Joyce © University of Maryland University College

All rights reserved. Reproduction of this book, in whole or in part, without written permission of the publisher, is prohibited.

Printed and bound in the United States of America.

The paper used in this publication meets the minimum requirements of American National Standard for Information Sciences—Permanence of Paper for Printed Library Materials, ANSI Z39.48-1992.

Library of Congress Cataloging-in-Publication Data

The Center for Intellectual Property handbook / edited by Kimberly M. Bonner and the staff of the Center for Intellectual Property.
      p. cm.
   Includes bibliographical references and index.
   ISBN 1-55570-561-8 (alk. paper)
   1. Copyright—United States. 2. Fair use (Copyright)—United States. I. Bonner, Kimberly M. II. Center for Intellectual Property in the Digital Environment.
   KF2994.C45 2006
   346.7304'82—dc22

                                        2006012456

►Dedications

I dedicate this book to my children, Cameron and Preston, who provide me with an endless supply of ideas and new ways of seeing the world.

K.B. Kelley

To my parents, Amos and Bessie Bonner, and my grandparents, Robert and Irma Allen. You were model educators who taught me the importance of access to a quality education and educational resources. Thanks for teaching me that with knowledge all things are possible.

K.M. Bonner

Contents

List of Figures   vii

Preface   ix

Acknowledgments   xiii

1   Copyright Basics   1
Kimberly B. Kelley and Kimberly M. Bonner

2   Instructional Materials and "Works Made for Hire" at Universities: Policies and Strategic Management of Copyright Ownership   15
Kenneth D. Crews

3   Fair Use and Licensing   39
Peggy E. Hoon and Cheryl L. Davis

4   Electronic Reserves and Copyright: A Collision Course?   55
Laura N. Gasaway

5   The TEACH Act: Will It Make a Difference for Colleges and Universities?   71
Kimberly M. Bonner

6   The Digital Millennium Copyright Act and the University Campus: A Safe Harbor?   87
Arnold P. Lutzker

7   Digital Rights Management (DRM) and Higher Education: Opportunities and Challenges   107
Kimberly B. Kelley, Kimberly M. Bonner, Clifford A. Lynch, and Jaehong Park

8   Copyright Education Programs   123
Olga François

9   Copyright Law, Intellectual Property Policy, and Academic Culture   153
Clifford A. Lynch

Appendices   175

    Chapter 1: Appendix A   177

    Chapter 2: Appendix B   181

    Chapter 3: Appendix C   191

    Chapter 4: Appendix D   199

    Chapter 6: Appendix E   205

    Chapter 8: Appendix F   227

Index   243

About the Center for Intellectual Property   252

About the Authors   253

▶ List of Figures

Figure 1.1: Chart of Works and the Public Domain   6

Figure 7.1: Top Four DCC Technologies   112

Figure 7.2: DCCS Goals   114

Figure 8.1: ACRL Information Literacy Standard Five with Highlighted
          Copyright Related Outcomes   126

Figure 8.2: Common Copyright Guidelines   134

Figure 8.3: Copyright and Learning Standards   136

Figure 8.4: Copyright Education   137

Figure 8.5: Sample Classroom Assignments   144

Figure 8.6: Resources for Copyright Quizzes, Questions, and Assessments   147

► Preface

Meeting the various challenges posed by digital distribution of legally protected materials has become a pressing issue in all arenas of academic life. The Center for Intellectual Property (CIP), an organization at University of Maryland University College (UMUC), is dedicated to easing these difficulties by providing information and other services about copyright issues to professionals at higher education institutions. The organization's staff has created *The Center for Intellectual Property Handbook* to offer a helpful and timely overview of current legal issues and propose potential solutions.

Why is there an increased need for information and education about these issues, particularly for those in academic fields? As more institutions offer a greater number of educational programs, classes, materials, or content online, the possibility of copyright infringement increases exponentially, as does the potential scope of its legal ramifications, including lawsuits and expensive out-of-court settlements. Confusion about what content can be utilized in online instruction has amplified greatly over the past decade. Mastering extremely complicated new legislation, such as the Digital Millennium Copyright Act (DMCA) and the Technology Education and Copyright Harmonization (TEACH) Act, presents daunting challenges. Understanding the conditions that must be met to comply with these congressional measures is often difficult for the layperson. Further, fair use, always a muddy concept, is all the more confusing when applied to digital works.

PURPOSE AND AUDIENCE

The goal of the *The Center for Intellectual Property Handbook* is to provide an insightful, accessible, and practical introduction to issues of copyright for a broad spectrum of individuals in the higher education community. Its potential readership within academe includes those engaged in every sphere of higher education, including:

- ► university presidents and provosts;
- ► college and university counsel;
- ► faculty and librarians;
- ► directors and managers of e-learning;
- ► corporate learning and education managers;
- ► knowledge management and information technology professionals;
- ► Web-based training specialists;
- ► instructional design managers;
- ► legal counsel;

► deans and directors of college and university academic and professional programs;

► students taking courses on legal issues.

It may even interest information consumers in the general public who are concerned about the effects of copyright on their day-to-day actions.

Individual chapter authors represent many different professional fields, including law, education, information technology, and librarianship. All tackle their particular subjects with the objective of presenting practical solutions that will lead readers toward the clear path of copyright compliance. They have drawn from the reservoir of CIP research as well as from the rich streams of other knowledge in the landscape of intellectual property issues. These contributing authors have been carefully selected for their individual expertise in particular facets of the complex, ever changing terrain that is copyright in the twenty-first century.

CHAPTER ORGANIZATION AND HOW TO USE THIS BOOK

In Chapter 1, "Copyright Basics," Kimberly B. Kelley and Kimberly M. Bonner introduce basic concepts, laws, and definitions relating to copyright and explain key ways they impact information exchange in higher education.

In Chapter 2, "Instructional Materials and 'Works Made for Hire' at Universities: Policies and Strategic Management of Copyright Ownership," Kenneth D. Crews examines the legal principles and institutional policies surrounding ownership of course materials. Summarizing current developments in this area in light of judicial decisions, Crews encourages educational institutions to reevaluate their copyright policies. He then discusses the options facing faculty and university administrators in allocating copyright ownership and offers helpful alternatives for avoiding ambiguity in these transactions.

In Chapter 3, "Fair Use and Licensing," Peggy E. Hoon and Cheryl L. Davis review the "fair use" doctrine—its purpose and the processes behind its use—and discuss recent judicial decisions and trends affecting this important concept. Their treatment of the topic focuses on the challenges to fair use posed by licensing educational materials in the digital environment, specifically in online instruction, and Web-enhanced education.

In Chapter 4, "Electronic Reserves," Laura N. Gasaway covers the history, purpose, and legal basis for e-reserves and how they have developed from traditional reserve collections. She also evaluates various existing attempts to guide faculty and library staff in the establishment and use of e-reserves.

In Chapter 5, "The TEACH Act: Will It Make a Difference for Colleges and Universities?" Kimberly M. Bonner reviews and analyzes the recently passed amendment to the Copyright Act, the Technology, Education, and Copyright Harmonization (TEACH) Act. Bonner examines key provisions of the act, sums up implications for universities, and looks at preliminary information from universities on whether or not the TEACH Act is being used as well as the underlying rationale for such use or nonuse.

In Chapter 6, "The Digital Millennium Copyright Act (DMCA) and the University Campus: A Safe Harbor?" Arnold P. Lutzker discusses the act and reviews the history of DMCA. In the process, he describes how this legislation, originally written to protect online service providers (OSPs) from liability resulting from the acts of their users, affects the university environment. Among other areas of immediate concern, Lutzker gives specific attention to the area of peer-to-peer file sharing.

Chapter 7, "Digital Rights Management (DRM) in Higher Education: Opportunities and Challenges" explains digital rights management (DRM) systems and discusses the results of a study about their implementation within the higher education community. The Center for Intellectual Property researchers—Kimberly B. Kelley, Kimberly M. Bonner, Clifford A. Lynch, and Jaehong Park—share the results of their investigation. Among other conclusions, they point to important findings about the types of DRM systems being employed by universities; whether and how institutions are using these technologies to control uses of and access to digital information; the level and extent of institutional compliance with certain technological mandates of the TEACH Act; policies for digital content management; and emerging trends in the use of DRM systems.

In Chapter 8, "Copyright Education Programs," Olga François examines the substance of programs that rely on the TEACH Act and the DMCA. François helps educators make sense of what a program must do to meet the legislatively mandated need for general "copyright education" and discusses information literacy standards. In doing so, she also describes best practices in copyright education at U.S. colleges and universities, offering recommendations for academic policy makers.

Chapter 9, "Copyright Law, Intellectual Property Policy, and Academic Culture," concludes *The Center for Intellectual Property Handbook*. Rather than being simply a summation of the current situation, Clifford A. Lynch looks toward the future of teaching and learning in light of trends in intellectual property and information access. Lynch expounds on the nature of the academic mission, discusses current and pending legislation, describes various academic scenarios, and makes a forecast of what the future might hold.

The staff of the Center for Intellectual Property hopes that this handbook will serve as a useful tool for educators, information professionals, and anyone else who handles or oversees the transmission and storage of information, fostering deeper understanding of the many different ways in which copyright law impacts their work. Far from restricting the educational mission of academic institutions, the CIP hopes that the policies, guidelines, and procedures discussed in the following chapters will advance communication, learning, and scholarship.

►Acknowledgments

The Center for Intellectual Property would like to express its earnest appreciation of the following individuals for their contributions of expertise needed to complete the Center's handbook: Kenneth Crews, Indiana University School of Law-Indianapolis; Laura "Lolly" Gasaway, University of North Carolina School of Law; Peggy Hoon, North Carolina State University Libraries' and Cheryl Davis; Arnie Lutzker, Lutzker, Lutzker & Settlemyer, LLP; Clifford Lynch, the Coalition for Networked Information (CNI). These authors represent the disciplines of education, law, information technology, and librarianship. Their writings convincingly speak to timely copyright issues that arise when digital works are a key component in delivering education worldwide.

Finally, the Center for Intellectual Property on behalf of Kimberly Kelley, Kimberly Bonner, and Olga Francois would like to acknowledge the efforts of the following CIP staff involved behind the scenes in the development of the project: Robert Burriesci, Michael VanderHeidjen, and Jack Boeve. The Center for Intellectual Property would like to thank the University of Maryland University College, the Center for Media and New Technology, Andy Joyce for his consistent artistic contributions and for the cover art of this book, and the Office of the Provost for their support of CIP's work. And of course, we thank all of the patrons and participants involved in the CIP's programming over the years.

1

COPYRIGHT BASICS

KIMBERLY B. KELLEY
KIMBERLY M. BONNER

This chapter discusses the following topics:
- ► The history and purpose of copyright
- ► Copyright basics
- ► Future trends in copyright law and policy

◄

INTRODUCTION

The Center for Intellectual Property Handbook (CIP Handbook) discusses various topics associated with the application of copyright law to the creation and use of digital works for teaching, learning, and scholarship. This chapter lays the necessary foundation for the discussions in the chapters of the CIP Handbook by reviewing the history and purpose of copyright law in the United States and the legal framework of copyright. A firm foundation in the history, purpose, and basics of copyright contributes to understanding and evaluating the changes in copyright law to adapt to new technologies; helps determine how to protect, use, and distribute works; and assists in avoiding legal liability.

THE HISTORY AND PURPOSE OF COPYRIGHT

Copyright in the United States is rooted in the British legal system. The British system for protecting printed works, with which American colonists were familiar, was originally promulgated to diminish the possibility of religious or political rebellion after the invention of the printing press. This system required all potential publishers to obtain a license and approval from the official censors, designated by the Crown, before a work could be published.[1] Eventually, the monopoly created by the censors was found to be an unacceptable bottleneck for the creation of new works, and through an act of Parliament, the law was revised and the first copyright law was created: The Statute of Anne. In 1710, the Statute of Anne, officially titled "An act for the encouragement of learning, by vesting the copies of printed books in the authors or purchasers of such copies, during the time therein mentioned," established a reformed approach to copyright law in England that was also used as the basis for setting policy in the United States Constitution.[2] The objective of the statute was to encourage the writing of "useful work" through granting authors the sole right to print their books for 14 years.[3]

The Statute of Anne was passed 255 years after the invention of the printing press and 233 years after William Caxton printed the first book in England.[4] Scholars contend that the Statute of Anne was a product of the technological innovations of the printing press even though more than two centuries passed between the two events.[5] The connection between innovations in technology and the development of new copyright laws continues today. As various authors in the CIP Handbook discuss, laws such as the Digital Millennium Copyright Act (DMCA) and the Technology, Education, and Copyright Harmonization (TEACH) Act are direct responses to changes in technology.

The United States Constitution

In framing the U.S. Constitution, the founding fathers determined that copyright law would fall under the purview of the national Congress and as such stated:

> The Congress shall have Power . . . To promote the Progress of Science and useful Arts, by securing for limited Times to Authors and Inventors exclusive Right to their respective Writings and Discoveries. (U.S. Constitution, art. I, § 8, cl. 8)

The copyright clause in the U.S. Constitution, similar to the Statute of Anne, was intended to promote the progress of science and the useful arts. Congress deemed that by providing authors exclusive rights for a limited period of time, there would be enough incentive to encourage the continued creation and dissemination of works for the betterment of society. However, the Constitution does not state that the exclusive rights of the creator should be held in perpetuity, and the wording "for limited times" was clearly designed to balance the need for incentives (providing for exclusive ownership and profit by that ownership) and the need for the free and open use of information for the purpose of a thriving democracy (by limiting the author's right of exclusive ownership to a set period of time).

The Copyright Clause in the U.S. Constitution has several guiding principles:

Principle 1: The purpose of copyright is to "give authors an economic incentive to create by giving authors exclusive control over their works."[6] Authors have exclusive control over the public use of their works for a limited time as an incentive to create more works.

Principle 2: Authors are given "exclusive rights to their creation for only a limited time so that after that time has expired, the public may reap the benefit of the author's work."[7] Both the Statute of Anne and the Copyright Clause have "limited time" language because of an appreciation for the need for public access to creative works.

Principle 3: Copyright is for the protection of the "author first and the publisher only second."[8] The Copyright Clause specifically refers to authors not publishers. Publishers may obtain copyright from authors through the bargaining process.

Principle 4: Copyright is designed to protect "creative expressions only."[9] Copyright is not designed to protect facts, ideas, or concepts, since those things are the building blocks of creative works.

Principle 5: To gain the protection of copyright law, "the author's work must have a modicum of creativity."[10] The law seeks to encourage creativity and innovation; therefore it requires that protection is only given to works that have some element of creativity.

The guiding principles listed above are enduring principles included in the Copyright Clause in the U.S. Constitution. As the details of modern U.S. copyright law are discussed in this chapter and others in the CIP Handbook, the reader should consider whether or not U.S. copyright law has upheld or strayed from the legal foundation and guiding general principles originally conceived and promulgated at the founding of the new nation.

COPYRIGHT BASICS

Copyrightable Works

Section 102(a) of the Copyright Act states that copyright protects original works of authorship "fixed in any tangible medium of expression."[11] The specific categories of authorship detailed in the Copyright Act include:

- ▶ literary works;[12]
- ▶ musical works, including accompanying words;[13]
- ▶ dramatic works, including accompanying music;[14]
- ▶ pantomimes and choreographic works;[15]
- ▶ pictoral, graphic and sculptural works;[16]
- ▶ motion pictures and other audiovisual works;[17]
- ▶ sound recordings;[18] and
- ▶ architectural works.[19]

The Copyright Act very clearly states in section 102(b) that copyright protection does not extend to ideas, procedures, processes, systems, methods and concepts.[20] For example, the theory of relativity would not merit copyright protection. However, a poem or story that told about the development of the theory does show sufficient original expression to merit copyright protection.

Originality and Fixation

The threshold requirements for copyright protection are *originality* and *fixation*. Originality, as articulated by the courts, includes two aspects: independent creation and a modest quantum of creativity.[21] Independent creation means that the work is not copied from another.[22] A very modest amount of creativity meets the deminimus standard that allows for a minimal amount of creativity, such as pictures on cake box labels, to merit copyright for a work.[23]

Once a work is fixed in a tangible medium, it is immediately afforded copyright protection. A final report for a course, an art project, a letter, or even a simple electronic mail message could be afforded copyright protection if each work meets the requirements of originality and fixation. Copyright protection is automatic and thus a copyright notice or registration with the U.S. Copyright Office is not required.[24] Therefore, copyright ownership should be assumed for all works unless there is a specific statement to the contrary. An owner would need to specifically state that s/he does not wish to retain his/her exclusive rights with a statement such as "you are free to copy, distribute, display, and perform the work and to make derivative works."[25] Otherwise, the creator is entitled to his or her exclusive rights for the time period set forth in the copyright law.

Because of the automatic nature of copyright in the United States, enormous amounts of works have copyright protection. The sheer volume of copyrighted works created and used on university campuses, due to the nature of U.S. copyright law, poses serious problems for universities and libraries. The problems arise from the fact that copyright gives the author certain exclusive rights in the work that are only limited specifically pursuant to the Copyright Act. Any uses of copyrighted works that are not pursuant to certain legal limitations are considered infringements. The increased possibility of massive copyright infringement, due to the use of digital networks to disseminate information, is a major concern for many university counsel, librarians, administrators, and presidents.

The Public Domain

As stated earlier, some works are not eligible for copyright protection; these are works of facts, ideas, concepts, principles, or discoveries. These works are often considered part of the public domain and are free to be used by the public. The term *public domain* is not defined in the Copyright Act of 1976 or later amendments. Jessica Litman has defined the term as "a commons that includes those aspects of copyrighted works which copyright does not protect . . ."[26] The public domain is generally considered to comprise the following categories of works:

Not Copyrightable: Works in the Public Domain

√ Ideas

√ Procedures

√ Processes

√ Systems

√ Concepts

√ Titles, short phrases, names, common symbols or designs, slight variations of type styles, lettering, or coloring, or lists of ingredients

Works containing only nonprotected material with no original authorship, such as lists of common facts, charts, or a plain calendar

---

▶ works ineligible for copyright protection because they do not meet the statutory definition for a copyrighted work;

▶ works in which the copyright term has expired;

▶ works which failed to meet historical requirements for copyright protection; and

▶ works produced by the federal government.

While the public domain is sometimes perceived to be of little value because many of the works are quite old, the free availability of works contributes to the creation of new knowledge and ensures access to works for use by everyone in society. The British realized the folly of giving any one entity exclusive rights over copyrighted works in perpetuity early in their history. The existence of the public domain is an important principle of copyright law and serves to ensure that no one person or organization may have an exclusive monopoly over copyrighted works to the detriment of society as a whole.

Once works are in the public domain, anyone may use the work and create derivative works without the permission of the original copyright holder. Using public domain works in new ways is not a violation of copyright. The public domain exists in order to permit new uses of works. These new uses often result in a benefit for the original creator of the work, while, at the same time, benefiting society. The public domain is critical to the higher education community. Without a vibrant public domain, research and teaching at universities could not occur. The public domain serves as the vital infrastructure and building blocks of all scholarship. Pamela Samuelson has identified several works in the public domain that directly impact teaching and learning:

▶ scientific principles, theorems, mathematical formulae, laws of nature, etc.;

▶ scientific and other methods, techniques, and processes;

▶ ideas, concepts, discoveries, theories, and hypotheses;

▶ facts, information, data, know-how, and knowledge;

▶ laws, regulations, judicial opinions, government documents, and legislative reports;

▶ works qualifying for intellectual property protection claimed or they expired;

▶ works that fail to qualify for intellectual property protection because they do not meet the requirements for patent, copyright, or trademark protection; and

▶ words, names, numbers, symbols, signs, rules of grammar, diction and punctuation.[27]

As this list by Professor Samuelson indicates, the public domain provides much of the critical information needed for higher education to function. The following chart outlines the term of copyright for works created at certain times. The public domain is heavily populated with works that have expired terms of copyright.

In light of the critical nature of public domain and lack of copyright liability for using public domain works, educators should be mindful of expired copyright terms for works that they want to use for teaching and research.

Duration of Copyright

The term of copyright protection has changed many times over the course of the history of copyright law in the United States. There are many factors that affect how long a work is under copyright. As a general rule, copyright is life of the

▶ FIGURE 1.1: Chart of Works and the Public Domain[28]

Works Published in the United States	Requirements	Term of Copyright
Before 1923	None	In the public domain
Between 1923 and 1 March 1978	Published *without* a copyright notice	In the public domain
Between 1923 and 1963	Published *with* notice but copyright was not renewed	In the public domain
Between 1923 and 1963	Published *with* notice *and* copyright was renewed	95 years after publication date
Between 1964 and 1977	Published *with* notice	28 years for the first term; now automatically extended for 67 years for a second term
Created on or after January 1, 1978	When work is fixed in a tangible medium of expression	70 years after the death of the author, or if the work is of corporate authorship, the shorter of 95 years from publication or 120 years from creation

author plus 70 years.[29] For works made for hire (i.e., works owned by corporate entities, anonymous, or pseudonymous works), the term is 95 years from the date of first publication or 120 years from the date of creation (whichever comes first).[30]

A recent extension to the length of copyright came in 1998 with the Sonny Bono Copyright Term Extension Act, which increased the term of copyright 20 years.[31] Whatever the motivation for extending copyright, recent efforts to find the extension of copyright unconstitutional have been unsuccessful.[32] In the Eldred case, the Supreme Court ruled that Congress did not violate the copyright clause when they extended the term of copyright, nor did Congress violate the First Amendment.[33] Therefore, the petitioner, Mr. Eldred, could not publish certain titles because they did not pass into the public domain after the passage of the act.

Copyright Ownership

The exclusive rights in copyright are initially given to the owner of the copyrighted work. Although the owner may transfer the copyright to someone else, any analysis of copyright ownership should begin with the principle that the author is the owner. Section 201 of the Copyright Act provides four categories for ownership: (1) author; (2) joint authors; (3) works made for hire; (4) collective works.[34] The primary exception to the "author is the owner" approach in U.S. copyright law is the work for hire category. When a work is made for hire, the employer, not an employee, is considered the owner/author of a work. Section 101 outlines two ways a work is made for hire: (1) the employee creates the work within the scope of his or her employment; or (2) the work meets the statutory criteria of being an independently contracted work made for hire.[35] The work for hire doctrine has always played a role in academic production. However, an exception to this rule was developed in the common law for such things as syllabi and lecture notes. In Chapter 2, Kenneth D. Crews discusses the details of the work for hire doctrine and the existence of the teacher's exception in recent case law.

Exclusive Rights

The exclusive rights of the creator are outlined in section 106 of the United States copyright law. The exclusive rights of the copyright owner are:
1. to reproduce the copyrighted work in copies or phonorecords;[36]
2. to prepare derivative works based upon the copyrighted work;[37]
3. to distribute copies . . . of the copyrighted work to the public by sale or other transfer of ownership, or by rental, lease or lending;[38]

4. to perform the work publicly, known as public performance, when the work is literary, musical, dramatic, choreographed, pantomimed, a motion picture or other type of audiovisual work;[39]

5. to display the work publicly (this applies to literary, musical, dramatic, choreographed, pantomimed, and pictorial, graphic, or sculptural works);[40] and

6. digital audio transmission of sound recordings (another form of public performance).[41]

Once an original work is created, it is instantaneously covered by copyright; the creator does not need to take any action or secure copyright registration. However, registration does carry certain benefits and is needed to bring a lawsuit.[42] In sum, reproduction, adaptation, distribution, performance display, and sound recording digital transmission rights are the bundle of rights included in copyright ownership. The exclusive rights reviewed briefly are:

▶ The reproduction right refers to fixing a copyrighted work in a tangible and relatively permanent form as stated in section 101 of the Copyright Act.

▶ The derivative right refers to a preexisting copyrighted work being reformed or adapted.

▶ The distribution right gives the copyright owner the right to control the first public distribution of the work. The distribution right enables the transfer to physical copies or phonorecords of works.

▶ The performance right includes the exclusive right to control public performances of a work. A performance would include acting a play, singing a song, or playing a DVD. To perform a work publicly includes performing in a public setting or any place where a substantial number of persons outside of a normal circle of a family and its social acquaintances are gathered.[43]

▶ The display right is the right to publicly show a copy of a work, either directly or by means of a film, slide, television image, or other device, and in the case of a motion picture or other audiovisual work, to show individual images non-sequentially.[44]

Even though these rights are the exclusive rights of the owner, the rights are subject to numerous limitations set forth in the Copyright Act and can be parsed and sold by the copyright owner. A person can violate one right or several rights simultaneously. Often the reproduction and distribution rights are violated in tandem. The statutory limitations on copyright ownership are set forth in sections 107–121 of the Copyright Act. This chapter will not discuss each of these limitations in detail because it would be too lengthy to explore. Instead, this chapter will highlight those limitations that are particularly relevant for teaching, learning, and research. Other chapters in the CIP Handbook, specifically Chapter 3 and Chapter 5 discuss sections 107, 110 (1)–(2), and 112(f) of the Copyright Act respectively.

Limits on the Exclusive Rights of the Copyright Holder

As stated previously, each exclusive right is subject to limitations set forth in sections 107–121. This section will discuss each limitation that accompanies the exclusive rights that are most relevant for teaching, learning, and research.

Ephemeral Recordings—section 112. This is a limitation on the reproduction and derivative right that enables copies and phonorecords of a copyrighted work to be made for transmission. Most recently, section 112 was amended to enable performances and displays of works in digital network transmission pursuant to the Technology, Education, and Copyright Harmonization Act that will be discussed in Chapter 5.

Fair Use — section 107. This is a limitation on the exclusive rights of copyright owners for purposes such as criticism, comment, news reporting, teaching (including multiple copies for classroom use), scholarship, or research. In order for a use to be considered fair, several factors must be considered. Those factors are set below.

Reproduction by Libraries and Archives—section 108. Libraries and archives may reproduce no more than one copy or phonorecord of a work under certain specified conditions listed in the section.

The First Sale Doctrine—section 109. This is a limitation on the distribution right that limits the copyright owner's control over copies of the work to their first sale or transfer.[47]

Educational Uses—section 110. This is a limitation on the performance and display right. Section 110(1) exempts performances of copyrighted works by instructors in a face-to-face teaching setting. Section 110(2) limits the performance and display for educational transmissions. Chapter 5 details each of these limitations.

Fair Use

Fair use is in a category unto itself. The Copyright Act refers to the fair use of a copyrighted work as not an infringement of copyright. Fair use enables the use of the copyright owner's exclusive rights for activities that serve the common good and foster debate, criticism, education, and scholarship. Fair use serves a unique role in balancing the rights of the copyright holder and the needs for a free and open society. Uses of copyrighted works, such as using portions of film to evaluate the film's merits, publishing portions of copyrighted works for criticism and debate, or using words of a song to parody the original work are essential elements of free and open discussion and contribute to an open and robust democracy. The fervor over the importance of fair use stems from its importance in contributing to an open society and its importance in ensuring political and religious freedom are maintained and flourish in support of an open society. Section 107 of the Copyright Act states:

> Notwithstanding the provisions of sections 106 and 106A, the fair use of a copyrighted work, including such use by reproduction in copies or phonorecords or by any other means specified by that section, for purposes such as criticism, comment, news reporting, teaching (including multiple copies for classroom use), scholarship, or research, is not an infringement of copyright.[48]

Section 107 goes on to state, "In determining whether the use made of a work in any particular case is a fair use the factors to be considered shall include:

- ▶ the *purpose* and character of the use, including whether such use is of a commercial nature or is for nonprofit educational purposes;
- ▶ the *nature* of the copyrighted work;
- ▶ the *amount* and *substantiality* of the portion used in relation to the copyrighted work as a whole; and
- ▶ the *effect* of the use upon the potential market for or value of the copyrighted work."[49]

Whether a use is fair is determined in a courtroom; it is not the outcome of legislation. The use of the four factors reflects an understanding that sometimes the letter of the law would violate the spirit of the law, and there must be some means to determine if an unauthorized use of a copyrighted work should be permitted. The four factors are used as one mechanism to determine whether a use is fair. However, the determination of when a use is fair depends on the specific case in question, the type of use, and the specific circumstances when the work was used. The four factors provide a general guideline, but it is not possible to determine whether a use is fair without a court decision that confirms a use was fair. That said, it is possible to know whether a use is more likely to be considered a fair use by evaluating the use through a checklist of factors based on the four fair use factors. Several excellent fair use checklists exist and make the determination much easier. The *Checklist for Fair Use* provides one excellent example.[50] A second example is the list from Central Missouri State University, which is an adaptation of the list developed at Indiana University.[51] There are many other notable examples that help determine whether a use is more or less likely to be considered fair. Peggy E. Hoon and Cheryl L. Davis detail the parameters of fair use and analyze recent case law in Chapter 3 of the CIP Handbook.

Infringement and Remedies

Use of copyrighted work without permission, unless it is covered by limitation in the Copyright Act, infringes on the exclusive rights of the author outlined in section

106 of the Copyright Act. Infringement can be direct, vicarious, or contributory. Direct infringement occurs when someone violates any of the exclusive rights of the copyright owner. Vicarious infringement occurs when one has the right to control the infringement of another or profits from infringement.[52] This type of liability is based on the relationship with the direct infringer. Contributory infringement occurs when a person has knowledge of infringing activity and/or induces, causes, or contributes to infringing conduct.[53] Educational institutions may be liable under all three types of liability. Because of this possibility, educational institutions were heavily involved in the liability limits in the Digital Millennium Copyright Act of 1998. Specifically, the DMCA limits liability for Internet service providers and provides safe harbors from liability for certain activities. In Chapter 6, Arnold P. Lutzker discusses the details of the DMCA and its application to college and university campuses.

CONCLUSION

This chapter outlined basic copyright principles and the copyright statutory regime so that the lay reader has a solid foundation for understanding the copyright issues discussed in greater detail in the remainder of the CIP Handbook. Although the Copyright Act is oftentimes very difficult to understand, chapter authors in the CIP Handbook have attempted to make the very complex more accessible to the layperson.

Trends and Developments in Copyright Law and Policy

Recent trends and developments in copyright law and policy include:

▶ The Sonny Bono Term Extension Act, which is the latest legislative amendment that extends the duration of copyright. The Sonny Bono Term Extension Act follows a trend internationally and within the United States to extend copyright protections for longer periods of time.

▶ Continual expansion of the types of works that can be copyrighted. Recent evidence of this trend is in the database protection legislation that has come before Congress in recent years. There is continual debate about what can be copyrighted and pressure from owners of works that are in the public domain to increase protections of their works.

▶ Greater complexity in amendments to the Copyright Act as a result of the complexities in technology and mechanisms for accessing copyrighted works. Generally, recent amendments, such as the Digital Millennium Copyright Act (DMCA) and the Technology, Education, and Copyright Harmonization (TEACH) Act place greater burdens on the users of works to guarantee a level of protection of these works and limit distribution through electronic means. The recent amendments attempt to manage digital works in a different manner than analog works and in doing so, create more confusion and place new burdens on users as a mechanism to stem piracy and ensure the exclusive rights of the owner remain intact.

▶ Greater recognition of specialized uses of copyrighted works such as those for libraries and educational institutions. The greater involvement of representative groups has contributed in great part to the growing recognition of these types of special needs. Advocacy and continual monitoring of the changes in copyright law represent an important aspect of having some involvement in creating new policy.

NEXT STEPS

▶ Develop copyright expertise at your college or university.
▶ Initiate copyright education efforts for faculty, staff, and students.
▶ Keep abreast of public policy developments related to copyright law.
▶ Develop and enforce a copyright policy.

ENDNOTES

[1] Marshall Leaffer, *Understanding Copyright Law* 4 (3d ed. 1999).

[2] Gretchen McCord Hoffman, *Copyright in Cyberspace: Questions and Answers for Librarians* 4 (2001).

[3] Leafer, *supra* note 1, at 5.

[4] Arlene Bielefield and Lawrence Cheeseman, *Technology and Copyright Law: A Guidebook for the Library, Research, and Teaching Professions* 4 (1997).

[5] *Id.* at 13 (It took that long "to experience the real impact of the invention," for legal concepts to be developed, and to bring the parties involved together).

[6] Center for Intellectual Property, University of Maryland University College, Copyright Primer 2 (2000) (This primer is also available in an online version at http://www-apps. umuc.edu/primer/enter.php#).

[7] *Id.*

[8] *Id.* at 3

[9] *Id.*

[10] *Id.* at 4.

[11] 17 U.S.C. § 102(a) (2000).

[12] 17 U.S.C. § 102(a)(1).

[13] 17 U.S.C. § 102(a)(2).

[14] 17 U.S.C. § 102(a)(3).

[15] 17 U.S.C. § 102(a)(4).

[16] 17 U.S.C. § 102(a)(5).

[17] 17 U.S.C. § 102(a)(6).

[18] 17 U.S.C. § 102(a)(7).

[19] 17 U.S.C. § 102(a)(8).

[20] 17 U.S.C. § 102(b).

[21] Feist Publ'ns, Inc. v. Rural Tel. Serv. Co., Inc, 499 U.S. 340, 345 (1990).

[22] Leaffer, *supra* note 1, at 56.

[23] Kitchens of Sara Lee, Inc. v. Nifty Foods Corp., 266 F.2d 541, 545 (2d Cir. 1959).

[24] The Berne Convention Implementation Act of 1988, Pub. L. No. 100-569, §§ 7, 9, 102 Stat. 2853, 2857-59, eliminated the need to register a work or provide a notice of copyright on the work in order to merit copyright protection. Since the Berne Convention Act, copyright is automatically applied to any work.

[25] See, e.g., Creative Commons, http://creativecommons.org/ (last visited Feb. 1, 2006).

[26] Jessica Litman, *The Public Domain*, 39 Emory L.J. 965–968 (1990).

[27] Pamela Samuelson, *Mapping the Digital Public Domain: Threats and Opportunities*, 66 Law & Contemp. Probs. 147, 151 (2003).

[28] Lolly Gasaway, When U.S. Works Pass into the Public Domain, http://www.unc.edu/~unclng/public-d.htm (last visited Feb. 1, 2006).

[29] 17 U.S.C. § 302(a) (2000).

[30] 17 U.S.C. § 302(c).

[31] Sonny Bono Copyright Term Extension Act, Pub. L. No. 105-298, 112 Stat. 2827 (1998).

[32] Eldred v. Ashcroft, 537 U.S. 186, 208 (2003).

[33] *Id.* at 209-18, 218-21.

[34] 17 U.S.C. § 201 (2000).

[35] 17 U.S.C. § 101 (2000 & Supp. II 2003).

[36] 17 U.S.C. § 106(1) (2000 & Supp. II 2003).

[37] 17 U.S.C. § 106(2).

[38] 17 U.S.C. § 106(3).

[39] 17 U.S.C. § 106(4).

[40] 17 U.S.C. § 106(5).

[41] 17 U.S.C. § 106(6).

[42] 17 U.S.C.§ 411(a).

[43] 17 U.S.C. § 101 (2000 & Supp. II 2003).

[44] 17 U.S.C. § 101.

[45] 17 U.S.C. § 107(a) (2000).

[46] 17 U.S.C. § 108(a) (2000).

[47] 17 U.S.C. § 109(a) (2000).

[48] 17 U.S.C. § 107 (2000).

[49] 17 U.S.C. § 107.

[50] Copyright Management Center, Indiana University—Purdue University, Checklist for Fair Use, http://www.copyright.iupui.edu/checklist.htm (last visited Feb. 1, 2006).

[51] Central Missouri State University, Fair Use Checklist, http://library.cmsu.edu/copyright/checklist.htm (last visited Feb. 1, 2006).

[52] MGM Studios Inc. v. Grokster, Ltd., 125 S. Ct. 2764, 2776 (2005) (citing Gershwin Pub. Corp. v. Columbia Artists Management, Inc., 443 F.2d 1159, 1162 (2d Cir. 1971)).

[53] *Id.* (citing Shapiro, Bernstein & Co., v. H. L. Green Co., 316 F.2d 304, 307 (2d Cir. 1963)) *Grokster* is distinguished from *Sony Corp. of America v. Universal City Studios, Inc.*, 464 U.S. 417 (1984) on the grounds that Grokster's "words and deeds go[] beyond distribution as such shows a purpose to cause and profit from third-party acts of copyright infringement." *Id.* at 2782.

▶2

INSTRUCTIONAL MATERIALS AND "WORKS MADE FOR HIRE" AT UNIVERSITIES:

POLICIES AND STRATEGIC MANAGEMENT OF COPYRIGHT OWNERSHIP

KENNETH D. CREWS

This chapter discusses the following topics:
- ▶ Copyright ownership of faculty works
- ▶ Works made for hire
- ▶ "Teacher's exception" to work made for hire
- ▶ University copyright policy development

INTRODUCTION

Ownership of copyrighted materials created at universities—especially application of the "work-made-for-hire" doctrine—has been the subject of much debate within higher education and among legal scholars. New studies have emerged with the growth of distance education and possible implications of copyright law for the control and use of instructional materials.[1] While many studies offer both an overview of the law and examination of its possible meaning for the academy, little has been written about the ultimate failure of the law to serve the extraordinarily nuanced needs of higher education. Similarly, few writings have examined the pitfalls of the law that may well render most existing policies at colleges and universities invalid.[2] Recent court rulings reveal serious gaps in existing studies.

The legal issues may revolve around statutory interpretation and the application of law to the changing and diverse conditions of educational institutions. Yet the debate sometimes centers on sharing revenues from the marketing of new works,[3] or the pressure on colleges and universities to derive new sources of income in the face of growing expenses.[4] Sometimes the controversy is about academic freedom and the potential control over academic work that a university might exercise should it possess the legal rights of the copyright owner.[5] Occasionally the discussion turns to the potential conflicts of interest or commitment that can arise amidst the struggle over ownership, revenue, and the dedication of faculty work time.[6] Continuing tensions within the educational community confirm the importance of these issues.

The importance of the copyright issues is not to be diminished. The concern may ultimately focus on intellectual inspiration or money, but copyright ownership can directly shape the ability to achieve those non-legal goals. Regardless of whether the analysis is about "work made for hire" or a "teacher's exception," copyright law is built around a fundamental premise of designating the owner of the copyright, who will hold the rights of ownership. Unless the parties otherwise agree, the owner gets all rights; determining ownership immediately shapes the implications and consequences of copyright law.

This chapter will ultimately propose that educational institutions should make a fresh evaluation of their policies in light of recent judicial decisions. It will also suggest that typical policies—as well as the law itself—seldom serve fundamental needs of higher education. Policies throughout the country may well merit a thorough reexamination.

THE PROBLEM: CONTROL OF EDUCATIONAL MATERIALS

Clarifying the matter of copyright ownership is vital, because copyright law can dictate the terms on which the creator of instructional materials, as well as the employing university, may use the works. As in many private companies and other organizations, the copyrighted works are a centerpiece of the university's fundamental pursuit: teaching, research, and service. These materials are simultaneously vital to the current and future productivity of the individual faculty member or other author. Compounding the difficulties, the individual and the institution usually need one another to achieve the greatest success. The institution has no instruction to offer without a talented faculty; the individual has neither support nor effective outlet for reaching students without the university.

To put this tension into a practical setting, consider the familiar example of online instructional materials and Web-based courses.[7] Professor Gomez works for ABC University. As part of his teaching duties, he prepares online modules to deliver fundamental instruction to students in his courses. He loads the materials on the university's Web server, where the students may access them. If Gomez holds the copyright to the materials, he effectively can assert several critical legal rights: to control how the students may use the works; to direct whether ABC may allow others to teach from the same materials; to revise the materials for future use or for incorporation into new publications and projects; and to license them for wider distribution—and to collect any revenue in exchange.[8]

Universities typically leave that roster of rights to the professor who creates teaching materials and similar works.[9] Yet seldom are the realities of modern situations so simple. Many online materials are today collaborative efforts. Perhaps Professor Gomez did create the substantive elements of the course, but he may have had help from Web designers to make the materials look right and function well. He may be using standard templates and other elements created at the university, and he enjoys the benefit of equipment and staff support provided by the university. The professor may also have created the course materials as part of a curricular initiative, perhaps to be part of a degree program and with special support or grants from the university. To place all the rights of control and use with Professor Gomez would mean that the university could not reliably pursue its objectives, and the professor alone could jeopardize the university's academic program. Professor Gomez could assert control over all elements of the project, even elements he did not actually create.[10]

Just as professors as copyright owners could undercut academic programming, so could the university—if it holds all rights—preclude professors from building future publications and other academic pursuits based on the course materials.[11] These possibilities are not only harmful to the individuals directly affected, but any time programs and scholarship are constrained, the entire academic enterprise suffers. Universities have had many good reasons for typically leaving copyrights with faculty authors. That approach may best foster academic freedom and motivate the strongest scholarship. Leaving copyright with the author is also appealing for practical reasons; universities are often not well positioned to hold and manage the plethora of papers, handouts, and other creative works generated each day on campus.

Arguments in support of granting the copyrights to either the author or the university can easily have merit. At the same time, granting all rights to one party is inherently detrimental to the other party, raising the prospect that sharing rights might be the better resolution of differences. The quandary in the quest for such an equitable outcome, however, is that neither law nor policy alone can produce the desired results. The law generally places ownership rights with only one party; the law by itself cannot create a sharing of rights.[12] University policies have attempted to achieve the desired results, but recent judicial rulings have raised serious questions about the validity of typical policies. The need for fresh evaluation has become imperative.

COPYRIGHT OWNERSHIP AND WORKS MADE FOR HIRE

Principles of Copyright Protection and Ownership

To comprehend the scope and magnitude of the issue, one must reckon with the vast range of copyright protected materials created at universities on a daily basis.[13] At the outset, one can generally assume that nearly everything that a professor creates and uses in his/her course is most likely protected by copyright, and that many of the uses—from scanning to transmitting—implicate rights that belong by law to the copyright owner. Hence, identifying the owner means establishing who has the authority to control the future uses of the materials in connection with teaching, publishing, and many other pursuits. Copyright protection vests automatically in nearly all works that are "original works of authorship" and that are "fixed in any tangible medium of expression."[14] Copyright protection applies to books, articles, essays, pictures, music, computer programming, Web sites, and more without any requirement of formal registration, copyright notice, or any other step.[15] With the scope of copyright drawn so broadly, the question of establishing ownership becomes even more crucial.

Works Made for Hire

While as a general rule copyright vests initially with the author or creator of the original work, the work-made-for-hire doctrine poses what may be called an exception to that general rule.[16] When the doctrine applies, it creates the outcome of legally declaring that the "author" of the work is actually the employer of the person who created it.[17] More important, the employer is also the holder of the copyright and all legal rights associated with the copyright. The employee who created the work has no rights under American copyright law.[18]

Scope of Employment

A work can be deemed to be "for hire" under either of two possible circumstances outlined in the Copyright Act. The most common possibility arises in the situation where an "employee" creates the work "within the scope of his or her employment."[19] This provision applies frequently in employment settings of all types. A software programmer creating the next Microsoft product or a copy editor drafting materials for a new promotional campaign is likely creating works that will deemed to be "for hire." Court rulings that apply this principle from copyright law draw upon centuries of legal development surrounding the definition of an "employee."[20] Courts do not simply look to labels, but look to details of the situation. For example, an employee is likely to be a person with a full-time job, receiving employment benefits, and using equipment and under the direction of an employer. A typical full-time faculty member at a college or university is likely to be deemed an employee.[21] By contrast, one who is hired to work on a particular project, or is paid simply an hourly rate for work as it progresses, or is given a fixed payment for a specific project may well be an "independent contractor," and this provision of the work-made-for-hire doctrine will not apply.

Whether the doctrine consequently applies to "employees" next depends upon whether the work performed is "within the scope of employment."[22] Legal analyses often diverge on this part of the analysis. Some commentators have argued that faculty members do not have specific duties to create individually identified research and teaching materials; therefore these products are not precisely within the scope of their employment.[23] Faculty members also do some of their creative work in the late of night and at home when they are not subject to direct supervision and perhaps not using university-owned equipment.[24] Countering these arguments, however, are court rulings that have applied the law when employees do their creative work at odd hours and times and without specific direction to generate each individual work that comes into existence.[25] Moreover, faculty members often itemize their individual works of scholarship as evidence of meeting career objectives and as support for continuation, pay raises, and promotion and tenure.[26]

A few early court rulings have suggested amid this uncertainty that a "teacher's exception" to the work-made-for-hire doctrine applies to teaching and research materials created by faculty members.[27] This possible exception, however, is simply too elusive for educators and universities to rely upon, with an assumption that it will clarify and resolve uncertainties in the law.[28] For example, some of the earliest cases predate Congress's vision of the law in 1976. When Congress revised the law, it included no reference to a "teacher's exception," leading to the inference that Congress did not mean to carry the doctrine into modern law.[29] Moreover, recent cases mentioning the possibility do so only in passing and as "dictum."[30] The courts may have discussed the possibility of the doctrine without needing to decide whether it really exists and might really apply in the case at hand. These are shaky grounds on which to base any conclusions about the ownership of the copyright to faculty work product.[31]

Independent Contractors

A second version of the work-made-for-hire doctrine offers somewhat more clarity, but it also requires deliberate compliance with detailed conditions in the law. This version generally applies to independent contractors when the employer and the contractor desire that the work be deemed "for hire" and that the copyright belong to the employer. In that case, the parties may agree in a written instrument signed by both of them that the work shall be treated as work made for hire. In addition, it must be "specially ordered or commissioned," and the creation must be among the specific categories listed in the relevant statute.[32] Among the works on the list that may be relevant to faculty is an "instructional text," but not all faculty projects will neatly fit into the statutory groups.[33]

Changing the Copyright Owner

Either of the two definitions of "work made for hire" establishes merely a "default" formulation of copyright ownership. If a work qualifies as "for hire," the copyright belongs to the employer—at least initially. The copyright statutes, however, add two tremendously important opportunities to change that result. The first possibility is a simple transfer of the copyright.[34] Any copyright owner may convey the copyright to another person. A valid transfer, however, must be evidenced by a written instrument and be signed by the transferor.[35] The specific statutory requirements again mean that general and unsigned university policies are not likely to effect a transfer.[36]

The second transfer possibility is a distinctive feature of the law of works for hire. The same statute specifying that the employer is the owner of all rights provides further that the creator of the work and the employer may agree to reallocate the rights between themselves.[37] That agreement, however, must also be in writing and signed by both parties.[38] This provision includes potential ambiguities and is occasionally mystifying. The plain language of the statute specifies that both parties must sign the agreement, while a simple transfer of copyright requires a signature only from the transferor. The language also makes clear that the resulting agreement effects only a transfer of the rights to the work. It therefore does not change its status as a "work made for hire." This outcome is of major significance. Rights in the work may well move to the employee. Indeed, the employee may end up as the owner in full of the copyright itself. But the work remains as it was at its inception: a work made for hire. Thus, the attributes of a work for hire remain applicable.[39]

One more possibility is possible under copyright law. The owner of the copyright may choose to transfer or license only some rights of ownership. The person designated as the owner under the law may continue to hold title and may hold some or most of the legal rights. The owner may, however, choose to grant to another person some of the rights associated with the copyright. In some situations, such a sharing or "unbundling" of rights is not unusual. An author of a book may hold the copyright but grant to a publisher rights to reproduce and distribute copies, or grant to a movie studio the right to make the motion picture. In the university setting, this same concept can allow a faculty author to hold the copyright, but grant to the university the right to include the instructional materials in an online degree program. A later section of this chapter will take a closer look at these possibilities for "unbundling" the rights of the copyright owner.

THE LATEST COURT RULINGS

In this context of ambiguous law and uncertain results, courts and commentators have found much to debate about the possible application of the work-made-for-hire doctrine to faculty work. The earlier court rulings were far from resolute.[40] The law of agency that defines "employee" and "scope of employment" is also susceptible to broad interpretation.[41] The gravity of the debate, however, appears to be shifting with more recent rulings from district courts. These decisions suggest a direction in which the law may be heading. Admittedly, the cases hardly settle the issues for universities. They give only short attention to the agency issues, finding relatively summarily that the works were within the "for-hire" doctrine. Only one of the cases is directly about the copyright in teaching materials; one is about a journal article; two are about the ownership of works by staff photographers. Yet the cases offered an opportunity for courts to scrutinize the doctrine of "work made for hire" in the educational setting and to explore the possibilities of a "teacher's exception." Certainly, the cases offered at least as strong an opportunity for dictum comparable to earlier decisions that stirred so much debate.[42]

These recent rulings instead take a considerably different tack. They deal with the ownership issue relatively briefly and unhesitatingly. They make little allusion to a "teacher's exception." Perhaps most important, the decisions raise serious doubts about the effectiveness of conventional university policies to create their intended results. These directions may or may not be good for the management of intellectual property, and any court ruling will produce both winners and losers. Nevertheless, these four rulings change considerably the direction of the legal analysis, and they include many new lessons for university policymakers.

University of Colorado Foundation, Inc. v. American Cyanamid, 880 F. Supp. 1387 (D.Colo. 1995).

> This case centered on a dispute over patent rights to a reformulated pharmaceutical developed in part by faculty researchers at the University of Colorado. The university argued that the defendant also copied portions of a published research article written by the researchers.[43] The copyright claim to the article was registered with the U.S. Copyright Office in the name of the university.[44] The defendant disputed the university's ownership, but the court rather summarily resolved that the article was a work made for hire created by employees within the scope of their employment.[45] The faculty authors also did not dispute the claim of ownership by the university. Because the court concluded that the university was the copyright owner, the university held all rights and could proceed with the infringement claim.[46]

Vanderhurst v. Colorado Mountain College District, 16 F. Supp. 2d 1297 (D.Colo. 1998).

> A professor of veterinary technology prepared an outline on his own time with his own materials for a course that he taught at the college.[47] After termination of his employment, the professor claimed ownership of the copyright to his course work. The court held that the creation of the outline by the professor should be fairly regarded as one method of carrying out the objectives of his employment.[48] Therefore, the outline was subject to the work-made-for-hire doctrine, and the rights belonged to the college.[49] Adding to the court's reasoning was a university policy specifying that the duties of faculty members included professional service activities such as development of courses, programs, and curricula.[50]

Manning v. Board of Trustees of Community College District No. 505 (Parkland College), 109 F. Supp. 2d 976 (C.D. Ill. 2000).

> After a community college had terminated the full-time employment of a staff photographer, both the college and the photographer claimed ownership of the copyrights to photographs taken for the college during the term of his employment.[51] The staff member alleged that he owned the copyrights, because a policy included in the college's policy manual sweepingly granted copyrights to employees who create new works.[52] The parties did not dispute that the photographs were works made for hire under the law, and the court held that a general policy was insufficient to meet the statutory requirements for changing the copyright ownership.[53] The Copyright Act sets forth a statutory presumption that the employer owns the copyright in a work made for hire, unless the parties have expressly agreed otherwise in a written and signed instrument.[54] The additional existence of a collective bargaining agreement and general employment agreement referencing the college policies did not meet the requirements for a valid transfer of rights.[55]

Forasté v. Brown University, 248 F. Supp. 2d 71 (D.R.I. 2003).

> This case is remarkably similar to *Manning* in that it involved the work of a professional staff photographer following termination of his employment, and the photographer claimed ownership of the copyrights.[56] The court appeared to have little trouble concluding that the photographer was an employee creating the works within the scope of his duties, and that therefore the works were "for hire" and belonged to the employer university.[57] The court also rejected the argument that the broad university policy designating that copyrights belonged to "the author or originator of the work" was sufficient to meet the statutory requirement of a writing signed by the parties.[58] Therefore, the employer held the copyrights.

These most recent cases make a few pointed suggestions about the state of copyright ownership in higher education. First, the fact that few cases have in relatively quick succession arisen in the courts suggests the growing importance of the issue and the tensions surrounding it. Copyright has become more important and more controversial in recent years, and the court rulings are a reminder that some disputes may actually lead to the expense and burden of litigation. Second, these cases address the legal issues of ownership with seeming haste. The courts are either not receiving or not heeding arguments about the complex implications of the law as applied to universities and the need to resolve some of the practical and historical subtleties. Thus, the courts make no mention whatsoever of a "teacher's exception," even in the *Vanderhurst* case involving instructional materials, where the exception might have had direct relevance.[59] Finally, the most recent two decisions reveal little tolerance for generic policies as a tool for redefining copyright ownership. When the Copyright Act specifies written and signed instruments of conveyance, the courts are not inclined to allow general policy positions as substitutes.

While the decisions undercut considerably the validity of general copyright policies in the context of works made for hire, the cases are also a reminder that institutions and individuals can effectively manage their intellectual property through properly devised and implemented agreements. The general policies may not work, but something else will. Through proper procedures, universities have the opportunity to exert deliberate and active management of intellectual property and to reorder copyright ownership for the benefit of the institutions and the individuals. Universities may have to develop more elaborate instruments related to copyright ownership, and they may have to create more systematic structures for implementation of policies and signed agreements. But the outcome can be more beneficial for institutions and individuals.

DIVISIBILITY OF COPYRIGHT AND "UNBUNDLING"

The policies and systems that a university may put into place can do much more than merely designate one party or the other as the copyright owner. With proper instruments, such a result is perfectly possible. In the university context, however, placing all rights with the institution or the individual sets up the conflict between the parties that copyright has engendered for years. On the other hand, the law provides a possibility for sharing rights and reducing conflicts, but only if the parties take the initiative and lay careful plans. The law will not yield a sharing of rights by itself; the parties have to enter into valid agreements or other arrangements. The opportunity to share rights among interested parties is a viable and important possibility under the law. This possibility may also be important for meeting the needs of higher education in the management of its copyrighted resources.

The concept is the "divisibility" of copyrights, and the principle is that a transfer of a copyright need not be complete. In other words, one may transfer the entire copyright to another party, but a copyright owner may also choose to transfer only select aspects of the rights associated with the copyright.[60] Consider the simple example of a novel. An author may own the copyright to the novel. Rather than transfer the copyright in full to a publisher, the author may transfer instead only reproduction and distribution rights to the publisher. In fact, the transfer could even be more specific, transferring those rights only in the context of preparing hardback copies distributed in North America for a designated period of years. The novelist may then transfer reproduction and distribution rights related to paperbacks to yet another publisher. The right to make derivative works may go to a film production company. The ability to parse the rights into detailed units for separate conveyance is limited only by the imagination and willingness of the parties.[61]

This divisibility of the copyright can prove to be of enormous importance to academic institutions, faculty members, staff, as well as publishers, researchers, and students who are affected by the copyright decisions. Consider these simple possibilities. The copyright policies in the *Manning* and *Forasté* cases generally stated a simple position that faculty and staff would hold the copyrights to the works they create. That position may have been well motivated by the desire to give authority to individuals who will benefit from holding the rights and will be motivated to do their best work. On the other hand, granting all rights to the individuals would have the effect of leaving the university with no rights. In the case of the staff photographers, the adverse consequences for the university are profound. The university would find itself under that policy unable to use its wealth of photographs in connection with teaching, research, community service, and promotional campaigns. If the photographer holds the copyright, the university with its clear need to use the photographs would find itself either committing copyright infringement or needing to secure permission to use the works that it paid to create in the first place. The "divisibility," or sharing, of the copyright can enable the university to hold rights of use that it needs, while simultaneously allowing the photographer to use the images for appropriate and agreeable purposes.

The same kinds of conflicts arise in the context of many instructional works. The modern example of online courses or distance education provides an important case in point. Imagine the common situation of a university seeking to create an online degree program. The dean may consult with a variety of faculty members and arrange for them to create individual modules that collectively become the overall academic program. If the copyrights belong in full to the faculty members, the university would need to be sure that it has secured rights from them for continued use of the materials. Each professor's ability to control the copyright also creates the risk that he or she could jeopardize the degree program by withdrawing rights to use the materials. By contrast, if all rights belong to the university, the professors are left with no control over their intellectual work. If a professor wants to incorporate that same material into future teaching or publications, the professor is left with the need to secure permission from the university. This situation creates the risk that the university could undercut the professor's future academic endeavors. A faculty member who recognizes that risk in advance may well be discouraged from contributing his or her best quality work to the project. That outcome would be a disaster for faculty, academic institutions, and the students and future researchers.

Tension and conflicts surrounding claims of ownership can be greatly relieved by pursuing a plan to "unbundle" the rights of copyright ownership and to share those rights among the interested parties. In the case of academic work product, if rights of use are carefully and specifically allocated between the university and the faculty member, the parties are likely to find that they can enjoy the rights of use that they need and avoid future conflicts as each party pursues academic programs, scholarship, and other creative ventures built upon the existing copyrighted materials. The law allows the parties to reach this result, but they need to be prepared to invest the time and energy in more creative and elaborate policies and related documents.

IMPLICATIONS FOR UNIVERSITY POLICYMAKING

Current Policies and Problems

Many university policies are built upon assumptions about the law and visions for the management of copyright in higher education that do not necessarily embrace complexities.[62] Policies that declare one party or the other to be the copyright owner may not be valid. They may be implicitly dependent on the dubious "teacher's exception" to make them valid. Most of all, few policies do more than identify different classes of works and name a copyright owner; they seldom comprehend the range of interests at stake and the benefits of allocating rights among different parties.

These problems with current policies are especially exacerbated by the recent cases suggesting more clearly than ever that a great deal of work created at colleges and universities will be treated as "work made for hire" with the copyright belonging to the employer. These legal developments also emphasize that general policy statements that are not specific to works in question and are not signed by the appropriate parties may not be adequate to change initial designation of copyright owners under the law. Recent developments in the law also weaken arguments for a "teacher's exception" to the work-made-for-hire doctrine. In the case of employees, such as most faculty members, the law also seems to have a tendency to diminish application of work made for hire when the professor happens to be working late at night or at home with a personal computer. Some critics will continue to argue that this analysis is wrong and that rights belong to the faculty authors. One can easily devise examples in which most people would rightly believe that the copyright in fact does belong to the faculty author. Nevertheless, current law is leaning toward either a trend of finding much academic work to be work for hire or creating greater uncertainty about the copyright status. In either case, the need for clear and creative university policymaking becomes increasingly important.

Thus, fresh rethinking of university policies should focus on two sets of issues. The first issues are procedural. The policy must be developed and adopted with proper authority from within the institution. The policy must also adhere to a proper method for enforceable application. The second group of issues is substantive. The policy should fundamentally address the identity of the named copyright owner of different types of works. More important, the policy must proceed in considerable detail to designate specifically which rights belong to which parties.[63] This last point is central to the successful application of copyright law. This unbundling or allocation of rights is an opportunity both to assure rights to different parties as well as to avoid tension and conflicts surrounding them. It is also an opportunity for the interested parties to anticipate their needs and to articulate them clearly. Keep in mind that the law of copyright addresses ownership rights only in broad and general terms. The law will not parse the issues in detail. The parties should therefore take the opportunity to consider specifically their desired outcomes and to do their best to secure those results in the language of the policy. Most of the remainder of this chapter will offer some details about these points.

Proposals for Policy Improvements

Structure of the Policy

Whatever the outcome that a university policy might seek to produce, one of the early decisions that policymakers must face is the structure or form of the policy and its implementation. For example, in the *Manning* and *Forasté* cases, the universities had fairly conventional policies that relatively simply declared individuals to be owners of copyrights. The policies were not specific to individual works and were not individually signed by faculty members, staff, and others affected by the terms of the document. Many universities routinely rely on such policies. To the extent that they are simply declarative of the law, they do not raise serious legal problems. For example, if a professor's independent publication is created outside the "scope of employment," the copyright should under the law belong to the faculty member; a policy to that effect makes no change in the legal result and at least does no harm. By contrast, if a work is created under circumstances that would have made it "for hire" under the law, a simple policy declaration vesting the copyright with the individual creator is not likely valid.

This predicament gives rise to the need for written instruments that comply with the requirements of the statutes. The university still needs a policy statement to clarify its position and the intended outcome of the copyright ownership question, but the policy may need to be supplemented with a written instrument of agreement or conveyance—properly signed by the appropriate parties—to make the intended result legally binding.

One more important possibility remains. The policy could be structured as a license. A nonexclusive license of the copyright or any of the separate rights need not be in writing or signed by any party.[64] A policy could state, for example, that while the university may hold the copyright to a work, it accordingly licenses the copyright to the faculty creator or another party. Such a license would likely be enforceable under copyright law.[65] Licenses may be less preferable as a management device, but they are easier than transfers to adopt and implement.

Methods for Sharing of Rights

The next strategic decision for policymakers is to structure the allocation of rights. The substantive position in the policy for the ownership of rights could be of a limitless variety.[66] Return to the familiar example of the professor developing an online course. The policy could assume a position at one end of the spectrum or the other and grant all rights to the faculty member, to the university, or to another party. Or the policy could identify one of the infinite points in the middle and designate some allocation of rights among parties. This paper already has emphasized the pitfalls of granting all rights to either the instructor or the institution; either decision will jeopardize the legitimate interests of the other party. Allocating rights, however, can allow each party to have defined rights to use the work—or portions of it—without necessarily undercutting the needs of the other.

In the case of the online course, the rights can be allocated in a variety of ways. For example, the finished "work" can be divided into its constituent parts. The instructor may have contributed the substantive elements and may want to retain rights to use them in future teaching and publication. The institution and other staff members may have contributed the template and programming to make the course effective as a teaching tool; the university likely needs control of those resources for building additional courses.

With respect to each element, the parties may also want to share rights of use. Clearly, if the university is to disseminate the online course, it needs at least certain specified rights to use the substantive content. If the instructor holds the copyright to those elements, the policy can provide for defined rights to be granted to the university; all other rights obviously remain with the professor. Similarly, if the professor is responsible for sharing the course, he or she will need authority from the university to use the elements to which it retains the copyright.

Exactly where one draws lines to allocate rights can vary greatly depending on the project, the needs of the parties, and their objectives. But the policy—and appurtenant agreements—can be the vehicle for validly defining the rights and assuring them to each individual or institution. The policy is also an opportunity to address issues that are not inherent in the law.[67] For example, the law provides the copyright owner with rights to reproduce and make certain other uses of the work. The law, however, does not specifically secure rights to revenue,[68] or a right of an author to have named credit,[69] or necessarily the right to prepare updates and supplements as the original content drifts out of date.[70]

Experiments with Implementation

Various experiments with policies and implementation—including detailed efforts to address the "unbundling" of copyright—have surfaced at some universities around the country. One extensive consortium of state universities has adopted such a strategy of "unbundling" the rights associated with the copyright and to allocate those rights among the interested parties, at least as between the individual authors and the home university. Known as the Consortium for Educational

Technology for University Systems (CETUS), the group comprises the multicampus systems of California State University, the State University of New York, and the City University of New York.[71] CETUS ultimately recommends to its members a sharing of rights—that not all rights associated with the copyright should necessarily be vested with one party.[72]

The CETUS recommendations received renewed endorsement in a November 2003 policy report from the Academic Senate of the California State University. After a fuller examination of the issues and possibilities, the CSU report concludes that the university should: "Establish a framework for allocating or 'unbundling' rights associated with new works in order to make them most widely available for teaching, learning, and research." The report anticipates the procedural complexity of such policymaking with this recommendation:

> Provide standard agreement forms (licenses) for the university and the creator(s) to enter into in order to set out and clarify the ownership of copyrights, and the allocation of rights associated with specific projects and the new works which are created. Such *written* agreements, at the onset of a collaborative project and clarifying the rights of all contributors to collaborative works, are especially helpful if one or more of the authors wishes to work with a third party.

A few universities have undertaken elaborate steps to implement such agreements. The campus of Indiana University Purdue University Indianapolis (IUPUI) has begun using a "Memorandum of Understanding" that details the sharing of rights as between faculty authors and the university.[73] The document specifically grants to faculty members broad rights to use their works for future teaching, research, and publication. The institution retains rights to use the materials in connection with educational programming. The "MOU" includes further details about named credit for authors, rights to make changes and updates, and a sharing of any revenues. The document is not formal policy, but instead is recommended for adoption and management at each school of the IUPUI campus. Faculty members may then voluntarily agree to make specific projects subject to the terms of the MOU. The document is used principally to address rights to modules and materials developed for online education with special support from the institution.

Other universities have examined the issues and have chosen to take a less complicated approach. The Massachusetts Institute of Technology has created an ambitious program, called "OpenCourseWare," to make instructional materials developed and used at MIT available to the world on the Internet.[74] Legal ownership of the materials is governed by the standing policy of MIT to leave copyrights to "textbooks" with the faculty authors.[75] As a condition to posting materials, however, MIT asks individual faculty members to enter into a licensing agreement that confirms their ownership, but that also grants rights to the public to use the materials for noncommercial educational purposes.[76] In effect, the individual author retains copyright ownership, but is voluntarily permitting the university to disseminate the materials and in turn is allowing the public to use and build on them.

Unlike many other university programs, MIT's initiative is not the systematic delivery of distance education; MIT is instead seeking simply to share the good work of its faculty. MIT, therefore, does not have the same interest that another institution might have in maintaining, updating, and deploying any individual course. Relatively simple terms for intellectual property rights may serve MIT well. At IUPUI and at California State University, by contrast, ambitious programs for distance learning heighten the university's interest in assured rights to the instructional materials. At any of these institutions, the individual faculty authors have comparable interests in the integrity of their works, credit for their efforts, and use of their materials in future projects. In all examples, a sharing of rights of use is the goal; the difference is in determining the precise balance of rights.[77]

CONCLUSION AND RECOMMENDATIONS

Many of the issues related to copyright ownership at universities have been debated for years, but the latest line of court rulings brings considerable focus to the controversies. The law of "employees" and "independent contractors" continues to offer ample ground for dispute and fine-tuning of legal doctrines. Whether works were created "within the scope of employment," and whether the "teacher's exception" survives, will also engender continued debate.

Latest developments in the law, however, offer something resembling an answer to some of these issues—or at least a direction that courts appear to be heading toward. The latest cases make no mention of the "teacher's exception," exactly when it might have applied. The latest cases also have drawn the "scope of employment" to include not merely the products of staff photographers, but also instructional materials and research journal articles. Finally, the latest cases have undercut the authority of general policies to meet the statutory requirements for altering the default of copyright ownership. A general policy in the university manual simply is not likely to satisfy the writing and signature requirements of copyright law.

Policymakers at universities are left to grapple with these legal and administrative issues:

The doctrine of "works made for hire" likely applies broadly. Much of the copyrighted material created in academia, from official photographs to new teaching materials, may well be within the scope of the doctrine, and the copyrights may belong to the employer—at least in the eyes of the judge.

Shifting the copyright ownership requires compliance with formalities of written instruments and signatures. Simple transfers of copyrights or of any rights associated with a work must be documented in written instruments and be signed by the transferor. Agreements between employers and employees that similarly change the ownership of a work for hire must also be in writing and signed. Standard policy statements alone will not likely satisfy those requirements.

Management of copyrights may need to migrate from policies to agreements. If the law requires written and signed instruments, universities may need to begin developing and implementing a system of signed documents governing the ownership of copyrights. Of course, such a transformation of the system of copyright management would be an enormous administrative responsibility. Documents would have to reach every affected person, with assurance that they are signed and returned. The process would invariably stir numerous questions. Moreover, peculiar situations will need special attention, raise requests for negotiated exceptions, and engender simple resistance. Universities must prepare to invest in staff time and training programs to make this stewardship of intellectual property successful.

Written agreements are increasingly critical for innovative instructional materials. The growth of online education and the need to manage the legal rights yield greater need for certainty. Certainty is best achieved through written agreements. Instructional materials are at the center of university activity, and they are fundamental to the scholarship agenda of the faculty member. Online education also reaches broad audiences of students, whether through university programs or commercial programming. The wider reach means a greater interest in assuring control. The likelihood of enhanced revenue and the involvement of commercial distributors—as well as various other parties—raise the need for resolving potential disputes before they can arise. Agreements are the best method to meet those objectives.

Written agreements provide the flexibility to "unbundle" rights and to meet the diverse and changing interests associated with the vast range of copyrighted works created at universities. Again, innovative instructional materials illustrate the point well. The collaborative nature of online education, the diversity of the works, and the future potential for teaching and scholarship all underscore the importance of finding a formula for sharing rights between the faculty authors and the university, as well as among collaborators and other interested parties.

None of these critical issues, however, addresses perhaps the most fundamental concerns of policymakers. Universities still need to make the substantive decisions related to categories of works affected, the persons governed by the policy, and the position that the university will take in asserting a claim of rights as well as reserving specific rights to individuals. For now, however, the most recent cases from district courts tell relatively clearly that the need to reach these decisions is upon us, and the means for implementing policy decisions must become better defined and more systematically adopted.

NEXT STEPS

▶ (Re)Evaluate and develop a copyright policy at the institution that serves the fundamental needs of higher education in light of recent judicial decisions:
  - ▶ the policy should be written and signed to comply with law and to withstand judicial challenge;
  - ▶ the policy should clearly distinguish the provisions that apply to "employees" as distinguished from "independent contractors";
  - ▶ the policy should clearly define "works made for hire" and the work that falls "within the scope of employment" and the provisions applicable to such works;
  - ▶ the policy should articulate the terms, if any, for transferring copyrights or any rights associated with a work and should provide for written agreements, if transfers are necessary or desirable; and
  - ▶ the policy should provide for written agreements that address divisibility and unbundling of rights associated with individual works or various types of works.

▶ Take notice that a "teacher's exception" to the work-made-for-hire doctrine is in debate and may no longer have legal validity; therefore, institutions and individuals should not rely on this concept in determining copyright ownership, and policies and agreements should reflect this development.

ENDNOTES

[1] This article focuses on the question of ownership of the copyright, or the rights associated with copyright, to new works created at colleges and universities. The issue in this context will focus on instructional materials, but it also extends to research materials and other works. The issue of copyright ownership also arises in connection with the management of rights to faculty works, such as the decision to assign copyright to publishers, at the risk of inhibiting access to scholarship. Those issues are obviously relevant, but are outside the scope of this paper. *See generally* Mark S. Frankel, *Seizing the Moment: Scientists' Authorship Rights in the Digital Age,* Report of a Study by the American Association for the Advancement of Science (2002). See also the work of the Zwolle Group, infra note 77.

[2] One of the few articles to note that contracts are increasingly important to make up for the legal deficiencies of general policies is: Kimberly B. Kelley et al., I*ntellectual Property, Ownership and Digital Course Materials: A Study of Intellectual Property Policies at Two- and Four-Year Colleges and Universities,* 2 Portal: Libr. & Acad. 255, 262–63 (2002). *See also* Andrea L. Johnson, *Reconciling Copyright Ownership Policies for Faculty-Authors in Distance Education,* 33 J.L. & Educ. 431, 453 (2004) (urging faculty members and institutions to "negotiate a separate written contractual arrangement" rather than rely on policy).

[3] *See, e.g.,* Ashley Packard, *Copyright or Copy Wrong: An Analysis of University Claims to Faculty Work,* 7 Comm. L. & Pol'y 275, 276 (2002) (setting up the controversy with a focus on

sharing revenue). Another study astutely describes the "spaces of commercialization" within universities. Elizabeth Townsend, *Legal and Policy Responses to the Disappearing "Teacher Exception," or Copyright Ownership in the 21st Century University*, 4 Minn. Intell. Prop. Rev. 209, 212–20 (2003).

[4] One article examines reasons for the new attention given to copyright ownership at universities, resolving "The answer is simple: money." Gregory Kent Laughlin, *Who Owns the Copyright to Faculty-Created Web Sites?: The Work-for-Hire Doctrine's Applicability to Internet Resources Created for Distance Learning and Traditional Classroom Courses*, 41 B.C. L. Rev. 549, 556 (2000).

[5] Among the writings emphasizing this point: Packard, *supra* note 3, at 287-293; Mark L. Meyer, *To Promote the Progress of Science and Useful Arts: The Protection of and Rights in Scientific Research*, 39 IDEA 1, 13–16 (1998); Chanani Sandler, *Copyright Ownership: A Fundamental Of 'Academic Freedom'*, 12 Alb. L.J. Sci. & Tech. 231 (2001).

[6] Sandler, *supra* note 5, at 256–59. A complete list of forces motivating examination of the issues would also have to include the appurtenant interests of faculty unions. Michele J. Le Moal-Gray, *Distance Education and Intellectual Property: The Realities of Copyright Law and the Culture of Higher Education*, 16 Touro L. Rev. 981, 1025–30 (2000). A recent court ruling from the Kansas Supreme Court has affirmed the authority of the faculty union to include intellectual property issues in collective bargaining. Pittsburg State Univ. v. Kan. Bd. of Regents, 122 P.2d 336, 348 (Kan. 2005).

[7] The growth of distance education, and the potential to reuse instructional materials, has stirred much of the new interest in copyright ownership at universities. It also provides an opportunity to examine some of the most important aspects of the debate, ranging from revenue to credit. *See generally* Le Moal-Gray, *supra* note 6, 981–86.

[8] The Copyright Act itself does not specifically allow to the copyright owner control of uses itemized here. Instead, the law gives to copyright owners certain broad rights, notably the right to make and distribute copies, to make derivatives, and the rights to make public performances and displays. Posting materials to a Web site, creating updates, and licensing uses to others are a means of exercising those legal rights, and the copyright owner is entitled to charge a fee for such uses, and hence earn revenue. 17 U.S.C. § 106 (2000 & Supp. II 2003).

[9] *See*, for example, the policies mentioned in the *Manning* and *Forasté* cases.

[10] *See* Laughlin, *supra* note 4, at 580.

[11] Compounding the problem is the common fact that many creative elements of the finished course are likely the contributions of Web designers and other individuals. To designate either the instructor or the institution as the owner of the legal rights to the entire work is to ignore their interests.

[12] This point is not to be confused with "joint" copyright ownership, which allows multiple authors to be the "owner." In that case, each of the joint owners has all rights, with accountability to one another. This paper is addressing the situation of multiple parties holding separate and discrete rights of use that do not necessarily overlap. For the statute on joint ownership, *see* 17 U.S.C. § 201(a) (2000).

[13] The present author has made this similar point in various other publications. *See, e.g.,* Kenneth D. Crews, New Copyright Law for Distance Education: The Meaning and Importance of the TEACH Act (2003), http://www.copyright.iupui.edu/teach_summary.htm. This article will not elaborate on copyright fundamentals, recognizing that the basics of copyright law are available in many publications, including the writings of the present author. *See* Kenneth D. Crews, Copyright Law for Librarians and Educators (2d ed. 2006).

[14] 17 U.S.C. § 102(a) (2000).

[15] 17 U.S.C. §§ 401(a), 408(a) (2000).

[16] 17 U.S.C. § 201(a), (b) (2000).

[17] 17 U.S.C. § 201(b) (2000).

[18] Application of the work-made-for-hire doctrine also yields other important consequences. For example, the duration of copyright protection is significantly different. In the case of a general copyrighted work, the copyright lasts for the life of the author plus 70 years. In the case of a work made for hire, the copyright lasts for the shorter of either 95 years from publication or 120 years from creation of the work. In addition, some more subtle consequences include: a work made for hire is barred from having "moral rights," and a transfer of a work made for hire is not subject to statutory termination. These issues are beyond the scope of this paper. *See* 17 U.S.C. §§ 101, 203(a), 302, 304(c) (2000 & Supp. II 2003).

[19] 17 U.S.C. § 101 (2000 & Supp. II 2003).

[20] The U.S. Supreme Court made clear that the concept of "employee" for this purpose should draw upon the general principles of agency law. Cmty. for Creative Non-Violence v. Reid, 490 U.S. 730, 739–40 (1989).

[21] On the other hand, an adjunct faculty member who is paid a stipulated amount to teach a specified course with no further obligations may well be an "independent contractor." The doctrine of work made for hire can also apply to independent contractors, as examined later in this paper. Nevertheless, by concluding that full-time faculty members are likely to be "employees," this paper does not examine in any detail the legal analysis that has attempted to define the circumstances under which a person is by law an employee or an independent contractor.

[22] 17 U.S.C. § 101 (2000 & Supp. II 2003).

[23] Among the articles generally sympathetic to this position: Georgia Holmes and Daniel A. Levin, *Who Owns Course Materials Prepared by a Teacher or Professor?: The Application of Copyright Law to Teaching Materials in the Internet Age,* 2000 BYU Educ. & L.J. 165, 186–89 (2000); and Stephanie L. Seeley, *Are Classroom Lectures Protected by Copyright Laws?: The Case for Professors' Intellectual Property Rights,* 51 Syracuse L. Rev. 163, 173–78 (2001).

[24] Laughlin, *supra* note 4, at 573–76 (concluding nevertheless that "it is hard to imagine that a court would find that faculty-created scholarly articles, books and teaching materials are not prepared within the scope of employment"). A recent case allowed for the possibility that a high-school teacher may be the owner of instructional materials not specifically created for his own school and created on his own time. Pavlica v. Behr, 397 F. Supp. 2d 519, 525–26 (S.D.N.Y. 2005).

[25] Among the articles generally taking this position: Rochelle Cooper Dreyfuss, *The Creative Employee and the Copyright Act of 1976*, 54 U. Chi. L. Rev. 590, 594–605 (1987); Le Moal-Gray, *supra* note 6, at 1000–03; Meyer, *supra* note 5, at 3–6,16–19; Sandler, *supra* note 5, at 250–52 (arguing that faculty work is generally not within the "scope of employment" under the law); Todd F. Simon, *Faculty Writings: Are They "Works Made for Hire" Under the 1976 Copyright Act?*, 9 J.C. & U.L. 485 (1982–83); and Russ VerSteeg, *Copyright and the Educational Process: The Right of Teacher Inception*, 75 Iowa L. Rev. 381, 397–407 (1990). *See also* Sandler, *supra* note 5, at 240–46 (arguing that the teacher's exception remains valid law, largely because it has not been explicitly repealed and is consistent with the demands of academic freedom).

[26] Among the analyses generally taking this position: Packard, *supra* note 3, at 280–81.

[27] Put more generally, the previous Copyright Act, enacted in 1909, allowed for employees to hold the copyrights to their works, if custom or other circumstances implied an agreement placing ownership with that party. Because teachers customarily retained their copyrights, the law might enforce that result. The current law, however, requires an explicit agreement, in writing, and signed by the parties. *See* Melville B. Nimmer and David Nimmer, Nimmer on Copyright, § 5.03[D] (2004). Elsewhere, Nimmer seems to refer sympathetically to the "teacher's exception," at least as it might have existed under prior law. *Id.* at § 5.03[B][1][b]. For an example of a case decided under the 1909 law, see *Sherrill v. Grieves*, 57 Wash. L. Rep. 286 (Dist. of Columbia Supreme Court 1929). In addition, a California court held that a professor retained common-law rights to lectures. Williams v. Weisser, 78 Cal. Rptr. 542, 545 (Ct. App. 1969).

[28] By contrast, one analysis concludes after elaborate examination of the legislative history of the 1976 Act that the "teacher's exception" survives despite no mention of it in the new law. Townsend, *supra* note 3, at 227. ("The best explanation of why it was not mentioned is that none of the testifying witnesses *believed* the exception was at issue.").

[29] Seeley, *supra* note 23, at 173–74.

[30] *See, e.g.*, Hays v. Sony Corp. of Am., 847 F.2d 412 (7th Cir. 1988) (suggesting the possibility of a teacher's exception to the doctrine). Somewhat more convincing is *Weinstein v. University of Illinois*, 811 F.2d 1091 (7th Cir. 1987) holding that the faculty members retain the copyright to a research article, but as a matter of university policy interpretation. *Id.* at 1093–95. *See also* Laughlin, *supra* note 4, at 577. ("Judge Posner's conclusions, however, are dictum and have no binding, precedential value.")

[31] Laughlin, *supra* note 4, at 578 ("there is nothing in the 1976 Act to support a teachers' exception."). Another study notes that many university policies allow faculty to hold the copyrights to works that are created without "substantial" university resources and attributes that position to an application of the teacher's exception. Kelley et al., *supra* note 2, at 263.

[32] Under the statute, the following works are eligible for this treatment: "a work specially ordered or commissioned for use as a contribution to a collective work, as a part of a motion picture or other audiovisual work, as a translation, as a supplementary work, as a compilation,

as an instructional text, as a test, as answer material for a test, or as an atlas, if the parties expressly agree in a written instrument signed by them that the work shall be considered a work made for hire." 17 U.S.C. § 101 (2000 & Supp. II 2003).

[33] The statute defines an "instructional text" as "a literary, pictorial, or graphic work prepared for publication and with the purpose of use in systematic instructional activities." 17 U.S.C. § 101 (2000 & Supp. II 2003).

[34] 17 U.S.C. § 201(d)(2) (2000).

[35] 17 U.S.C. § 204 (2000).

[36] This point will be examined more closely later in this paper in connection with analysis of recent court rulings.

[37] 17 U.S.C. § 201(b) (2000).

[38] 17 U.S.C. § 201(b). Some commentators have raised concerns about the possibility that general university policies may not satisfy the specific requirements for written instruments and signatures that appear in the Copyright Act. *See, e.g.,* Roberta Rosenthal Kwall, *Copyright Issues in Online Courses: Ownership, Authorship and Conflict,* 18 Santa Clara Computer & High Tech. L.J. 1, 4 n.13, 5 n.17 (2001).

[39] Confirming this interpretation of section 201(b) is *Forasté v. Brown University,* 290 F.Supp.2d 234, 237–39 (D.R.I. 2003). For an explanation of the attributes of a work made for his, see *supra* notes 16–18.

[40] *See* cases at *supra* note 27.

[41] *See Reid,* 490 U.S. 730.

[42] At least one more case reinforces the trends identified in the four cases highlighted here, although it is not about higher education. In *Shaul v. Cherry Valley-Springfield Central School District,* 363 F. 3d 177 (2d Cir. 2004), the court ruled that instructional materials prepared by a school teacher are works made for hire and therefore belong to the employer. *Id.* at 185–6. The court also refused to apply an "academic" exception to the rule, suggesting that earlier cases limited such a concept to journal articles for publication, as opposed to instructional materials, and asserting that the exception applied only when an institutional policy provided for it. *Id.*

[43] Univ. of Colo. Found., Inc. v. Am. Cyanamid, 880 F. Supp. 1387, 1400–03 (D. Colo. 1995).

[44] *Id.* at 1400.

[45] *Id.*

[46] One can speculate why the faculty members may not have disputed the university's claim of ownership. One possibility would be if the faculty members owned the copyright individually, then they will be responsible for hiring expensive legal counsel to pursue the litigation on the infringement issue. Further, evidence in the case indicates that the article was written and infringed in 1981. It was not accepted for publication in a journal until the following year, at which time the copyright was assigned to the publisher. Once properly assigned, the faculty members gave up their rights anyway, so perhaps they saw little merit in claiming that they held the ownership for the year or so before executing the publication agreement. *Id.* at 1400 n.2.

[47] Vanderhurst v. Colo. Mountain Coll. Dist., 16 F. Supp. 2d 1297, 1307 (D. Colo. 1998).

[48] *Id.*

[49] *Id.*

[50] *Id.*

[51] Manning v. Bd. of Trs. of Cmty Coll. Dist. No. 505 (Parkland College), 109 F. Supp. 2d 976, 978–79 (C.D. Ill. 2000).

[52] *Id.*

[53] *Id.* at 979.

[54] *Id.* at 980.

[55] *Id.* at 980–81.

[56] Forasté v. Brown Univ., 248 F. Supp. 2d 71, 73–5 (D. R.I. 2003). For further, relevant litigation on in this case, see *Forasté v. Brown University*, 290 F.Supp.2d 234 (D.R.I. 2003).

[57] *Forasté*, 248 F.Supp.2d at 79–81.

[58] *Id.* at 81. In later litigation in the same case, the court more clearly emphasized the insufficiency of a general policy statement as a means for transferring copyrights. Forasté v. Brown Univ., 290 F. Supp. 2d 234, 239–41 (D.R.I. 2003).

[59] Subsequent litigation in one case made mention of such an exception, but did not adopt it as a rule of law. Forasté v. Brown Univ., 290 F. Supp. 2d 234, 239 (D.R.I. 2003) (calling it a "faculty exception").

[60] 17 U.S.C. § 201(d)(2) (2000).

[61] The ability to exploit the divisibility of the copyright is also subject to the writing and signature requirements of transfers. 17 U.S.C. § 204 (2000).

[62] For a general suggestion of the need for innovative policies, see Georgia Harper, *Developing a Comprehensive Copyright Policy to Facilitate Online Learning*, 27 J.C. & U.L. 5–12 (2000). This article will not give detailed attention to many individual policies, but will only examine a few by way of example. Other articles that take closer looks at some policies include: Kelley et al., *supra* note 2, at 255–66; Packard, *supra* note 3, at 293–309 (systematic analysis of policies from 70 universities); Townsend, *supra* note 3, at 244–74 (qualitative examination of several policies). *See also* Michael W. Klein, *"The Equitable Rule": Copyright Ownership of Distance-Education Courses*, 31 J.C. & U.L. 143, 175 (2004) ("The written document should be a comprehensive one that delineates not just ownership, but the rights and methods for using a work as well.").

[63] One study offers some insightful "guidelines" for policies on these issues, suggesting for example that institutions consider joint ownership of work, a "shop right" allowing the institutions to use new works, and more. Philip T.K. Daniel & Patrick D. Pauken, *The Impact of the Electronic Media on Instructor Creativity and Institutional Ownership within Copyright Law*, 132 Educ. L. Rep. 1, 18–20 (1999).

[64] Section 204 of the Copyright Act imposes a writing requirement for transfers, which are defined to include exclusive licenses, but not nonexclusive licenses. 17 U.S.C. § 204 (2000). The definition of "transfer" is at *id.*, § 101. The parties in the university example, however, may not be satisfied with a nonexclusive license. For example, if the law deems a

faculty work to be "for hire," the policy can license rights of use to the faculty author. However, if the license is nonexclusive, the university could grant the same rights to others—surely to the chagrin of the faculty author.

[65] The validity of such a license may be subject to contract principles or the law of employment relations, but those issues are outside the scope of this paper. In addition to the license possibility, a policy position granting certain rights to someone other than the copyright owner may have some legal validity under estoppel or other equitable doctrine that might bar the university from seeking rights that it had granted to someone under a properly adopted policy.

[66] For example, one commentator concludes that the "teacher's exception" survives today in policy statements, rather than in the law. Townsend, *supra* note 3, at 210.

[67] The fundamental rights of the copyright owner are listed at 17 U.S.C. § 106 (2000 & Supp. II 2003).

[68] Copyright owners generally derive revenue by granting to others the ability to exercise the legal rights, in exchange for payment of a fee, often called a royalty.

[69] Limited rights to have credit associated with a copyrighted work only recently have become part of the law. In 1990, Congress added limited "moral rights" that included the right of an artist to prevent removal of his or her name on some works of art, 17 U.S.C. § 106A (2000). In 1998, Congress added a right to prevent under some circumstances the removal of "copyright management information," which could include the author's name, 17 U.S.C. § 1202 (2000). Outside of copyright law, authors have occasionally asserted with some success under trademark law or the law of unfair competition a right to be named on a work.

[70] Depending on circumstances, the updates or supplements may be "derivative works" and thus within the rights of the copyright owner. Whether any particular planned update is or is not a derivative work, detailing the right of the faculty member or institution to make updates would be an important point to clarify under the terms of the policy.

[71] For the original studies prepared by CETUS in the 1990s, *see* CETUS: Consortium for Educational Technology in University Systems, http://www.cetus.org/ (last visited Sept. 7, 2005). More recently, California State University has prepared an updated and revised version of the studies on copyright law. For that report, *see The Academic Senate of the Cal. State Univ., Intellectual Property, Fair Use, and the Unbundling of Ownership Rights* (2003), http://www.calstate.edu/AcadSen/Records/Reports/Intellectual_Prop_Final.pdf. The present author was a consultant to this project and wrote significant portions of the copyright papers.

[72] For a more detailed examination of the CETUS position, see Townsend, *supra* note 3, at 246–51.

[73] For information about the MOU, *see* Copyright Management Center, Managing the Rights to Use Works Created at the University, http://www.copyright.iupui.edu/dl_faq.htm (last visited Sept. 7, 2005).

[74] For information about OpenCourseWare, *see* MIT OpenCourseWare, http://ocw.mit.edu/index.html (last visited Sept. 7, 2005).

[75] MIT Policies and Procedures, Section 13.1.2. According to the FAQs associated with OpenCourseWare, "Faculty retain ownership of most materials prepared for MIT OCW, following the MIT policy on textbook authorship. MIT retains ownership only when significant use has been made of the Institute's resources." *See* MIT OpenCourseWare, MIT OCW Help, http://ocw.mit.edu/OcwWeb/Global/OCWHelp/help.htm#FAQ3 (last visited Sept. 7, 2005).

[76] The license is modeled on terms developed by the Creative Commons initiative. *See* MIT OpenCourseWare, License: Creative Commons—MIT Open CourseWare License 1.0, http://ocw.mit.edu/OcwWeb/Global/license.htm (last visited Sept. 7, 2005).

[77] The "Zwolle Group" is an international project, promoting the creation of policies that adapt ownership interest to the variable balance of interests among various parties. *See* SURF, Copyright Management for Scholarship, http://www.surf.nl/copyright/ (last visited Sept. 7, 2005).

▶3

FAIR USE AND LICENSING

PEGGY E. HOON
CHERYL L. DAVIS

This chapter discusses the following topics:
- ▶ An overview of fair use—its purposes and the decision-making processes involved in its determination
- ▶ A review of relevant court decisions with an analysis of fair use factors in light of judicial trends
- ▶ The application of fair use to materials that are licensed, but not owned
- ▶ The challenges posed by licensing copyrighted materials in the digital environment, specifically for online instruction

INTRODUCTION

A faculty member decides to enhance a copyrighted musical score with additional instrumentation for a concert. An assistant copies an entire journal each month for everyone in the chemistry department. An academic librarian provides electronic access to a journal article for a class in anthropology. A graduate student wants to include some photographs of the 1982 World's Fair in her dissertation. Are these uses of copyrighted materials fair ones, or are they infringing on the rights of the copyright owners?

Fair use is a concept that advances the intent of copyright law, to "promote the progress of science and the useful arts"[1] by allowing the copying and use of copyrighted materials in certain circumstances. Until the Copyright Act was revised in 1976, fair use determinations were made by the courts, with each case outcome depending on its own specific fact situation. This is still true. Although now codified, fair use remains fact-based and dependent on individual circumstances. While this can seem daunting, it does provide some assurance that each case can be analyzed and decided within its own context.

Fair use is a valuable tool and one that is often misunderstood and misapplied. It is a gray area, where some invoke fair use for nearly every use and others refuse to assert it under any circumstances. When faced with the additional challenge of determining fair use of licensed materials, it can be tempting to give up on it altogether. It is, however, deserving of close consideration by those who use copyrighted materials, whether in a classroom, on a Web site, in a new work, or elsewhere. This chapter will explain the purposes of fair use, describe the decision-making processes involved, and analyze the application of fair use to materials that are licensed but not owned.

THE FAIR USE STATUTE

When the fair use doctrine was made part of the Copyright Act in 1976, Congress provided general guidelines that both the courts and users of copyrighted information can use to decide whether a particular use is a fair one or if it is copyright infringement. Congress intentionally avoided establishing strict boundaries to fair use and instead passed into law the factors upon which the courts had come to rely.[2] It is left up to the user, then, to decide whether the use she has in mind will be a fair one, and to the courts to resolve the issue should the copyright owner disagree. Fortunately, both the user and the courts are operating with the same set of factors.

The statute is short, but not simple:

§ 107. Limitations on exclusive rights: Fair use

Notwithstanding the provisions of sections 106 and 106A, the fair use of a copyrighted work, including such use by reproduction in copies or phonorecords or by any other means specified by that section, for purposes such as criticism, comment, news reporting, teaching (including multiple copies for classroom use), scholarship, or research, is not an infringement of copyright. In determining whether the use made of a work in any particular case is a fair use the factors to be considered shall include—

(1) the purpose and character of the use, including whether such use is of a commercial nature or is for nonprofit educational purposes;

(2) the nature of the copyrighted work;

(3) the amount and substantiality of the portion used in relation to the copyrighted work as a whole; and

(4) the effect of the use upon the potential market for or value of the copyrighted work.

The fact that a work is unpublished shall not itself bar a finding of fair use if such finding is made upon consideration of all the above factors.[3]

Each of the four factors must be considered in order to make a decision about a particular use. The statute does not favor any particular factor (although some courts do), and failing to find fair use for any factor will not defeat the use—it is all a matter of balance. An explanation of each factor follows, with examples that demonstrate how courts have treated specific fact situations. Examined separately, the factors concentrate on various issues of copyright ownership and public bene-fit; taken together, they provide a means to balance these often conflicting notions.

THE FIRST FACTOR: PURPOSE AND CHARACTER OF THE USE

This factor applies to the proposed use of the material. Is it going to be used for educational, nonprofit purposes? In an academic setting, the use will most often be educational, but that does not end the inquiry. The simple fact that a use takes place on a college or university campus does not make it fair—an educational use can also be commercial, as in the case of a textbook authored by a faculty member. The amount used may be too substantial. In an extreme case involving Internet piracy, fair use was used as a defense for a file-sharing service that offered illegal copies of commercial software. The defendants, known as "Pirates With Attitude," or PWA, claimed educational fair use and used as proof the fact that a professor was involved in its activities, the students were learning about the software, and the project was housed on a university campus. The court was not persuaded. Not only did the other fair use factors fail to support PWA's activities, but the professor in-volved had taken pains to hide the project server in a closet. The university was un-aware of his activities.[4]

Most educational fair use issues do not involve such radical activities, but faculty understanding of fair use can nonetheless be critical. A faculty member who posts an entire textbook, chapter by chapter, within a password-protected class Web site can be as culpable as the professor who worked with the PWA. Educational use alone will not support fair use.

In some situations, the concept of "transformative use" may come into play, which refers to the second prong of this factor, the "character" of the use. Trans-formative use adds new content or meaning to a work, thereby creating a different sort of work, for example, a work of parody or a critical review. The more transfor-mative the use, the more likely the use will be considered a fair one.

An example of transformative use is found in the case of *Faulkner v. National Geographic Society*.[5] The Society had created a poster consisting of past magazine covers to celebrate its anniversary, and Faulkner, a freelance photographer who held the copyright to some of the cover art used, objected. Along with weighing the other three fair use factors, the court found the poster to be a transformative use of the past covers and therefore a fair use. On appeal, the court's decision was largely upheld, except as to seven photographs that were protected by specific contractual language.

THE SECOND FACTOR: NATURE OF THE COPYRIGHTED WORK

To evaluate the second factor, determine whether the copyrighted work is artistic and creative, as in a work of fiction, or factual, as in a scholarly article. It is easier to assert fair use in factual works than in creative ones. Also important is whether the work has been published. Works that are published are more easily subjected to fair use than unpublished works, since the right of a creator to decide when to publish a work is highly valued in copyright law. A case involving reclusive author J.D. Salinger analyzes both of these aspects of the nature of a work.

In 1986, Salinger sued to enjoin the publication of an unauthorized biography of his life. In writing the biography, author Ian Hamilton had quoted extensively from unpublished letters written by Salinger that had been donated to libraries by their recipients. The court held that Hamilton's use of the letters was not fair use, and the opinion of the court is instructive to researchers similarly inclined. First, Hamilton could have recited facts as he found them in the letters, but he preferred to quote directly and closely paraphrase Salinger's words, which the court considered to be Salinger's copyrightable expression rather than simple facts. Second, Salinger's decision not to publish his letters was compelling—his right to decide when, where, or if to publish them outweighed Hamilton's right to make fair use of them.[6]

THE THIRD FACTOR: AMOUNT AND SUBSTANTIALITY

How much of the work is being used? Is it one chapter from a book, or most of the book? Is it one stanza of a song or the entire song? How should fair use be gauged with respect to photographs?

This factor requires consideration of how much of the work as a whole is being used. Naturally, the decision that a use is fair becomes easier as the portion of the work used grows smaller, but it is possible that even an entire photograph can be subject to fair use, as in the National Geographic case discussed earlier.

The outcome of this factor relies heavily on the specific facts of each use. It applies not only to the actual amount used from the copyrighted work, but how much of the work as a whole is being used. Since works vary greatly, from short poems to full-length treatises, the amount that can be used has been the subject of several attempts to define just how much use is fair use.

One of these is commonly known as the Classroom Guidelines. Found in a House Report incorporated into the 1976 Copyright Act, the "Agreement on Guidelines for Classroom Copying in Not-for-Profit Educational Institutions"[7] provides some fairly strict, and not very practical, limits for classroom copying.

Although quite detailed, they do not effectively serve the needs of colleges and universities, since many readings assigned to undergraduates and graduate students will far exceed their limits. While the House Report acknowledges this limited value, describing their purpose as "stat[ing] the minimum and not the maximum standards of educational fair use,"[8] timid users are unlikely to reach beyond the stated boundaries.

The Classroom Guidelines also do not address the problems that arise when using electronic resources, and a subsequent attempt to design guidelines for the digital era found more disagreement than consensus. From 1994 to 1998, a working group consisting of universities, publishers, library associations, scholarly societies, government agencies, and other organizations held a series of meetings in an effort to create guidelines for fair use as applied to digital images, distance learning, educational multimedia, electronic reserves, interlibrary loan, and the use of computer software in libraries. Their work, known as the Conference on Fair Use, or CONFU, was summarized in a final report in 1998.[9]

No agreement was reached on guidelines, but the report contains proposals for digital images, distance learning, and educational multimedia. Limitations are set for the proportion of material used, for how long, and to whom the copies are distributed.[10] While CONFU was instructive in discovering the problems inherent in devising limits for fair use in electronic media, the usefulness of the proposals is quite limited; since no consensus was reached, they do not provide the safe harbor that many had hoped for.

THE FOURTH FACTOR: EFFECT OF USE ON POTENTIAL MARKET FOR OR VALUE OF WORK

Although Congress intended that none of the four factors weigh more heavily than the others, market effect is certainly one of the most discussed. Fortunately, few fair use cases directly address academic activities, but two merit discussion. The first is *Princeton University Press v. Michigan Document Services (MDS)*.[11] MDS copied and sold "course-packs," collections of copyrighted materials chosen by professors for particular classes. It did not ask for permission to copy from the copyright owners, nor did it pay permission fees, as did other copy shops. MDS lost on every factor, but the case is important for the court's treatment of the fourth factor—it found that the potential market for the works from the collection of permission fees would be damaged if the practices of MDS became widespread.[12]

American Geophysical Union v. Texaco, Inc.[13] dealt with a practice uncomfortably familiar to most academics, the copying of articles for one's own personal research use, but the practices complained of in the case can be distinguished from those of most researchers. There, the court found an "institutional, systematic, archival multiplication of copies"[14] that threatened journal subscriptions and revenue from permission fees. The case is important for its focus on the availability of licensing entities, such as the Copyright Clearance Center, when considering market impact, but it did leave room for academic researchers to continue to copy articles. The scientists in Texaco were working on research in a for-profit setting. In its decision, the court noted that it was not dealing with individual copying by a professor or scientist for personal research; fair use is still available so long as the analysis of the four factors can reasonably be supported.

The Supreme Court has said that the effect of a use on the potential market for or value of a copyrighted work is the single most important element of fair use,[15] but it is important to remember that balancing the four factors must still occur; it is still possible to "lose" the fourth factor and "win" the other three to reach a conclusion of fair use.

FAIR USE IN THE LEGISLATURE

Vast changes in technology have occurred since the legislature made fair use part of the Copyright Act in 1976, and in attempting to keep pace with these changes, Congress often acts in ways that negatively affect fair use. For example, the Digital Millennium Copyright Act of 1998 was ostensibly intended to amend the Copyright Act to conform with international treaties, but it contains "anticircumvention" provisions that make fair use not only difficult, but unlawful.[16] Although a provision of the law asserts that it will not affect fair use, the reality is that the practice of copying a small portion of a work, if made impossible by technology, is also made unlawful if that technology is circumvented.

In March 2005, a bill was introduced in the House of Representatives that would restore fair use to the works protected by the DMCA. If passed, which is by no means guaranteed, the bill would remove the penalties for circumvention for non-infringing uses, such as fair use.[17] This scenario of passing a new law to fix problems with an old one is not unusual, and it illustrates how difficult it is for legislation to effectively keep up with technological advances.

FAIR USE AND DIGITAL MATERIALS

The notion of fair use has now gone far beyond photocopying journal articles or showing recorded video clips; with more information available digitally, libraries and faculty members can reach their audiences across time and space. Libraries make fair use of materials they place on reserve, including those in e-reserves. But what use is fair use? The Association of College and Research Libraries has posted on its Web site a "Statement on Fair Use and Electronic Reserves," which explains the operation of fair use in this particular electronic environment.[18]

Libraries are also some of the greatest providers of digital collections, whether they are small collections for the use of a faculty member in an art or architecture class or a large special collection of items owned by the institution. Certainly there is reliance on fair use in making these collections available to scholars and researchers. Institutions take various steps to ensure that users understand the limits of fair use. For example, the Indiana University's Digital Images Delivered Online contains over 320,000 images; availability is limited to those with an Indiana University ID and password.[19] SPIRO, at the University of California, Berkeley, provides thumbnail images to all users, and larger images to members of the UC community.[20] Both universities provide users with copyright information and terms of use.

Outside the library, faculty members use course management systems such as Blackboard or WebCT to present class materials, including copyrighted materials. Use of such systems is likely to grow. In a 2003 study of the University of Wisconsin system, 80 percent of the responding faculty used a course management system to supplement face-to-face learning, and two-thirds reported increasing their use as they gained experience with the system.[21] Because the content is accessible only to those enrolled in a particular course, it is impossible to know how much material is presented using these systems, or even if some faculty members don't realize that they would be infringing if not for fair use.

Many institutions have policies in place to encourage fair use, which not only provide guidance but also may offer some protection to their members. Section 504(c)(2) of the Copyright Act authorizes the remission of statutory damages if the infringer honestly believes that his/her use was a fair use and is acting as an employee of a nonprofit educational institution, library, or archives.[22]

The Copyright Act is intended to be technology-neutral. In fact, the language of the act is deliberately broad enough to encompass any form of fixation "now known or later developed" (17 U.S.C. § 102(a) [2000]). Using works from the Web and placing works on the Web are governed by the same fair use considerations and the same fair use analysis as using their print counterparts.[23]

FAIR USE AND LICENSING

No discussion of fair use and the online digital environment of higher education would be complete without addressing the ever-increasing role of licensing in the access to and use of copyrighted works. In the past, materials used on campuses were primarily in print format (or film, i.e., not digital), the physical copies were almost always purchased, and they typically did not come with licenses governing their uses. Purchased materials, as opposed to licensed materials, are generally subject only to the Copyright Act rather than specific license terms. Use of these materials for teaching or research purposes was governed by the Copyright Act and case law interpreting its provisions. Uses on campus were, therefore, generally pursuant to section 107 (Fair Use), section 108 (the library provisions), and section 110 (the performance and display exemptions) of the Copyright Act.[24] Face-to-face classroom performances and displays of copyrighted materials have been, and continue to be, covered by section 110(1), while transmissions of performances and displays fall within the more restrictive Section 110(2). Before the advent of online classes, such transmissions were largely conducted through televised classes, and some of the materials transmitted via this route were undoubtedly covered by a license. Another common use of licenses on campus before the Internet involved the public performance of copyrighted music outside the classroom setting. Generally, most campuses had long-standing license agreements in place with ASCAP or BMI[25] for use of music in public performances of plays, concerts, choirs, and the like. Licenses, however, were not particularly prevalent in other campus locations such as the library or in the classroom.

The last 15 to 20 years have seen a tremendous increase in the use of licenses and licensed materials on campuses, particularly in the library but also in the context of the push to place more courses and course materials online. According to the Association of Research Libraries (ARL), as of 2002–2003, expenditures for electronic resources consumed, on average, 25 percent of ARL institutions' library budgets, amounting to some $228 million spent annually.[26] In fact, ARL library spending on electronic serials had increased 171 percent since the 1999–2000 survey and by more than 1800 percent since such spending was first reported in 1994–1995.[27] The authors' own institution, the NCSU Libraries, owned or leased just 21 electronic resources in 1993–1994. Ten years later, that figure was 267,172.[28]

Significantly, most, if not all, of the electronic resources accessible online through library subscriptions are now leased, rather than owned. This is a huge shift from past and current practice for print materials. That is, when a library acquires print materials, either journals or books, it owns the physical copy, and it owns it forever. Under the First Sale doctrine of copyright law (section 109), the library can loan its copy to whomever it chooses.[29] If the copy becomes lost, damaged, deteriorated, obsolete, or is stolen, section 108 allows a replacement copy to be made under certain conditions.[30] The materials are owned, not leased pursuant to a license.

The use of third party copyrighted materials by other entities on campus has also grown as more and more faculty move their courses or portions of their courses online. These activities may well intersect with licensing in several ways. First, the faculty member may seek permission to post the copyrighted work online, and this permission may take the form of a license. Alternately, the faculty member may simply desire to repost material originally accessed or obtained through one of the library's licensed resources. Or the faculty member may want to repost materials found at another Web site that has terms and conditions of use that may or may not require an express act of acceptance (click-wrap vs. browse-wrap).

So how does licensing affect rights, like fair use, already present under the Copyright Act?

LICENSING IN THE LIBRARY

Focusing first on the lion's share of third party materials accessed and used on campuses brings one squarely to the library's electronic resources, largely electronic journals and databases. The primary mode of acquisition for these materials is via a license between a vendor and the library or its parent institution. (Academic libraries are not usually separate legal entities capable of entering into a binding license agreement; at best they may have been delegated signature authority and can act in these circumstances on behalf of the parent institution.)

Although termed "licenses," which may also simply be a permission to engage in certain behavior including the use of property, the library's electronic resource agreements are more accurately labeled "contracts." If the required elements of a contract are present, including offer, acceptance, and consideration, it is reasonable to assume, as a starting point, that the contract is probably enforceable. It is also reasonable and prudent for the library to actively interact with the proposed license, i.e., negotiate it. "Negotiate," in a broad sense, should include reading and understanding the license; reconciling the permissions granted with the information needs (access and use) of the library's users now and in the future; and being willing and able to comply with any obligations imposed on the library itself. It is critical, then, that the library negotiator(s) has a thorough and working knowledge of the qualities and characteristics of the resource being licensed as well as how the users need to use it. This will allow the negotiator to make better decisions concerning what license terms are acceptable and what terms are not.

In developing its negotiating position, the library is well advised to consult any of the various library licensing principles and guidelines that have been devised in recent years by library associations and organizations. ARL's Principles for Licensing Electronic Resources was developed by multiple major library associations and is an excellent resource.[31] Similarly, the Statement of Current Perspective and Preferred Practices for the Selection of Electronic Information developed by the International Coalition of Library Consortia (ICOLC)[32] and the licensing principles promulgated by the International Federation of Library Associations (IFLA)[33] provide bedrock guidance for libraries in the licensing arena. These general principles, as well as licensing workshops, online materials, Webcasts, and other written materials like Yale's Liblicense site (http://www.library.yale.edu/~llicense/index.shtml), are the library community's response to the rapidly accelerating proliferation of licensed materials in the library.[34] Such resources represent the recognition that today's acquisitions librarian must quickly develop a skill set that includes some legal knowledge and understanding of common contract terms as well as an ability to bargain effectively. In fact, consultation with the institution's legal counsel over specific language in the license may or may not be required by policy, but is often a good idea.

In particular, the library needs to scrutinize the sections of a proposed license that address authorized uses of the material to ensure that uses otherwise permitted by law are not lost or given up. Do any "use" restrictions in the license encroach upon rights granted by the Copyright Act such as fair use, performance and display rights or the library exemptions? Are these "use" restrictions enforced by technological control measures such as print controls? Such restrictions in a negotiated, bargained-for, signed contract will govern the use of the materials—not copyright law. If the library makes a bad bargain, it will be stuck with it.

Look carefully at licensing terms that only permit printing a single copy, for example, or ones that forbid sharing in any format with someone outside the authorized users. Beware of clauses that prohibit electronic reserves or limit electronic interlibrary loans, and so on. Remember, fair use is a right that can be easily contracted away, and libraries should not assume that both parties to the license will necessarily act with the public's best interest in mind.

Therefore, strike or remove restrictive use language at odds with fair use. At a minimum, insert specific fair use language, such as "Nothing in this license shall in any way exclude, modify, or affect any of the Licensee's statutory or common law rights under the Copyright law of the United States." Many licensors will agree to this language and, in fact, a copyright holder may attempt to require a user to contract out of fair use. A contract that specifically prohibits fair use may be impermissible under the doctrine of federal preemption.[35]

In addition to including language that specifically preserves fair use, the library should remove language that would make it responsible for the behavior of its users. This should be intuitive, since the library has no meaningful ability to prospectively control the behavior of library users and should not promise that it will. It cannot "protect the intellectual property" of the licensor or promise that its users will not breach any of the license terms (the users are not parties to the license anyway). The most the library can undertake are "reasonable" efforts to inform its users of the general terms and then engage in a cooperative investigation should a user allegedly exceed fair use. Finally, the library should recognize that many vendors are fully capable of tracking uses and downloads that may exceed the license terms.

LICENSING BEYOND THE LIBRARY

Similar concerns should control in situations where a faculty member or other campus entity negotiates a license for use of copyrighted materials. However, locations outside the library are often not as aware of copyright and fair use rights and may benefit from online informational licensing resources. As a general proposition, fair use and other rights should not be given away without a compelling reason.

Faculty members who wish to repost material on their course Web site that they obtained from their library's licensed resource need to consult their librarian before doing so. Many licenses for electronic resources specifically forbid this, and it is very difficult to rectify this term.

CLICK-THROUGHS AND BROWSE-WRAPS

Sometimes libraries acquire materials, physically or online, that are accompanied by an electronic license agreement. In order to access, use, and/or install the materials, some express manifestation of assent to the terms—like clicking "I Accept" or "I Agree"—is required. Are these agreements enforceable? Who has the authority to "click" on behalf of the library or the parent institution? What happens if the electronic license screen comes up as the library is setting up access to a resource already covered by a fully negotiated and executed license—which license controls?

The law concerning the validity or enforceability of click-through (sometimes called "click-wraps") licenses is still evolving, although they are more likely to be upheld if the following conditions are present. These conditions were compiled by the Working Group on Electronic Contracting Practices from the Business Law Section of the American Bar Association in 2001.[36]

▶ **Opportunity to Review Terms**
The intended licensee should have a meaningful opportunity to review the license terms, and this review should happen before the intended licensee can access the licensed materials. The terms should be easy to read at the licensee's own pace and viewable throughout the entire assent process.

▶ **Display of Terms**
The electronic license must be as legally proper and sufficient as the analogous paper license in terms of applicable law concerning layout, conspicuousness, notice requirements, and so forth. For example, various statutes and regulations like the Uniform Commercial Code may specify disclosure language, legible font size, and format of assent. It should also be consistent with other content on the site or with the product.

▶ **Acceptance or Rejection of Terms**
There should be a clear method for actively choosing to accept or decline the terms. Access to the licensed material must be conditioned upon acceptance, and this should be clear to the licensee in advance.

▶ **Opportunity to Correct Errors**
A reasonable opportunity to correct likely errors should be part of the process if the individual is assenting to an agreement involving multiple choices or input of information. Providing an online summary of order specifications would be such an error correction mechanism.

▶ **Keep Records to Prove Assent**
Records showing the format and content of the electronic license, as well as the acceptance process, in successive versions should be kept, particularly in accordance

with any records retention laws that may apply. If records concerning a particular licensee's acceptance are maintained, compliance with privacy laws is important. Licensees should be able to print and store a copy of the license and their acceptance.

While these recommended practices by the ABA would enhance the enforceability of a click-through license, the absence of any of these conditions should not lead the library licensee to assume the license is invalid and, therefore, that the terms can be safely ignored. It is important to treat all of these licenses as potentially enforceable, although the ability to negotiate the terms may be nil. It is also important for librarians and faculty members to have a clear understanding of their institution's position on who has authority to bind the institution and how that authority is properly exercised. An employee without signature authority is, generally speaking, not able to commit the institution to a contract. It follows that only those authorized to commit on behalf of the institution in print should be able to commit the institution electronically through clicking the "I Accept" button. The unauthorized "clicker" may have only bound him or herself and not the institution. Depending on how the situation is corrected, this may affect the user's ability to access the resource. The authors' library, for example, does not acquire electronic resources through electronic click-through licenses. Since we do not have authority to sign for the institution, we also do not have authority to "click" on behalf of the institution.

If the library has already negotiated the license for a particular resource and a second "standard" (and likely inconsistent) click-through license appears when setting up access to the resource, the library should not click through. Stop the access process and clarify with the licensor in writing that the negotiated license is the controlling document and remove the click-through. Although there is a good chance that the negotiated license terms would prevail should a dispute arise, it is better to be sure at the outset.

Lastly, more and more faculty are finding and using third party copyrighted materials from online Web sites with no click-through agreements in place. It is quite common for Web sites to simply post terms and conditions of use on a page linked from the Web site's homepage. These are "browse-wrap" agreements, where agreement is implied by simply continuing to access the Web pages. The terms and conditions of use are intended to describe permitted as well as prohibited types of uses and conditions that might be imposed. For example, many sites allow their materials to be used for nonprofit educational uses, but not for commercial purposes. Some may require proper attribution or notification of use. Any number of conditions can be enumerated. Indeed, a widely publicized effort to encourage copyright holders to allow certain uses of their works for free resulted in the establishment of the nonprofit organization Creative Commons[37] in 2001. Very early on

Creative Commons released a set of copyright licenses free for public use with an online tool that allowed users to select license term features and, in effect, design their own licenses.

Are such browse-wrap licenses enforceable? They are certainly ubiquitous and can even be found on university library Web sites, particularly when special collections have been digitized and placed online. Such collections are usually limited to scholarly and research purposes and prohibit commercial uses. Are prohibitions against commercial use of the site materials enforceable? Without the express consent to terms evidenced by clicking on an "I Accept" or "I Agree" button, is there sufficient evidence that a user has had an opportunity to read and consent to a site's terms? The cases in this area are few, divided, and limited to their facts. Two early cases upholding the enforceability of a browse-wrap agreement involved the unsympathetic practice by one commercial entity of methodically "screen scraping" information from the site of its competitor.[38] On the other hand, a leading case rejected the validity of a browse-wrap agreement in which the individual being sued was invited by the site in question to download software. The opportunity to download came at a point on the Web page where the otherwise inconspicuous terms and conditions link was not even visible without scrolling.[39]

Analyzing and extrapolating from these cases, the ABA working group has suggested the following practices to increase the likelihood of a browse-wrap agreement's enforceability:[40]

▶ provide the user with adequate notice of the existence of the proposed terms;

▶ give the user a meaningful opportunity to review the proposed terms;

▶ provide the user with adequate notice that taking a specified action (like use of the site) manifests assent to the terms; and

▶ note that the user takes the action specified in the notice.

CONCLUSION

There is very little reason to doubt that we now live in a world where every digital bit of information can and may well be licensed. The ability of licensors to remotely monitor and track both uses and potential license term violations will continue to grow. Technological rights control measures will become increasingly sophisticated and will enable licensors to prospectively enforce the terms of the license. Terms that are legitimately subject to different interpretations by reasonable minds, such as "fair use," are particularly at risk. It will not matter much that a license permits fair use if the licensee thinks two copies of an article is fair use but the licensor sets a printing control for one.

Academics and librarians have long assumed the role of champions for fair use rights both in practice and in the legislative arena. Legislation is consistently introduced, and occasionally passed, that significantly strengthens the rights of copyright holders at the expense of fair use. Without sustained awareness and vigilance, fair use will continue to shrink either through restrictive licenses or the intended or unintended consequences of congressional law-making activity. Through careful attention to license terms, firm retention of fair use rights, and an active awareness of proposed changes to the law that restructures either, academics and librarians can extend the life expectancy of fair use in the digital world.

NEXT STEPS

▶ Develop and disseminate an institutional policy on who has authority to negotiate, accept, and exercise the terms of any license agreements for materials and resources.

▶ Develop a policy on click-through and browse-wrap agreements.

▶ Understand the parameters of fair use and protect fair uses; remain informed and vigilant about challenges to fair use, both in practice and the legislative arenas.

ENDNOTES

[1] U.S. CONST. art. I, § 8.

[2] That the House Report intended section 107 to allow for individual determinations is clear: "Indeed, since the doctrine is an equitable rule of reason, no generally applicable definition is possible, and each case raising the question must be decided on its own facts. On the other hand, the courts have evolved a set of criteria which, though in no case definitive or determinative, provide some gauge for balancing the equities." H.R. Rep. No. 94–1476 (1976).

[3] 17 U.S.C. § 107 (2000 & Supp. II 2003).

[4] *United States v. Slater*, 348 F.3d 666 (7th Cir. 2003).

[5] 294 F. Supp. 2d 523 (S.D.N.Y. 2003), *aff'd* in part, *rev'd* in part, and *remanded*, 409 F.3d 26 (2d Cir. 2005), *cert denied* 126 S. Ct. 833 (2005).

[6] *Salinger v. Random House, Inc.*, 811 F.2d 90 (2d Cir. 1987).

[7] H.R. Rep. No. 94-1476 (1976).

[8] *Id.*

[9] Bruce A. Lehman, *The Conference on Fair Use: Final Report to the Commissioner on the Conclusion of the Conference on Fair Use* (1998), *available at* http://www.uspto.gov/web/offices/dcom/olia/confu/confurep.pdf.

[10] An excellent overview of the proposed guidelines for multimedia use is provided by the University of Texas. Copyright Crash Course, Fair Use Guidelines for Educational Multimedia, http://www.utsystem.edu/ogc/intellectualproperty/ccmguid.htm (last visited Aug. 31, 2005).

[11] 99 F.3d 1381 (6th Cir. 1996).

[12] *Id.* at 1387.

[13] 60 F.3d 913 (2d Cir. 1994).

[14] *Id.* at 931.

[15] *Harper & Row, Publishers, Inc. v. Nation Enters.*, 471 U.S. 539 (1985).

[16] 17 U.S.C. § 1201 (2000).

[17] Digital Media Consumers' Rights Act of 2005, H.R. 1201, 109th Cong. (2005). The United States Copyright Office maintains a list of bills that affect copyright law on its Web site, at http://www.copyright.gov/legislation/.

[18] *Ass'n of College and Research Libraries, Statement on Fair Use and Electronic Reserves* (2003), http://www.ala.org/ala/acrl/acrlpubs/whitepapers/statementfair.htm.

[19] Indiana University, DIDO: Digital Images Delivered Online, http://www.dlib.indiana.edu/collections/dido/index.html (last visited Aug. 31, 2005).

[20] University of California, Berkeley, SPIRO, Architecture Visual Resources Library Image Database, http://shanana.berkeley.edu/spiro/ (last visited Aug. 31, 2005).

[21] Glenda Morgan, *Educause Ctr. for Applied Research, Key Findings: Faculty Use of Course Management Systems* (2003), *available at* http://www.educause.edu/ir/library/pdf/ecar_so/ers/ers0302/ekf0302.pdf.

[22] "The court shall remit statutory damages in any case where an infringer believed and had reasonable grounds for believing that his or her use of the copyrighted work was a fair use under section 107, if the infringer was: (i) an employee or agent of a nonprofit educational institution, library, or archives acting within the scope of his or her employment who, or such institution, library, or archives itself, which infringed by reproducing the work in copies or phonorecords . . ." 17 U.S.C. § 504(c)(2) (2000).

[23] There are many fair use resources available on the Web. These include: North Carolina State University Libraries, Fair Use Considerations Worksheet, http://www.lib.ncsu.edu/scc/copyright/worksheet.pdf (last visited Aug. 25, 2005); Stanford University Libraries, Copyright and Fair Use, http://fairuse.stanford.edu/ (last visited Aug. 25, 2005); and University of Texas, Fair Use of Copyrighted Materials, http://www.utsystem.edu/ogc/intellectualproperty/copypol2.htm (last visited Aug. 25, 2005).

[24] 17 U.S.C. §§ 107, 108, 110 (2000 & Supp. II 2003).

[25] ASCAP is the American Society of Composers, Authors and Publishers (www.ascap.com) and licenses the right to perform songs and musical works owned by their members. BMI is Broadcast Music, Inc. (www.bmi.com) and also licenses performance rights on behalf of its members.

[26] Mark Young and Martha Kyrillidon, *Ass'n of Research Libraries, ARL Supplementary Statistics 2002–03 5* (2004), http://www.arl.org/stats/sup/index.html.

[27] *Id.*

[28] North Carolina State University Libraries 2001–2004 Progress Report.

[29] 17 U.S.C. § 109 (2000).

[30] 17 U.S.C. § 108 (2000).

[31] ARL's Principles for Licensing Resources was released in 1997 and was developed by the American Association of Law Libraries, the American Library Association, ARL, the Special Libraries Association, the Medical Library Association and the Association of Academic Health Sciences Libraries. *Am. Ass'n of Law Libraries et al.*, *Principles for Licensing Electronic Resources* (1997), http://www.arl.org/scomm/licensing/principles.html

[32] ICOLC's Statement of Current Perspective and Preferred Practices for Selection and Purchase of Electronic Information, released in October 2004, specifically emphasized the importance of educational use "exceptions" and the need for those to remain intact in the electronic environment. Arnold Hirshon et al., *International Coaltion of Library Consortia Statement of Current Perspective and Preferred Practices for the Selection and Purchase of Electronic Information* (1998), http://www.library.yale.edu/consortia/statement.html.

[33] Comm. on Copyright and Other Legal Matters, Int'l Fed. of Library Ass'ns & Insts., Licensing Principles (2001), http://www.ifla.org/V/ebpd/copy.htm.

[34] ARL has conducted licensing workshops for years. *See generally*, Ass'n of Research Libraries, Licensing Issues, http://www.arl.org/scomm/licensing/index.html (last visited Aug. 25, 2005). It has recently moved into workshops exploring how libraries can keep track of licenses and their terms. Ass'n of Research Libraries, Reaching and Mapping Licensing Language for Electronic Resource Management: A Pilot ARL/DLF Workshop, http://www.arl.org/stats/work/mapping.html (last visited Aug. 25, 2005).

[35] For an interesting discussion of copyright, contracts, and federal preemption, *see generally*, David Nimmer et al., *The Metamorphosis of Contract into Expand*, 87 CAL. L. REV. 17 (1999).

[36] *See* Christina L. Kunz et al., *Click-Through Agreements: Strategies for Avoiding Disputes on Validity of Assent*, 57 BUS. LAW. 401 (2001).

[37] Creative Commons licenses address such options as attribution, commercial vs. noncommercial uses, derivatives, and share alike. The license selected is provided in machine-readable code, human-readable, and lawyer-readable. Other licenses available include sampling, music sharing, and dedication to the public domain. *See* Creative Commons, http://www.creativecommons.org (last visited Aug. 25, 2005).

[38] *Register.com, Inc. v. Verio, Inc.*, 126 F. Supp. 2d 238 (S.D.N.Y. 2000); *Pollster v. Gigmania Ltd.*, 170 F. Supp. 2d 974 (E.D. Cal. 2000).

[39] *Specht v. Netscape Commc'ns Corp.*, 150 F. Supp. 2d 585 (S.D.N.Y. 2001), *aff'd*, 306 F.3d 17 (2d Cir. 2002).

[40] Christina L. Kunz et al., *Browse-Wrap Agreements: Validity of Implied Assent in Electronic Form Agreements*, 59 BUS. LAW. 279, 279–312 (2003).

ELECTRONIC RESERVES AND COPYRIGHT:

A COLLISION COURSE?

LAURA N. GASAWAY

This chapter discusses the following topics:
- ▶ The purpose of e-reserves
- ▶ The legal basis for e-reserves
- ▶ E-reserve guidelines
- ▶ Views from publishers and libraries

INTRODUCTION

The promise of making large collections of materials available to users electronically is now a reality for many libraries. Not only do libraries acquire digital access to never-before-held materials, they also make digital copies of works held in analog format for specific purposes, such as preservation. Publishers increasingly offer digital content to libraries through license agreements, some content that the library previously owned in print or other analog form but also to works that are new to the library. Reserve collections in libraries have also entered the digital environment.

Prior to the introduction of photocopy equipment, library users and researchers had to take notes from copyrighted works by hand. Reproduction technology in libraries changed the research methodology and greatly facilitated the review of scholarly materials for research. No longer did researchers have to take laborious notes; instead, they could highlight reproductions of articles, make notes in the margins, etc.

When libraries removed a volume from the circulating collection and placed it in a restricted circulation collection, such as library reserves, no copyright issues were raised by this activity. The photocopier made it possible to reproduce materials and place those reproductions in a restricted collection so that the original volume could remain in the collection available to other users. Under certain conditions, photocopies of copyrighted articles and chapters generally were considered by libraries to be fair use.

Now libraries are digitizing materials that previously would have been on photocopy reserves and creating electronic reserve collections (e-reserves). Copyright owners have serious concerns about digital reproduction of analog materials for e-reserves, access to these digital materials through the library's Web site, whether and to what extent fair use applies to this activity at all, and whether and at what point permission should be sought and royalties paid.

TRADITIONAL RESERVES IN LIBRARIES

Pre-Technology Library Reserves

After centuries as nonlending collections, libraries slowly became lending libraries. Naturally, some materials were in greater demand than others, so as budgets permitted, libraries acquired multiple copies of these works. When even multiple copies could not meet the demand for these works, reserve collections were established with shorter lending periods.

Creating a separate reserve collection served two purposes: (1) more users could have access to the work if the circulation period was made very short; and (2) the materials themselves were protected. The circulation period was often only a few hours or, after a certain time, such as 9:00 p.m., they could be checked out overnight and were due for return early the next morning. Libraries called these collections "permanent reserves," meaning that the library itself had selected the materials for this restricted circulation collection and that they would remain in the reserve collection indefinitely. In addition to reference materials, academic libraries sometimes placed a copy of assigned textbooks on reserve to assist students who forgot to bring their copies on a particular day or for students who could not afford to purchase the assigned textbook. Others put textbooks on reserve only if they were not assigned as the textbook for the course.

Permanent reserve collections raise no copyright concerns. In the United States, there is no restriction on the right to read, and copyright holders are not entitled to any royalties when libraries lend books from their collection.[1] Under section 109(a) of the Copyright Act, anyone who possesses a copy of a work may dispose of that copy without any further royalties to the copyright holder. Called the "first sale doctrine," this section of the statute permits libraries to lend works to users or even to rent them to library patrons. Thus, placing original works on reserve and lending them to users is permitted under the first sale doctrine. Copyright concerns arise when materials are *reproduced* for library reserve collections.

Then faculty members began to request that particular books and journal volumes be placed on reserve as supplemental readings for students. The first mention of a reserve room in library literature was in 1878 when Harvard College reported that professors commonly gave the library a list of books to which they intended to refer their students during the class term. The library would then remove these books from the circulating collection to reserve their use for the class.[2] With the advent of the photocopier for course reserves, libraries were eager to substitute a photocopy for the original volumes. If the class size was sufficiently large, then multiple copies were reproduced for course reserves. While some copyright holders objected to this practice, it became a ubiquitous practice among academic libraries. Many librarians recognized that making multiple copies for reserve collections might cause copyright problems; at the request of librarians, the American Library Association issued a model policy for reserves in 1982.[3] A considerable number of libraries followed the recommendations contained in this document. With photocopy reserves, a student requests the item at the reserve desk and then may read the photocopy checked out, or the student may reproduce the photocopy to read later.

Even prior to electronic reserves there were reports by publishers of abuses of traditional reserves. For example, to substitute for a textbook or a coursepack, some faculty members began to place photocopies of all of the readings for a course on reserve. Thus, reserve collections grew tremendously, and the original purpose of such collections was altered. Complaints about abuse of reserve collections are not new. In 1938, the following complaint was published:

> In my humble judgment, some professors have simply lost their sense of proportion. They have become so enamored of the reserved book system that they feel they could not give their favorite course unless there were from 500–1000 books on reserve, specifically ticketed with the name and number of their course.[4]

Background Issues for Photocopy Reserves

Most library issues are covered in the library exemption, section 108. Library reserves are governed by section 107, fair use. Often called the "safety valve" of copyright, fair use excuses activity that normally would be infringement. If a use is a fair use, no permission must be sought from the copyright holder, and no royalties are due. The law simply recognizes that some uses of copyrighted works have a significant enough value to justify being excused. Section 107 of the Copyright Act provides that:

> . . . [T]he fair use of a copyrighted work, including such use by reproduction in copies . . . for purposes such as criticism, comment, news reporting, teaching (including multiple copies for classroom use), scholarship, or research, is not an infringement of copyright . . .[5]

In order to determine whether a use is fair, the statute directs that the following factors be considered: (1) purpose and character of the use; (2) nature of the copyrighted work; (3) amount and substantiality used; and (4) effect on the potential market for or value of the work.[6] One of the difficulties with fair use is that only a court can determine authoritatively whether a particular use is fair. Thus, it is not only a limitation on the exclusive rights of the copyright holder, but it is also a defense to copyright infringement. Unfortunately for libraries and library users, there are no "bright line" rules for judging fair use. Courts balance these four factors to make fair use determinations.

The first factor, *purpose and character of the use*, focuses on the use itself. Nonprofit educational uses are favored but not automatically exempted as fair uses, but are more favored than uses for commercial gain.[7] Courts also favor so-called productive or transformative uses over simple reproductions. An example of a transformative use is when a critic quotes extensively from a book in a literary criticism of the book.[8] "Transformative use" is a term of art and really means that the second author is using the quoted portion of the copyrighted work for a different purpose or in a different manner than that of the original author. Thus, the second use adds some value to the original work. Clearly, photocopying materials for reserve collections involves no such transformative use, but the use is for nonprofit educational purposes. So, the reproduction for reserve collections satisfies one prong of the first factor but not the other; however, this may be sufficient.

Nature of the copyrighted work, the second fair use factor, looks at the work itself. It requires an examination of the work, and each work must be judged separately on this factor. As a general rule, uses of factual works are more likely to be a fair use than are uses of creative works.[9] Another important consideration for this factor is whether the work is unpublished or is out of print.[10]

The third factor, *amount and substantiality used*, is both a quantitative and a qualitative test. Generally, the smaller the amount used, the more likely the use will be found to be a fair use. Section 108(d) indicates that libraries can reproduce a single copy of an article from a periodical issue or other contribution from a collective work. One certainly could argue that this should also apply to library reserves under section 107, but the *American Geophysical Union v. Texaco*[11] decision held that an individual article is an independent, copyrighted work in itself.[12] Thus, reproducing the entire article would constitute reproducing an entire copyrighted work.[13] For reserves, the entire article or chapter is usually reproduced. Amount and substantiality is a qualitative test as well. If the alleged infringer takes the heart of the work, regardless of the amount used quantitatively, the use will not be a fair one. [14]

The final fair use factor, *market effect*, focuses on the effect the use has on the potential market for or value of the use. This is the economic test for the copyright holder. A series of cases indicates that publishers have an economic interest in the right to license to photocopy and that avoiding paying those royalties even for research and educational uses is not a fair use.[15]

When the Copyright Act was being debated, a negotiated agreement from representatives of publishers, authors, and educational associations was presented to Congress. Called the "Classroom Guidelines," the agreement covers classroom handouts, i.e., reproducing and distributing photocopies of book chapters and periodical articles for classes in nonprofit educational institutions.[16]

The Guidelines detail conditions and tests that should be met when a teacher reproduces multiple copies of copyrighted works to use in the classroom. The Guidelines also deal with single copying by teachers for their own use in teaching and research,[17] but for purposes of this chapter, it is the multiple copying portions of the Guidelines that are important. Teachers are permitted to make multiple copies of copyrighted works and distribute one copy to each student in the class if certain tests are satisfied: (1) brevity; (2) spontaneity; (3) cumulative effects; (4) notice of copyright on each item; and (5) no charge to students beyond the actual cost of making the copies.[18] The test of most concern to library reserves is cumulative effects, a portion of which states that the teacher may not repeat copying with respect to the same item from term to term. Such repeated copying cannot meet the spontaneity test for use of the same material in subsequent class terms.[19]

Copyright Issues for Photocopy Reserves

The American Library Association's *Model Policy Concerning College and University Photocopying for Classroom, Research and Library Reserve Use*[20] was developed by ALA legal counsel. Unlike the Classroom Guidelines, the Model Policy[21] does not represent negotiated guidelines nor does it have any stamp of Congress. While publishers often criticize the guidelines contained in the policy because they are not negotiated guidelines, there has been no litigation concerning the Model Policy.[22]

The Model Policy begins with a statement that libraries may photocopy and place materials on reserve "in accordance with guidelines similar to those governing formal classroom distribution for face-to-face teaching . . .,"[23] although the Register of Copyrights specifically rejected this assertion.[24] The ALA Guidelines adopt the premise that the library reserves function as an extension of the classroom and that photocopying for reserve for convenience of the student simply reflects the individual student's right to copy materials for private research and study, which is a traditional fair use. The Guidelines state that, in general, materials photocopied for reserve should follow the "standard guidelines," meaning the Classroom Guidelines. The following criteria from the Classroom Guidelines are repeated:

1. The distribution of the same materials does not occur every semester.
2. Only one copy is distributed for each student.
3. The material includes a copyright notice on the first page of the portion of the material photocopied.

4. The students are not assessed any fee beyond the actual cost of the photo-copying.[25]

The most important part of the Model Policy deals with requests to place multiple copies on reserve. The criteria for course reserves are unique except for number three:

1. The amount of material should be reasonable in relation to the total amount of material assigned for one term of a course taking into account the nature of the course, its subject matter, and level, 17 U.S.C. § 107(1) and (3).
2. The number of copies should be reasonable in light of the number of students enrolled, the difficulty and timing of assignments, and the number of other courses which may assign the same material, 17 U.S.C. § 107(1) and (3).
3. The material should contain a notice of copyright, see 17 U.S.C. § 401.
4. The effect of photocopying the material should not be detrimental to the market for the work. (In general, the library should own at least one copy of the work.) 17 U.S.C. § 107(4).[26]

Under the ALA Model Policy, it is clear that reserves are not meant to replace a textbook or a coursepack reproduced with permission and royalties. Implicit in the criteria is that materials placed on reserve by faculty are not intended to constitute all of the materials assigned for the course. The Model Policy has been adopted and implemented by many libraries, but others object to the limitation on use for only one semester/term without additional permission, as well as the restriction on the amount of material that may be reproduced for reserve. Some libraries have simply ignored these criteria and placed all of the materials for the course on reserve, including coursepacks.

Despite the fact that many libraries have complied with the ALA Model Policy and other libraries attempted to comply with fair use for reserve copying, publishers point out that they never agreed to the Model Policy. Additionally, some believe that reproducing entire articles is too much.[27]

ELECTRONIC RESERVES

Background and Benefits

Librarians have always turned to technology to solve various challenges ranging from cataloging and acquisitions to maintenance of circulation systems and records. Naturally, technology was viewed as solving some of the problems presented by course reserves, such as lack of space, keeping up with photocopies, having to copy materials multiple times, tracking permissions, and evaluating the use of reserve materials.

Digitizing the materials for course reserves that were formerly held as photocopies offers many advantages to libraries: (1) space concerns are greatly eased;

(2) scanning has to be done only once; (3) managing the collection is easier electronically; and (4) no staff member is needed to assist users by checking out and checking in reserve materials for each use. Students using e-reserves have increased access to the materials, whether physically present in the library or not, have enhanced search capability, and have the ability to download the materials to use for study and note-taking.

E-Reserves Copyright Concerns

The same copyright concerns exist for e-reserves as existed for photocopy reserve collections. Libraries took a variety of approaches in dealing with copyright issues: (1) some libraries sought permission for each item digitized and placed on e-reserve; (2) some followed the ALA Model Policy as a way to deal with copyright issues; (3) some libraries placed nothing on e-reserve other than items in the public domain or in which the requesting faculty member held the copyright; (4) some used articles only from licensed full-text journals for e-reserves; and (5) still others digitized articles and chapters for e-reserves and sought no permissions, believing that the activity was protected as a fair use.

E-reserves also raise some unique copyright problems. With photocopy reserves, clearly students make additional photocopies from the photocopies on reserve. With digitized materials, however, copies are made not only when the work is printed or downloaded, but whenever it is read on a computer screen.[28] Thus, just by the way an e-reserve system functions, more copies of a work are made than in a photocopy reserve collection. Another important difference is that copies reproduced from a digital copy are basically originals or perfect copies. There is no denigration in the quality of the copies.

Publishers fear lost sales due to the availability of their works even on password-protected e-reserve systems. In the past, faculty members required students to purchase scholarly monographs for their classes. Today, many faculty members place several chapters from these monographs on e-reserve, and publishers claim that the sales they would have made in the past have been lost.[29] Moreover, publishers also fear the loss of control over their copyrighted works due to e-reserve reproduction at a magnitude simply not possible with print reserves. They believe students are likely to upload reserve items onto listservs, and, "with a few keystrokes, transmit the work to 100,000 people."[30]

An e-reserve item viewed in a public library could also infringe a copyright owner's right of public display. It is unlikely, however, that other students will be particularly interested in what reserve items a fellow student is viewing on a computer screen. If the digitized item is a sound recording or a portion of a motion picture, and if a student is listening to or viewing the item in a public area, then the copyright owner's right of public performance may be infringed.

Libraries certainly can take steps to allay or at least reduce copyright holders' concerns. For example, a library can restrict access to the materials reproduced in the system to students, faculty, and staff of the institution or to students who are actually enrolled in that particular course. Further, libraries can create and monitor systems for obtaining permissions, paying royalties and tracking use. Some scholars believe that e-reserves should be used only to support the basic texts assigned for a course and never in lieu of a textbook.[31] Moreover, when the same item is used by a professor term after term, the argument for fair use is weaker with each use.[32]

When a library obtains a work in digital format (as opposed to converting a paper copy to digital format), the license agreement that accompanies the digital version will control whether portions of the work can be included in an e-reserve system. The library section of the Copyright Act contains a statement that nothing "[A]ffects any contractual obligations assumed at any time by the library or archives when it obtained a copy or phonorecord of a work in its collection."[33]

Publishers also are very concerned about declining sales and blame it on the growth of e-reserves, at least to some extent. The Association of American Publishers (AAP) reports that the percentage of growth of sales by higher education publishers grew in 2004 by only 1.8 percent after growing by 3.6 percent in 2003 and 12.9 percent in 2002. Publishers worry that declining sales are due to the uncompensated use of electronic course materials. However, it is difficult for publishers to verify the extent to which this is true, because e-reserve systems are behind firewalls.[34]

In 2005, there were news reports of a dispute between the AAP and the University of California-San Diego concerning publishers' objections to the e-reserve system at the institution. At this writing, the matter has not been resolved. A series of letters has been exchanged between Allan Adler, AAP Vice President for Legal and Government Affairs, and UC-San Diego attorney Mary McDonald. Ms. McDonald indicates that the correspondence with the AAP states that the institution has not followed fair use in its e-reserve system, and she worries that this portends litigation over the matter despite the institution's comprehensive response in early 2005.[35] She believes that the AAP clearly sees this as a national issue and that this is an opportunity to challenge e-reserves.[36] Mr. Adler has admitted that UC-San Diego was chosen because the AAP has more data about e-reserves at that institution than from others, the data being provided to the AAP from someone within the university community itself.[37] It is unclear whether the AAP will actually file suit, but according to Mr. Adler, it has not been ruled out.[38]

Attempts to Create Guidelines

In the mid-1990s, the Conference on Fair Use (CONFU)[39] was convened to determine whether it was possible to develop guidelines for the fair use of copyrighted works in the digital environment.[40] Most participants assumed that e-reserves would be one of the areas in which negotiated guidelines would be likely. From October 1994 to the spring of 1997, CONFU met regularly and worked on a series of guidelines, with one small working group developing the Electronic-Reserve Guidelines.

Early in the process it appeared that Electronic Reserve Guidelines would be adopted, and some organizations did so, including the American Council of Learned Societies, the American Association of Law Libraries, Special Libraries Association, and the Association of American University Presses.[41] Most other library associations and the Association of American Publishers (AAP) did not endorse them.[42] The nonendorsing library associations believed that the Guidelines were too restrictive on libraries, while the AAP criticized them as going far beyond fair use since they permit reproduction of entire articles and chapters, rather than small excerpts.[43] Interestingly, the AAP now believes that it was a mistake to oppose these Guidelines.[44]

The Guidelines were based on the ALA Model Policy and adapted for e-reserves. Moreover, the Guidelines applied only to complementary or supplementary readings for a course, such as copyrighted articles and chapters and all of the materials assigned for a course, such as a coursepack. The Guidelines permitted digitizing the material that could have been placed on reserve under the ALA Guidelines. As Peter Grenquist, then Executive Director of the Association of American University Presses, stated, "There are costs on both sides. Publishers will have to bear some of the costs and so will libraries."[45] Under the CONFU Guidelines, publishers would have relinquished receipt of royalties for one-term use in the e-reserve system, and libraries would bear the cost of managing the system and implementing the restrictions found in the Guidelines.

Libraries would be limited to use of an article or chapter in an e-reserve system for only one term without obtaining permission from the copyright holder, just as under the ALA Guidelines. They would also be required to restrict access to the e-reserve materials to students enrolled in the course, to include admonishments that no further distribution of the material is permitted, and to provide no more detailed bibliographic access to the material than is provided for other journal articles and book chapters.

Although the ALA Model Policy did not directly restrict access to students enrolled in the course, the Electronic Reserve Guidelines went back to the Classroom Guidelines and incorporated this limitation. While this does not eliminate the possibility of abuse, it does reduce the potential for abuse, since the number of users is controlled. This left the method for such restriction up to the individual institution and could be as simple as assigning each course an access number that was distributed only to students in the course.

As was found in both the Classroom and the ALA Guidelines, the Electronic Reserve Guidelines dictated that each copyrighted item in the digital system should contain notice of copyright. Based on concerns of publishers, the Electronic Reserve Guidelines went further and recommended the inclusion of an additional statement, perhaps in the initial e-reserve screen, to the effect that "further transmission of this work is prohibited." This alerts students that further transmission or copying is also an infringement of copyright.

The Electronic Reserve Guidelines dictated that libraries should provide bibliographic access at the same level of detail that is given for other journal articles and book chapters. Today this means that the bibliographic access should be limited to course name and number and the name of the faculty member. It is hoped that this will reduce the likelihood that other students not enrolled in the course will be encouraged to seek access to the materials.

Potential Solutions to Copyright Problems

The Copyright Clearance Center (CCC) has established the Electronic Course Content service to cover e-reserves, e-coursepacks, and e-learning.[46] Many libraries have used the CCC for e-reserves when they have determined that it is appropriate to pay royalties. While this is only a partial solution, the CCC does provide an easy way to seek permissions and pay royalties once the library has exceeded fair use for e-reserve materials.

One potential solution is the new joint statement by library associations, which takes an entirely different approach. The American Library Association itself has tried to disassociate itself from the Model Policy. In November 2003, the ALA, along with the other major library associations, produced a statement on e-reserves.[47] The new ALA statement recommends that libraries simply apply the four fair use factors to determine whether digitizing works and repeatedly placing them on e-reserve is permissible.

Another solution is to restrict e-reserve materials to (1) public domain materials; (2) works in which the faculty member or the institution holds the copyright; and (3) those for which the institution already has a license. Then the library can link to specific articles and chapters covered by the license or, if the license agreement permits, copy the materials into the e-reserve system. For several years, libraries have asked the Association of American University Presses to offer a blanket license to universities and colleges for monograph chapters and journal articles. Virtually every academic institution would take the license, and university presses would be guaranteed an annual license fee. The license would cover not only copies for e-reserves but also coursepacks. To date the AAUP has been unable to reach internal agreement on this issue, and no such license is yet available to higher education.

Libraries themselves should develop a copyright policy that includes addressing e-reserves. Some institutions are more willing than others to risk being sued; the policy should reflect this level of comfort.[48]

Another possible solution may be found in amending the statute to include e-reserves in the library section. In early 2005, a section 108 study group was created by the Library of Congress' National Digital Information Infrastructure and Preservation Program, in cooperation with the U.S. Copyright Office. The group consists of 19 individuals appointed because of their knowledge of copyright law and of particular segments of the library or copyright holder communities. The study group is charged with reviewing all library copyright issues, whether currently found in section 108 or not, and developing "balanced, solid recommendations for revisions"[49] to the act by mid-2006. One of the issues this group is likely to address is e-reserves.

COURSEPACKS, E-RESERVES, AND MATERIALS POSTED BY FACULTY ON COURSE MANAGEMENT SOFTWARE

Conflation of Reserves and Other Electronic Access

While it is possible to distinguish e-reserves from e-coursepacks and from materials uploaded into course management software, from the publishers' viewpoint, there is little difference. Publishers view these digital copies as lost sales and/or lost royalty income. Moreover, there is some data, as well as anecdotal evidence, to support this view.

Publishers are concerned that libraries often have exceeded the traditional notion of library reserves by putting excessive amounts of materials per course into e-reserve systems. Instead of supplementary or complementary readings only, some faculty have asked that all of the materials for their courses be available to students free through the e-reserve system, and some libraries have acceded to their requests. By contrast, many libraries have obtained permission and paid royalties as requested, while others have employed a fair use analysis and maintained that if it is fair use to put the materials into the e-reserve system for one semester, it is fair use for all subsequent semesters.

Faculty members now have an additional choice in making materials available electronically to students. Course management software, such as Blackboard and WebCT, creates the ability for faculty to upload copyrighted articles and chapters and make them available to students. This is not covered by the TEACH Act, since it involves neither performance nor display. Instead, it is a simple reproduction and distribution of copyrighted works.[50] Libraries are seldom involved in this activity, and it clearly is not e-reserves. To a publisher, however, there is little difference between the two. Of course, faculty members may link to licensed resources without duplicating the materials into the course management system, and the library should be involved in helping faculty to identify these materials.

Another similar issue is the creation of e-coursepacks for which the Copyright Clearance Center can provide a license. Publishers argue that if all of the materials for a course are placed on e-reserve, an e-coursepack has been created. Thus, to the publishing community, electronic reserves, coursepacks, and making materials available to users through course management software is all the same.

MEDIA ON E-RESERVES

The remainder of this chapter focuses on print, text, and images (photographs) that are digitized for e-reserve collections. Increasingly, libraries are being asked to digitize portions of videos and sound recordings for particular classes. Libraries then stream the works for students as a part of e-reserves. The copyright concerns for this material include all of the issues discussed in the preceding. There are, however, unique copyright issues associated with digitizing this material.

Sound Recordings

The Guidelines on the Educational Use of Music accompanied the Copyright Act of 1976 and were published in the House Report.[51] They actually permit duplication of a single copy of portions of sound recordings: "A single copy of a sound recording (such as a tape, disc, or cassette) of copyrighted music may be made from sound recordings owned by an educational institution or an individual teacher for the purpose of constructing aural exercises or examinations and may be retained by the educational institution or individual teacher." Based on this, libraries have placed this material on reserve. Faculty often have asked that multiple copies of the CD made under the Music Guidelines be placed on reserve. The Guidelines, however, limit the number of copies to one. Therefore, streaming the sound recording via the e-reserve system allows the library to rely on only one copy. A number of music libraries have developed their own guidelines for providing access to assigned listening music.[52] Interestingly, to date, the Recording Industry Association of America (RIAA) has not complained about the duplication of sound recordings for e-reserves made available to students through streaming, perhaps because it is difficult to download from the stream.

Videos

Libraries are now being asked to digitize portions of videos on VHS and DVD and make them available through streaming via the e-reserve system. If the original format is VHS, then copying small portions and placing them on reserve in VHS format is no different from other analog reserve issues. Copying small portions of a VHS and burning them onto a DVD is an e-reserve issue, but it is no different than the sound recording issue discussed above. The DVD could be checked out from a reserve collection for viewing within a restricted circulation period.

When the video is originally acquired in DVD format, and the library wishes to reproduce short portions of the DVD for e-reserves, not only are the same issues present as for streaming sound recordings, but also the anti-circumvention provision of the Copyright Act is invoked.[53] The anti-circumvention provision creates liability for interfering with the technological access controls, such as encryption, that a copyright holder places on a copyrighted work. To copy portions of the DVD, one may be interfering with technological controls. At present, it is still possible for a library to acquire most videos in VHS format so that it can digitize small portions for reserve, but when VHS becomes an obsolete format, the only available format will be DVD with its concomitant access controls. Thus, some change in the statute is critical for libraries that place video clips on e-reserve and stream them to users.

CONCLUSION

As libraries have moved into the digital age and created electronic reserve collections, they are faced with a myriad of copyright problems. Some may be easy to solve, but others may prove much more difficult. There must be some way to permit digitizing for e-reserves while still protecting the rights of the copyright owner. Let us hope that some solution, or a combination of the potential ones, either solves the problem or at least makes it bearable for all concerned.

NEXT STEPS

▶ Assess whether your reserves (traditional and electronic) comply with legislation, accepted guidelines, and institutional/organizational policies.
▶ Determine whether individuals are properly using reserve collections, particularly faculty in and for classroom use. Develop a copyright policy that includes e-reserves and that also reflects your institution's/organization's risk tolerance.
▶ Design and implement educational initiatives to inform everyone at your institution/organization about the laws and policies governing copyright.
▶ Develop a program and policy for the proper identification and use of materials for course management software

---

ENDNOTES

[1] 17 U.S.C. § 109(a) (2000). In several European countries, there is a public lending right which generates royalties for copyright holders. The United States has not enacted such a provision; nor is it likely to do so. For a discussion of the public lending right abroad *see* Laura N. Gasaway and Sarah K. Wiant, *Libraries and Copyright: A Guide to Copyright Law in the 1990's* 199–216 (1994).

[2] 3 Libr. J. 271, 271 (1878).

[3] *See Am. Library Ass'n, Model Policy Concerning College and University Photocopying for Classroom, Research and Library Reserve Use* (1982), *reprinted* in 43 C. & Res. Libr. News 127 (1982), *available at* http://www.unc.edu/~unclng/ALA-modelpolicy.htm [hereinafter Reserve Guidelines]. The policy is discussed in detail beginning at note 22 below.

[4] Theodore W. Koch, A Symposium on the Reserve Book System, in *College and University Library Service: Trends, Standards, Appraisal, Problems; Papers Presented at the 1937 Midwinter Meeting of the American Library Association* 73, 74 (A.F. Kuhlman ed., 1938).

[5] 17 U.S.C. § 107 (2000 & Supp. II 2003).

[6] 17 U.S.C. § 107.

[7] 2 Paul Goldstein, *Copyright* §10.2.2.1 (2d. 1996) [hereinafter Goldstein].

[8] Am. Geophysical Union v. Texaco, Inc., 60 F.3d 913, 922-25 (2d Cir. 1994).

[9] *Id.* at 925.

[10] S. Rep. No. 976, 93-976 (1974), *reprinted in* 13 *Omnibus Copyright Revision Legislative History* 117 (1977).

[11] 60 F.3d 913 (2d Cir. 1994).

[12] *Id.*

[13] *Id.*

[14] *See Harper & Row, Publishers, Inc. v. The Nation Enters.*, 471 U.S. 539, 566 (1985) (a case for which the qualitative part of this factor was critical to the holding that the use was not a fair one).

[15] *See Texaco* 37 F.3d at 881 and the coursepack cases, *Basic Books, Inc. v. Kinko's Graphics Corp.*, 758 F. Supp. 1522 (S.D.N.Y. 1991), and *Princeton Univ. Press v. Mich. Documents Serv.*, 99 F.3d 1381 (6th Cir. 1996).

[16] H.R. Rep. No. 94-1467 (1976), *reprinted in Omnibus Copyright Law Revision Legislation* 68–71 (1977). Congress recognized the agreement concerning fair use contained in this agreement by publishing them in the House Report.

[17] *Id.* at 68.

[18] *Id.* at 68–69.

[19] *Id.*

[20] Reserve Guidelines, *supra* note 3.

[21] The terms "Model Policy" and "Reserve Guidelines" are used interchangeably in this chapter.

[22] See Laura N. Gasaway and Sarah K. Wiant, *Libraries and Copyright: A Guide to Copyright Law in the 1990's* 148–49 (1994).

[23] Reserve Guidelines, *supra* note 3, at 127.

[24] James D. Heller and Sarah K. Wiant, *Copyright Handbook* 28–29.(1984).

[25] Reserve Guidelines, *supra* note 3, at 129.

[26] *Id.*

[27] The statements were made by publishers' representatives, including Carol Risher of the Association of American Publishers and Harriet Goldberg of Simon and Schuster at various sessions of the Conference on Fair Use, October, 1994–November, 1996.

[28] *See* MAI Sys. Corp. v. Peak Computer, Inc., 991 F.2d 511 (9th Cir. 1993).

[29] Peter Givler, Executive Dir. of the Am. Assoc'n of Univ. Presses, Statement at the Section 108 Study Group meeting at the Library of Congress (April 15, 2005).

[30] Carol Risher, Vice President for Copyright, Assoc'n of Am. Publishers, Statement at the Conference on Fair Use (January 4, 1995).

[31] Donna L. Ferullo, *The Challenge of E-Reserves*, Libr. J. Net Connect, Summer 2002, at 33, 35.

[32] *Id.*

[33] 17 U.S.C. § 108(f)(4) (2000).

[34] Vauhini Vara, *Publishers are Clashing with Professors*, Wall St. J., April 27, 2005, at B3.

[35] Scott Carlson, *Legal Battle Brews over Texts on Electronic Reserves at U. of California Libraries*, Chron. Higher Educ. (Wash. D.C.), April 22, 2005, at A36, *available at* http://chronicle. com/weekly/v51/i33/33a03601.htm.

[36] Marty Graham, *Sides Clash over Online Library*, Nat'l L.J., April 29, 2005, *available at* Law.com, http://www.law.com/jsp/article.jsp?id=1114679112558.

[37] Vara, *supra* note 34.

[38] Carlson, *supra* note 35.

[39] *Intellectual Property and the National Information Infrastructure: Report of the Working Group on Intellectual Property Rights* (1995).

[40] *Id.* at 83–84.

[41] Though never adopted by CONFU, the 1996 draft electronic reserve guidelines are available on several Web sites, *see, e.g.*, Fair Use Guidelines for Reserve Systems, http://www.ut-system.edu/ogc/intellectualproperty/rsrvguid.htm (last visited Sept. 2, 2005) and Am. Library Assoc'n., Library Reserve Guidelines, http://www.unc.edu/~unclng/ALA-mod-elpolicy.htm (last visited Sept. 2, 2005) and are *reprinted in Growing Pains: Adapting Copyright for Libraries, Education and Society* 499 (Laura N. Gasaway ed., 1997).

[42] Ass'n of Am. Publishers, Inc., Statement on E-Reserves presented at CONFU: The Conference on Fair Use (May 26, 1996).

[43] *Id.*

[44] Conversation with Allan Adler, Legal Counsel for the AAP on December 17, 2003, in Washington, D.C.

[45] Peter Grequist, Statement at CONFU: The Conference on Fair Use meeting, Washington, D.C. (May 30, 1996).

[46] Copyright.com, Electronic Course Content Service, http:// www.copyright.com/ccc/do/viewPage?pageCode=ac5-n (last visited Sept. 2, 2005).

[47] *See Ass'n of Research Libraries, Applying Fair Use in the Development of Electronic Reserves Systems* (2003), http://www.arl.org/access/eres/eresfinalstmt.shtml; Am. Library Assoc'n, Fair Use and Electronic Reserves (2004), http://www.ala.org/ala/washoff/WOissues/copy-rightb/fairuseandelectronicreserves/ereservesFU.htm#sum.

[48] Ferullo, *supra* note 31, at 35.

[49] Press Release, Library of Cong., Section 108 Study Group Convenes to Discuss Exceptions to Copyright Law for Libraries and Archives (May 13, 2005), http://www.digitalpreservation.

gov/about/pr 051305.html. Note that the author of this chapter is one of the co-chairs of the Study Group.

[50] It is possible to upload photographs, movie clips and sound recordings too, but these would be covered under the TEACH Act, discussed in chapter 5.

[51] H.R. REP. NO. 94-1476 (1976), *available at* http://www.utsystem.edu/ogc/intellectual-property/musguid.htm.

[52] *E.g.*, Iowa State University Library, Audio Streaming Policy, http://www.lib.iastate.edu/class/ers/avstreamingpolicy.html (last visited Aug. 30, 2005).

[53] 17 U.S.C. § 1201 (2000).

▶5

THE TEACH ACT:

WILL IT MAKE A DIFFERENCE FOR COLLEGES AND UNIVERSITIES?

KIMBERLY M. BONNER

This chapter discusses the following topics:
- ▶ The rise of digital distance education
- ▶ The history and background of the TEACH Act
- ▶ The education exemptions
- ▶ Analysis of the TEACH Act
- ▶ Influence of the TEACH Act

INTRODUCTION

This chapter highlights a recent amendment to U.S. copyright law for educational transmissions of copyrighted works. The Technology, Education, and Copyright Harmonization Act, or TEACH Act,[1] was promoted as a welcome modernization of U.S. copyright law, adapting it to new technologies for delivering education. The TEACH Act amends two sections of the U.S. copyright law, sections 110(2) and 112(f), permitting educators to perform and display third-party copyrighted works in educational transmissions, including those associated with Web-based instruction. Specifically, if an instructor needs copyrighted movie or audio clips included in an online course, the TEACH Act enables the instructor to use those works subject to several conditions and requirements.

This chapter compares and contrasts the education exemptions for face-to-face teaching and educational transmissions and reviews the rationale for amending the educational transmissions exemption. This chapter also analyzes the TEACH Act and preliminary information from universities on whether or not the TEACH Act is used by the higher education community. Although the TEACH Act was lauded by members of the educational, publishing, and library communities, few educational institutions are taking advantage of the new law. This chapter discusses possible reasons why.

The Growth of Digital Distance Education

The use of the Internet to disseminate knowledge, educate, and learn is steadily increasing. Over 2.3 million students took at least one online course in the fall of 2004.[2] Ninety-five percent of public institutions agree or are neutral when asked if online learning is critical to the long-term strategy of their institution.[3] The growth rate for online enrollment remains "both substantial and steady."[4]

The increase in digital distance education is due to many factors. One possible reason for the increase is the greater flexibility that digital distance education provides for administrators, faculty, and students. For example, digital distance education is far more scalable than traditional face-to-face instruction. Administrators are not limited by brick-and-mortar classroom space capacity when providing courses online. Faculty can provide interactive discussion and possibly enhanced individual instruction to students in the online classroom. Additionally, Web-based resources may be accessed in the classroom and interwoven in the course design, making the course much more resource- and media-rich than a traditional face-to-face course. Students have enhanced flexibility because they can take online courses wherever and whenever their schedule permits. The Report on Copyright and Digital Distance Education by the U.S. Copyright Office (hereinafter, Copyright Office Report) states that the growth in distance education is in large part due to its appeal to an older, nontraditional student population.[5] Online education students are working adults who cannot attend face-to-face classes during normal working hours.[6] Digital distance education provides a way for students to continue working while they obtain their degrees. The time/place/resource flexibility is an enormous advantage for online education, and this advantage will continue making online education a very attractive option for administrators, faculty, and students.

Although online learning has many potential advantages, there are also disadvantages. Securing rights to use copyrighted materials is one of the highest costs of providing quality digital distance education. University of Maryland University College reports spending $1200 to place an article from the *Washington Post* in its electronic reserves for a course.[7] A print copy of the same article would have cost only $50.[8] A major research university spent a large amount of money securing rights for film content for use in an online course. The clip was less than one minute in duration. However, the university abandoned its efforts when it was unable to secure the rights.[9] Although many costs are associated with delivering digital distance education, securing rights to use copyrighted materials is certainly one of the primary costs. Because of the costs associated with securing rights to digital content and the inadequacy of the education exemption in the Copyright Act of 1976 to deal with digital network transmissions, the higher education community lobbied to broaden and modernize the educational transmission exemption in the late 1990s.

BACKGROUND OF THE TEACH ACT: THE COPYRIGHT FRAMEWORK

Educational institutions have historically been one of the primary beneficiaries of the copyright legal framework in the United States. This framework is based on the mandate in the U.S. Constitution that Congress has the power to "promote the Progress of Science and useful Arts, by securing for limited Times to Authors and Inventors the exclusive Right to their respective Writings and Discoveries."[10] The Copyright Clause has its roots in the Statute of Anne. The Statute of Anne was entitled "An Act for the Encouragement of Learning, by Vesting the Copies of Printed Books in the Authors or Purchasers of such Copies, during the Times therein mentioned."[11] Although never applied under English law to the American colonies, twelve of the thirteen original states enacted copyright laws based upon this English law.[12] As the text of the Copyright Clause and the title of the Statute of Anne suggests, the ultimate goal of copyright law is to promote learning.

Copyright vests automatically for works that are "original works of authorship" and "fixed in any tangible medium of expression."[13] Books, journals, art, graphics, slides, even possibly e-mail and the postings in learning content management systems are copyrighted if they meet the statutory definition. Copyright owners have certain rights in copyrighted works that include:

▶ the right "to reproduce a copyrighted work in copies or phonorecords";[14]

▶ the right "to prepare derivative works based upon the copyrighted work";[15]

▶ the right "to distribute copies or phonorecords of the copyrighted work to the public by sale or other transfer of ownership, or by rental, lease, or lending";[16]

▶ the right, "in the case of literary, musical, dramatic, and choreographic works, pantomimes, and motion pictures and other audiovisual works, to perform the copyrighted work publicly";[17]

▶ the right, "in the case of literary, musical, dramatic, and choreographic works, pantomimes, and pictorial, graphic, or sculptural works, including the individual images of a motion picture or other audiovisual work, display the copyrighted work publicly;[18] and"

▶ the right, "in the case of sound recordings, to perform the copyrighted work publicly by means of a digital audio transmission."[19]

Professors, students and staff can violate the aforementioned rights easily in the course of teaching, learning, and conducting research. Making copies of literary works and images for courses, showing films, performing plays and songs in classes would certainly breach copyright if no exceptions in the law existed. If no exemptions existed within copyright law to accommodate educational uses of copyrighted work, the cost associated with education would be considerably higher, and many of the activities involved in higher education would probably cease to occur. Because of this and because the fundamental Constitutional goal of copyright law is to promote learning, U.S. copyright law has several limitations on the exclusive rights of copyright owners that favor educational uses. These include fair use,[20] the library photocopying and related exemptions,[21] first sale,[22] and education exemptions.[23]

THE OLD EDUCATION-RELATED EXEMPTIONS: COMPARE AND CONTRAST

Specific exemptions related to education are located in section 110 of the Copyright Act. Section 110(1) addresses face-to-face teaching and section 110(2) addresses educational transmissions. Section 110 focuses on the rights of *public performance* and *public display* and does not address other rights such as reproduction or distribution. Examples of public display include showing a picture, page of text, or book cover to a class. Examples of public performance would include showing a motion picture with accompanying sound, singing a song, or reciting a poem to a class.[24]

Section 110(1), the face- to-face teaching exemption, permits teachers and students in nonprofit educational institutions to perform or display any work in the classroom without seeking permission from the copyright owner. The primary limitations are the institution must be nonprofit, the performance or display must be in a classroom or similar place of instruction, and, if the work is an audiovisual or motion picture, it must have been lawfully obtained. The exemption for face-to-face teaching in 110(1) is very simple and relatively broad.

The old section 110(2) was developed during the 1970s, when the primary mode of distance education delivery was via television. Former section 110(2) was very narrowly tailored for this type of instructional delivery. Moreover, former section 110(2) applied to a narrower class of works than the face-to-face exemption. The former section 110(2) applied to only "performance of a nondramatic literary or musical work or display of any work."[25] Thus, performance of dramatic works and dramatic musical works, such as operas, musical comedies, and motion pictures were per se excluded from the exemption.[26] Addtionally, former section 110(2) had other restrictions:

▶ "the performance or display is a regular part of the systematic instructional activities of a governmental body or nonprofit educational institution;[27] and"

▶ "the performance or display is directly related and of material assistance to the teaching content of the transmission;[28] and"

▶ "the transmission had to be made primarily for reception in classrooms or similar places devoted to instruction; or reception by persons to whom the transmission is directed because their disabilities or other special circumstances prevent their attendance in classroom or similar places devoted to instruction; or reception by officers or employees of governmental bodies as part of their official duties or employment."[29]

Copyright Office Recommendations

Section 110(2) originally focused on the technology of television and satellite transmissions for delivering educational content. Telecourses and closed-circuit television have had large audiences since the 1950s and are still used in various higher education institutions.[30] However, by the late 1990s, the Internet was becoming the dominant medium to deliver courses at a distance. The Copyright Office acknowledged this shift and observed that the technological characteristics of digital transmissions in the late 1990s "rendered the language of section 110(2) inapplicable to the most advanced delivery method for systematic instruction."[31]

The inadequacy of section 110(2) was the subject of extensive public debate prior to the passage of the Digital Millennium Copyright Act (DMCA). Even though these discussions were conducted during Congress' consideration of the DMCA, no conclusion was reached.[32] In 1998, Congress directed the Copyright Office to "consult with representatives of copyright owners, nonprofit educational institutions, and nonprofit libraries and archives" and submit to Congress "recommendations on how to promote distance education through digital technologies, including interactive digital networks, while maintaining an appropriate balance between the rights of copyright owners and the needs of users of copyrighted works."[33] As a result, the Copyright Office Report was developed. The Copyright Office determined that:

> Where a statutory provision intended to implement a particular policy is written in such a way that it becomes obsolete due to changes in technology, the provision may require updating if that policy is to continue. Doing so may be seen not as preempting a new market, but as accommodating existing markets that are being tapped by new methods. In the view of the Copyright Office, section 110(2) represents an example of this phenomenon.[34]

The Copyright Office Report recommended many changes to the old educational transmission exemption including:

▷ eliminate the requirement of a physical classroom;
▷ clarify that the term transmission covers digital transmissions;
▷ expand the rights covered by the exemption to include those needed to accomplish network transmissions;
▷ emphasize [the] concept of mediated instruction;

- ▶ maintain [the] existing standards of eligibility;
- ▶ require use of lawful copies;
- ▶ expand the category of works exempted from the performance rights beyond the coverage of nondramatic literary and musical works;
- ▶ create new safeguards to counteract the risks imposed by digital transmissions; and
- ▶ add new ephemeral recordings exemption.[35]

The Copyright Office's recommendations were in large part placed in the original bill that was introduced in the Senate by Senators Hatch and Leahy. That bill contained several conditions and requirements. Most notably, the bill would have required institutions to apply "technological measures that reasonably prevent unauthorized access to and dissemination of the work and, does not intentionally interfere with technological measures used by the copyright owner to protect the work."[36] Publishers desired increased technological protection and thought the protection in the Hatch/Leahy bill was insufficient.[37]

The Technology, Education, and Copyright Harmonization Act implemented many of the Copyright Office recommendations and was officially signed into law by President George W. Bush on November 2, 2002. One of the major changes from the Senate Bill was the duty placed on institutions to apply technological protection measures that reasonably prevent unauthorized retention and dissemination of copyrighted works. As Kristine H. Hutchinson notes,

> [r]equiring institutions to prevent retention of copyright works provides greater protection of copyright owners' markets while imposing a significantly higher burden on institutions. Copyright owners believed and educators eventually agreed that this higher standard of protection was necessary to ensure that online educators' and their students' uses of the copyrighted works do not cause significant harms to the markets for their copyrighted works.[38]

The next section details the requirements and conditions of the new law.

THE TECHNOLOGY, EDUCATION, AND COPYRIGHT HARMONIZATION ACT OF 2002

The principal sponsors of TEACH in Congress stated that the TEACH Act is designed to update the distance education provisions of the Copyright Act for the twenty-first century and achieve certain goals:

- ▶ To promote distance learning by preventing students and teachers from running afoul of U.S. copyright law and implement the recommendations from the May 1999 report from the Register of Copyrights;
- ▶ To enable increased educational access to a variety of types of students in urban and rural areas; and

▶ To update the old distance education exemption by:
  ▶ eliminating the physical classroom requirement;
  ▶ covering temporary copies of works made in transmission; and
  ▶ permitting transmission of expanded classes of works, such as audiovisual works and sound recordings.[39]

The TEACH Act is a technical piece of legislation that does not have the simplicity of the face-to-face teaching exemption or, relatively speaking, of fair use. Specifically, the TEACH Act has several conditions that must be met prior to asserting the exemption as a rationale for use of copyrighted works in educational transmissions.

Types of Works

Excluded Classes of Works

The TEACH Act does not apply to works that are unlawfully acquired and the institution "knew or had reason to believe" the works were not lawfully made and acquired. The TEACH Act also does not apply to works produced or marketed for performance or display as part of mediated instructional activities transmitted via digital networks.

Included Classes of Works

The TEACH Act does exempt the following categories of works:
  ▶ the public performance of a nondramatic literary work or musical work; or
  ▶ reasonable and limited portions of any other work; or
  ▶ the public display of a work in an amount comparable to that which is typically displayed in the course of a live class session.[40]

Most notably, the TEACH Act does expand the uses of copyrighted works in digital distance education. However, entire audiovisual works such as films still cannot be performed in digital distance education. These expanded possible uses in distance education environments are subject to numerous conditions that must be met. These conditions highlight the publishers' concern, valid or not, that their works would be widely disseminated in the digital environment. If a professor wants to invoke the TEACH Act in defense of a claim of copyright infringement, the professor would have to meet all the threshold conditions and requirements of the TEACH Act.

Conditions for Performance or Display

The performance or display must be:
  ▶ made at the direction of, or under the actual supervision of an instructor;[41]
  ▶ an integral part of class session;[42]
  ▶ part of systematic mediated instructional activities;[43]

▶ made by an accredited nonprofit educational institution or governmental body; and[44]

▶ directly related and of material assistance to the teaching content of the transmission.[45]

The Senate Report indicates that the "actual supervision" requirement does not require constant supervision or approval by the instructor. The term mediated instructional activity is defined according to the Senate Report as:

> activities that use [copyrighted materials] . . . integral to the class experience, controlled by or under the actual supervision of the instructor and analogous to the type of performance or display that would take place in a live classroom setting. The term does not refer to activities that use, in 1 or more class sessions of a single course, such works as textbooks, coursepacks, or other material in any media, copies or phonorecords of which are typically purchased or acquired by the students in higher education for their independent use and retention or are typically purchased or acquired for elementary and secondary students for their possession and independent use.[46]

According to the Senate Report, the mediated instructional activity requirement was intended to prevent the TEACH Act from displacing textbooks, coursepacks, or other material that are typically purchased by students for their independent use. The TEACH Act was not intended to address student use of "supplemental" or research materials such as electronic coursepacks, e-reserves, and digital library resources. The requirement that the performance or display must be integral to the class session is related to the concept of "mediated instructional activity" in that the performance or display must not be a supplemental or ancillary use of the copyrighted work. The Senate Report defines class session as the period during which a student is logged on to the server of the institution making the display or performance and is likely to vary with the needs of the course. However, a class session cannot last for the entire semester.

It is interesting to note that authors of the TEACH Act used traditional face-to-face teaching as the conceptual model for understanding terms like class session. For example, the Senate Report states that class session is intended "to describe the equivalent of an actual single face-to-face mediated class session."[47] In light of the time/space/resource flexibility that digital distance education provides, as discussed in the introduction of this chapter, the author finds it rather perplexing that the conceptual model used to develop TEACH was so restrictive. Perhaps this was because the drafters were relatively unfamiliar with online education. However, the face-to-face teaching model is an incongruent one to use for describing a distance education class session. Depending on the type of course, independent study, graduate fieldwork, etc., the class session could in fact be the entire semester and work would need to be accessed for an extended period of time. Again, the face-to-face teaching analogy that is used throughout the TEACH Act was restrictive and, in the author's opinion, a conceptual error that makes the new law seem at once new and archaic.

The TEACH Act further limits the nature of the educational transmission such that the transmission must be made solely for and is limited to:

- students officially "enrolled in the course for which the transmission is made;[48] or"
- governmental employees or officers for their duties or employment.[49]

The TEACH Act also imposes requirements for the institution or transmitting body that must be met. These requirements include:

- copyright policy development and implementation;[50]
- providing information to faculty, students, and staff that accurately describes and promotes compliance with copyright law;[51]
- providing notice to students that information may be copyrighted;[52]
- for digital transmissions, applying technological measures that reasonably prevent retention of the work in accessible form by recipients of the transmission for longer than the "class session";[53]
- for digital transmissions, applying technological measures that reasonably prevent unauthorized further dissemination of the work in accessible form;[54] and
- for digital transmissions, not engaging in conduct that could reasonably be expected to interfere with technological measures used by copyright owners to prevent retention and further unauthorized dissemination.[55]

According to the House Report, the additional responsibilities of instituting copyright policies and providing information to students are intended to "promote an environment of compliance with the law, inform recipients of their responsibilities under copyright law, and decrease the likelihood of unintentional and uninformed acts of infringement."[56] The House Report also states that the technological measures used to "reasonably prevent" retention of a work for longer than a class session and unauthorized further dissemination of the work in accessible form need not be perfect.[57] However, reasonable prevention is an objective standard of reasonableness regarding the ability of a technological protection measure to achieve its purpose. The House Report lists streaming technologies, digital rights management systems that limit access to or use encrypted material downloaded onto a computer as examples of technological measures referred to by the TEACH Act.[58] The House Report also suggests that the requirement of technological measures that "reasonably prevent" may evolve because of evolutions in technology or the "availability of a hack" that can be readily used by the public.[59] Additionally, these technological controls must reasonably prevent retention of the work for "longer than the class session." This class session language again refers to the analogous face-to-face sessions.

The TEACH Act also includes an amendment to section 112(f) that authorizes educators to make the copies needed to display and perform works in the educational transmission. Section 112(f) permits those authorized to perform and display works pursuant to 110(2) to copy digital works and digitize analog works. This is subject to the following conditions:

▶ copies are retained only by the institutions and are used pursuant to 110(2); and

▶ if digitizing analog works, no digital version of the works is available at the institution or the available digital version of the work is subject to technological protection measures that prevent its use under 110(2).

USE OF THE TEACH ACT

In October 2004, the Center for Intellectual Property conducted a survey of Research 1 and Liberal Arts Colleges to determine the use of digital rights management systems in use at higher education institutions. The survey asked, among other matters, about institutional compliance with the TEACH Act. The survey was sent to chief information officers, library directors, and directors of distance or continuing education. A total of 1437 individuals received the survey and a total of 771 institutions were surveyed.[60] Moreover, of the respondents, only 7.8 percent stated that their institution was taking advantage of the TEACH Act.[61] Approximately two years after the passage of the TEACH Act, few institutions are taking advantage of the new law. The survey findings confirm earlier reports that the law was not being widely used by higher education institutions.[62] The CIP's study did not identify any overarching reason for nonuse.

There are many possible reasons for the nonuse of the TEACH Act. Perhaps institutions need more than two years to complete a cost-benefit analysis of the new law. Perhaps the TEACH Act provisions are too complex. Perhaps institutional decision-makers do not have enough knowledge or are not aware of the TEACH Act. Of the respondents to the CIP survey, 52.9 percent indicated that they were either very or somewhat knowledgeable about the TEACH Act.[63] And 41.4 percent indicated that they were not very knowledgeable or not knowledgeable at all.[64]

In his article "Regulatory Copyright," Joseph Liu gives a possible reason why the TEACH Act is not widely used. As stated earlier, compared to the original sections 110(2) and 110(1), the TEACH Act has far more conditions than earlier exemptions. Liu notes that the trend in recent copyright legislation is for more detailed and complex statutes as he states:

> [T]he increasing complexity of the Copyright Act has become the subject of bemused humor among copyright scholars and others. Comparisons to the tax code are becoming increasingly frequent. . . . Many commentators have become concerned that the complexity of the code is making it more difficult for individuals to understand and comply with its provisions.[65]

Liu goes on to state:

The trend [in recent copyright legislation] is such that this mode of "regulatory copyright" is now arguably the dominant mode of copyright lawmaking. . . . The great strength of the regulatory approach in copyright is that it permits far more detailed and precise tailoring of rights and responsibilities in response to specific industry structures. . . . At the same time, the regulatory approach, as currently implemented in the copyright context, suffers from a number of weaknesses. The regulatory approach is more complex and therefore more costly to administer. The complexity makes copyright law less coherent and less transparent. . . . As currently implemented, the regulatory approach in copyright lacks flexibility, and thus presents the risk of locking in existing industry structures. The current approach also makes insufficient use of expertise and empirical data in the policymaking process.

. . .

[W]here the case for market failure is not so clear, where there is significant uncertainty about technology and/or the future structure of the market and where there are new entrants, a property based model may be preferable. This suggests that recent attempts to apply a regulatory model to digital copyright issues are ill-advised.[66]

The TEACH Act has been touted by many to be a welcome modernization of the copyright law. It certainly modernizes the old section 110(2) and brings it up to date with the technologies that are presently used to deliver digital distance education. However, the TEACH Act continues a trend in regulatory copyright that provides for a very detailed statutory provision that is costly to administer. The TEACH Act is a textbook example of the type of regulatory copyright to which Liu refers.

The TEACH Act has some benefits in that it updates former 110(2); is the result of compromises by education, library, and publishing communities; permits the expansion of possible types of works in classes; expands the possible locations for receipt of educational transmissions; and permits digitizing analog works. The weaknesses of the TEACH Act are the incongruous conceptual model used to develop the exception, the exacting requirements for instructors and institutions, and the lack of clear meaning of key terms that are critical to the exemption, like class session and reasonably prevent. The TEACH Act does not permit the use of an entire video/movie, and requires greater institutional roles and responsibility for controlling retention and dissemination of digital content. According to Liu, greater institutional roles and responsibilities translate into increased costs for institutions. Additionally, some contend that the failure of the TEACH Act to cover e-reserves is also a deficiency of the law.

Presently, few institutions comply with its provisions. Ultimately, every university or college thinking about taking advantage of the TEACH Act must do a cost-benefit analysis. The time and energy needed to analyze the statute and determine whether or not it applies to instructional and institutional needs are costs. Building and maintaining any required compliance program is a cost.[67] Training faculty, staff, and students is yet another cost.[68] K. Matthew Dames succinctly evaluates the cost-benefit analysis for the TEACH Act and concludes:

> Using and implementing the TEACH Act effectively will require collaboration with a copyright specialist—perhaps also the university's legal counsel—and healthy doses of vigilance and patience. Given these costs, an educator should ask, "Is parsing through the TEACH Act worth the time, energy, effort, and money that is required for compliance?" Some educators may decide that the increased resource commitments needed to comply with the TEACH Act outweigh the alleged diminished copyright infringement risk . . . In the end, and despite Congress' best efforts, the TEACH Act may not be the balanced, fair copyright limitation it is intended to be.[69]

FAIR USE

If an institution and/or instructor finds that compliance with the TEACH Act is not worth the costs, other options remain. Fair use has been a primary limitation in copyright law used to deliver copyrighted works to both educators and students. Chapter 3 discusses the details of fair use. Nevertheless, the fair use provision should be recited here. Moreover, Congress intended for fair use to fill gaps in areas covered inadequately by the TEACH Act.[70]

> Fair use is a critical part of the distance education landscape. Not only instructional performances and displays, but also other educational uses of works, such as the provision of supplementary materials or student downloading of course materials, will continue to be subject to the fair use doctrine. Fair use could apply as well to instructional transmissions not covered by the changes in 110(2) . . .[71]

Fair use is a limitation of the exclusive rights of the copyright owner that applies to all classes of copyrighted works. If a use is considered fair, permission and payment of licensing fees are not needed. Pursuant to section 107, fair use was created to further certain public uses such as "criticism, comment, news reporting, teaching (including multiple copies for classroom use), scholarship, or research."[72] Specifically, section 107 states four criteria that must be used to determine whether or not a use is fair. Ultimately, a court of law must evaluate four criteria stated in section 107 to determine a fair use:

- ▶ the purpose and character of the use, including whether such use is of a commercial nature or is for nonprofit educational purposes;[73]
- ▶ the nature of the copyrighted work;[74]
- ▶ the amount and substantiality of the portion used in relation to the copyrighted work as a whole;[75] and
- ▶ the effect of the use on the potential market for or value of the copyrighted work.[76]

Fair use determinations are made on a case by case basis depending on the facts of a given situation. Since the TEACH Act has several limitations for use and also does not cover copying and other uses, fair use will continue to be used in the development of online education; however, risks exist. The final decision on whether a use is fair or not must be made by a court of law. There is little certainty that a court will apply the facts of a given situation similar to educational institutions. Some courts may draw the boundaries of fair use in a more restrictive manner than educational institutions. That uncertainty makes fair use less appealing for many academic enterprises. Chapter 3 goes into further detail about each factor and relevant case law. As an initial matter, any teacher or administrator considering using the TEACH Act should also review fair use to determine if both limitations will effectively help deliver educational content via digital network transmissions.

CONCLUSION

The TEACH Act continues a trend in regulatory copyright. Whether that approach to the changing technologies involved in transferring information and knowledge is wise remains to be seen. The TEACH Act is an improvement over the previous section 110(2) in that it expands the types of copyrighted works used in digital distance education and can be applied to digital network transmissions of educational content. The TEACH Act is not an improvement over the previous section 110(2) in that the conditions of use are numerous, greater burdens and responsibilities are placed on institutions, and critical concepts are either unclear or improperly defined. Although these reasons have not been definitively identified as the primary reasons for noncompliance with the law, it is fair to assume that some variation of these reasons may explain why. Any institution or instructor thinking about complying with the TEACH Act should do a cost-benefit analysis to determine whether the TEACH Act is worth the costs. Institutions and instructors should also recognize that fair use, with its simple yet complex four factors, is still available when the TEACH Act does not provide the needed coverage for certain uses of copyrighted works in digital distance education.

NEXT STEPS

▶ Assemble a team at your institution to conduct a cost-benefit analysis of the TEACH Act. Members of the team should include information technologists, librarians, faculty, legal counsel, and a distance education coordinator or dean.
▶ After the cost-benefit analysis is completed and you determine that TEACH is beneficial for your institution, you should do the following:
  ▶ develop a copyright use policy;
  ▶ provide accurate information to faculty, students, and staff about copyright;

- ► include notices that materials may be protected by copyright;
- ► make sure systems do not interfere with technological controls on the materials to be use;
- ► determine if materials may only be accessed by students enrolled in the course;
- ► provide technology that reasonably limits the students' ability to retain or disseminate materials;
- ► make the materials only available to students for a period of time pertinent to the class session;
- ► store materials on secure servers and transmit portions allowed by law;
- ► do not make any copies other than the one needed to make the transmission;
- ► determine whether materials are of the proper type and amount;
- ► determine whether materials are not among those the law specifically excludes from coverage; and
- ► if using an analog original, determine that the amount copied is the amount you are authorized to copy and there is no digital copy of the work available except with technological protections that prevent use for the class the way the statute authorizes.[77]

ENDNOTES

[1] Technology, Education, and Copyright Harmonization Act of 2002, Pub. L. No. 107-273, § 13301, 116 Stat. 1758, 1911-14 (codified at 17 U.S.C. §§ 110(2), 112(f) (Supp. II 2003)).

[2] I. Elaine Allen and Jeff Seaman, *Growing by Degrees: Online Education in the United States*, 2005 3, 5 (2005), *available at* http://www.sloan-c.org/resources/growing_by_degrees.pdf.

[3] *Id.* at 11.

[4] *Id.* at 20.

[5] U.S. Copyright Office, Report on Copyright and Digital Distance Education 20 (1999) [hereinafter Copyright Office Report], *available at* http://www.copyright.gov/reports/de_rprt.pdf.

[6] *Id.*

[7] University of Maryland University College, Promotion of Distance Education through Digital Technologies 4 (Feb. 5, 1999) (written submission to the Copyright Office). The TEACH Act ultimately does not address the e-reserve issue asserted by UMUC in its written submission.

[8] *Id.*

[9] *Promoting Technology and Education: Turbocharging the School Buses on the Information Superhighway: Hearing on S. 487 Before the S. Comm. on the Judiciary*, 107th Cong. 19 (2001) (statement of Gerald A. Heeger, President of University of Maryland University College).

[10] U.S. Const. Art 1, § 8, cl 8.

[11] Copyright Act of 1709 (Statute of Anne), 8 Anne, c. 19.

[12] Arlene Bielefield, *Technology and Copyright Law: A Guidebook for the Library* 19 (1996).

[13] 17 U.S.C. § 102(a) (2000).

[14] 17 U.S.C. § 106(1) (2000 & Supp. II 2003).

[15] 17 U.S.C. § 106(2).

[16] 17 U.S.C. § 106(3).

[17] 17 U.S.C. § 106(4).

[18] 17 U.S.C. § 106(5).

[19] 17 U.S.C. § 106(6).

[20] 17 U.S.C. § 107 (2000).

[21] 17 U.S.C. § 108 (2000).

[22] 17 U.S.C. § 109 (2000).

[23] 17 U.S.C. § 110 (Supp. II 2003).

[24] *See* 17 U.S.C. §§ 101, 106(4), 106(5) (2000 & Supp. II 2003).

[25] 17 U.S.C. § 110(2) (2000).

[26] H.R. Rep. No. 94-1476, at 83 (1976), *as reprinted in* 1995 U.S.C.C.A.N. 5659, 5697.

[27] 17 U.S.C. § 110(2)(A) (2000).

[28] 17 U.S.C. § 110(2)(B).

[29] 17 U.S.C. § 110(2)(C).

[30] Copyright Office Report, *supra* note 5, at 13.

[31] *Id.* at xv.

[32] S. Rep. No. 107-31, at 5 (2001).

[33] S. Rep. No. 107-31, at 5

[34] Copyright Office Report, *supra* note 5, at xv.

[35] *Id.* at 146–61.

[36] 147 Cong. Rec. S 2006, 2008 (daily ed. Mar. 7, 2001); *see also* Copyright Office Report, *supra* note 5, at 150–52.

[37] *Promoting Technology and Education: Turbocharging the School Buses on the Information Super-highway: Hearing on S. 487 Before the S. Comm. on the Judiciary*, 107th Cong. 22-23 (2001) (statement of Allan R. Adler, Vice President for Legal and Governmental Affairs, Association of American Publishers).

[38] Kristine H. Hutchinson, *The TEACH Act: Copyright Law and Online Education*, 78 N.Y.U. L. Rev. 2204, 2222–23 (2003).

[39] S. Rep. No. 107-31 at 4-5 (2001).

[40] 17 U.S.C. § 110(2) (2000 & Supp. II 2003).

[41] 17 U.S.C. § 110(2)(A).

[42] 17 U.S.C. § 110(2)(A).

[43] 17 U.S.C. § 110(2)(A).

[44] 17 U.S.C. § 110(2)(A).

[45] 17 U.S.C. § 110(2)(B).

[46] S. Rep. No. 107-31, at 2 (2001).

[47] S. Rep. No.107-31, at 12 (2001).

[48] 17 U.S.C. § 110(2)(C)(i).

[49] 17 U.S.C. § 110(2)(C)(ii).

[50] 17 U.S.C. § 110(2)(D)(i).

[51] 17 U.S.C. § 110(2)(D)(i).

[52] 17 U.S.C. § 110(2)(D)(i).

[53] 17 U.S.C. § 110(2)(D)(ii)(I)(aa).

[54] 17 U.S.C. § 110(2)(D)(ii)(I)(bb).

[55] 17 U.S.C. § 110(2)(D)(ii)(II).

[56] H.R. Rep No. 107-687, at 11–12 (2002).

[57] H.R. Rep No. 107-687, at 13

[58] H.R. Rep No. 107-687, at 13.

[59] H.R. Rep No. 107-687, at 13.

[60] Center for Intellectual Property in the Digital Environment, University of Maryland University College, *Digital Rights Management (DRM) and Higher Education: Opportunities and Challenges* 19–20 (Oct. 31, 2005) [hereinafter Mellon DRM Report] (final report prepared for The Andrew W. Mellon Foundation, Teaching and Technology / Scholarly Communications Program).

[61] *Id.* at 43-44.

[62] *See* Dan Carnevale, *Slow Start for Long-Awaited Easing of Copyright Restriction*, Chron. Higher Educ., Mar 28, 2003, at A29.

[63] Mellon DRM Report, *supra* note 60, at 42.

[64] *Id.*

[65] Joseph P. Liu, *Regulatory Copyright*, 83 N.C. L. Rev. 87, 88 (2004).

[66] *Id.* at 91-93.

[67] K. Matthew Dames, *Copyright Clearances: Navigating the TEACH Act*, Online, Mar./Apr. 2005, at 29.

[68] *Id.*

[69] *Id.*

[70] S. Rep. No 107-31 at 14-15 (2001).

[71] *Id.*

[72] 17 U.S.C. § 107 (2000).

[73] 17 U.S.C. § 107(1).

[74] 17 U.S.C. § 107(2).

[75] 17 U.S.C. § 107(3).

[76] 17 U.S.C. § 107(4).

[77] Georgia Harper, *The TEACH Act Finally Becomes Law*, http://www.utsystem.edu/ogc/intellectualproperty/teachact.htm#actsummary (last visited Nov. 18, 2005).

▶6

THE DIGITAL MILLENNIUM COPYRIGHT ACT AND THE UNIVERSITY CAMPUS:

A SAFE HARBOR?

ARNOLD P. LUTZKER

This chapter discusses the following topics:
▶ A review of DMCA history and how the DMCA was originally written to provide online service providers protection for liability resulting from the acts of their user communities
▶ Concepts of OSP and Safe Harbor
▶ Legislative developments and recent DMCA judicial opinions concerned with the responsibilities institutions have as OSPs, particularly regarding peer-to-peer file sharing.

THE DMCA: AN OVERVIEW

The Digital Millennium Copyright Act (DMCA), enacted into law in 1998, was the most substantial overhaul of copyright laws in a generation. Copyright, the set of rules that govern ownership and use of creative works, is recognized in the U.S. Constitution and made manifest in a series of statutes that date back to the first Congress. Over the past two and one-quarter centuries, copyright laws have adapted to the advent of the printing press, photography, phonographs, radio, television, the photocopy machine, and the VCR. Recognizing the impact of digital technology on all creative works and the growing importance of the Internet as a medium for sharing digital files, Congress concluded that legislation was needed to strengthen legal protections against the potential for massive digital piracy and enacted the DMCA.

To understand the DMCA issues affecting universities today, it is useful to recognize that educational institutions were crucial to the development and growth of the

Internet throughout its formative years (the 1960s through the early 1990s). Originally conceived by the Defense Department as a way of internetworking government computers, the digital medium was embraced by universities first as an efficient and later as an indispensable means for disseminating research and information. Thus, any rules that affect the Internet and digital technology impact on educators.

The progress of the DMCA can be divided into three stages. First, when Bill Clinton became president, his administration initiated a study of the National Information Infrastructure (NII). Among other things, the NII Agenda for Action led to several detailed reports that analyzed changes needed to tailor copyright law to the Internet. Second, since the Internet had become synonymous with a *global network of computers*, as a preliminary step to U.S. law reform, the Clinton administration pushed for amendments to the Berne Convention, the pre-eminent international treaty that establishes rules for copyright cooperation. The effort culminated in the adoption of two World Intellectual Property Organization (WIPO) treaties in 1996. Third, for the United States to accede to the WIPO Treaties, certain changes were needed in its copyright law. These changes constituted a core motivation for passage of the DMCA.

The key statutory elements of the DMCA are rules: (1) to prohibit circumvention of technological measures designed to control access to digital copyrighted works; (2) to publish and protect copyright management information; and (3) to limit the liability of online service providers. As the congressional debate opened the copyright law to intense scrutiny, the DMCA incorporated certain additional amendments that were advocated by various interests, including an update of the limitations on copying supervised by libraries. In addition, the DMCA debate laid the foundation for legislation subsequently adopted to reform distance education (the TEACH Act of 2002). Another provision ultimately deemed too controversial to be included in the final version of the DMCA would have created a new legal regime to regulate exploitation of databases. To this day, database legislation, an important goal of many content publishers, remains hotly contested. On a parallel track, but adopted in separate legislation, was a 20-year extension of the copyright term. While several of these topics are dealt with elsewhere in this publication, this chapter will focus on the limitation of liability for online service providers and its application to universities.

ONLINE SERVICE PROVIDER LIMITATION ON LIABILITY FOR COPYRIGHT INFRINGEMENT—GENERALLY

The Problem—Contributory and Vicarious Copyright Infringement

One of the persistent problems associated with the Internet that sparked concern during consideration of the DMCA and remains of vital importance to content owners was the fact that copyrighted works, such as musical CDs and feature films, were being posted at renegade sites for anyone to download. Content owners expressed fear that their system of commercial distribution of digital works would be jeopardized if unauthorized digital duplication was not curtailed. However, since the cyberspace perpetrator of the infringement may reside outside the United States, may operate under a different legal regime, or may be judgment-proof or simply untraceable, the content owners, relying on the principle of vicarious and contributory infringement, directed their legal complaints to the online service providers that link subscribers to these sites.

Briefly, under copyright law, if someone copies, publicly distributes, or publicly displays a copyrighted work without authority of the copyright owner or its agent, then a direct violation of law has occurred; even innocent infringements are subject to penalties. If someone has the right and ability to supervise the infringing actions of another, then that person may be "vicariously" liable for the infringement of the other person. Vicarious liability often involves a direct financial interest or benefit, and may be found even without the supervisor having actual knowledge of what is taking place. The principle has been applied to hold dancehall operators liable for copyright infringements caused by bands they hire (*Dreamland Ball Room, Inc., v. Shapiro, Bernstein & Co.*, 36 F.2d 354 [7th Cir. 1929]). Contributory infringement, by contrast, is found when one who, with knowledge of the infringement induces, causes, or materially contributes to the infringement (*Gershwin Publ'g Corp. v. Columbia Artists Mgt, Inc.* 443 F.2d 1159 [2d Cir. 1971]). A contributory infringer is connected to the infringement in a material way and does not need to be a direct infringer. Providing services or equipment can be enough of a connection.

In two cases involving online Bulletin Board Services (BBS) or entities that provide online access—Online Service Providers or "OSPs"—courts ruled that the unauthorized uploading and downloading of digitized works, such as photographic images or electronic games, constituted copyright infringement by the BBS operator when reproduction by BBS subscribers was unauthorized.[1]

These BBS cases contrasted with another ruling that framed the DMCA debate and ultimately the solution for OSPs. In a nuanced analysis, *Religious Technology Center v. Netcom On-Line Communications Services, Inc.*, 907 F. Supp. 1361 (N.D. Cal. 1995), the court held that the service provider was not liable for copyright infringement when a subscriber transmitted copyrighted documents without authority, because the OSP had no knowledge of its particular contents and merely provided the facilities for automatic transmissions.

For OSP services, the possibility of liability for copyright infringement due to contributory or vicarious actions created a potentially huge and unpredictable legal exposure, because if the service were responsible for the infringing actions of its subscribers, hundreds, if not thousands, of infringements could be occurring daily without direct participation or control of the OSP. Since copyright law permits the copyright owner prevailing in an infringement action to receive actual damages and profits of the infringer, or, in the alternative, "statutory damages" (currently $750–$30,000 per work infringed; up to $150,000 per work in cases of willful infringement) plus attorneys' fees, the potential exposure for OSPs is gigantic. Thus, as the DMCA debate began, OSPs rose in unified opposition to the charge of contributory copyright infringer and sought legislative protection. Their defense relied upon their passive role as an intermediary, unaware of what content is being communicated over their facilities. Among the most steadfast proponents of the OSPs' position were representatives of universities, colleges and libraries, whose sophisticated digital networks were beginning to be blamed for much of the infringing activities.

Traditionally, common carriers have been explicitly exempt from liability for copyright infringement because they merely provide the facilities that link sender and receiver and have no control over the actual content of the transmissions.[2] For libraries and educational institutions, this passive role properly described their functions for patrons, students, and faculty in connection with the Internet. Nevertheless, in their capacity as service providers, educational institutions actually do more than simply link users to servers. Like other OSPs, they provide software to link users to sites, they store information on their servers, and they facilitate recordings and displays by subscribers. Each of these activities is a function that may be characterized as implicating the exclusive copyright of content owners, and, under the theories of contributory and vicarious copyright infringement explained above, relief from liability was needed. The fact that an institution is "not for profit" does not eliminate exposure to the copyright infringement claim.

The Solution—A Safe Harbor for Limiting Liability

To remedy this exposure, commercial and nonprofit OSPs sought a limitation under copyright law. After two years of negotiations, the Online Copyright Infringement Liability Limitation was approved by Congress as part of the DMCA.[3] The limitation is not a free pass; rather, it creates a "safe harbor" from the most onerous impact of liability—it eliminates exposure to money damages. The rules do *not* exempt an OSP from being sued or having to comply with an injunction. Still, as a safe harbor, it serves as a first line of defense against a claim of copyright infringement and is, in addition to other copyright defenses and limitations, like fair use.

The rules governing the OSP limitation on liability identify four categories of services and prescribe conditions that must be met for the limitation to apply in a particular category. There are also strict deadlines which, if ignored, may undo the limitation. Unless legal requirements are met, an OSP, even a nonprofit institution, faces loss of the exemption and exposure to potentially large copyright damage claims. To manage risks, libraries and educational institutions that operate as service providers must establish internal mechanisms to ensure compliance, and they should monitor their efforts regularly.

DETAILS OF THE OSP LIMITATION

Categories of Services

The new provision recognizes four separate and distinct functions of most transitory digital network operations and establishes criteria for establishing a safe harbor for each function. Specifically, the categories of services are:

- ▶ transmitting, routing, or providing connections for infringing material;[4]
- ▶ system caching or the intermediate and temporary storage of material on a system or network controlled or operated by the OSP;[5]
- ▶ placing information on a system or network at the direction of users;[6] and
- ▶ linking users to infringing sites or using information location tools, *such as directories, indexes, and hypertext links.*[7]

SERVICE PROVIDER DEFINED

The statute has two definitions of "service provider." The first is particularly applicable to those OSPs providing transmitting, routing, and connection services; the other applies to all services. The copyright law defines a service provider as follows:

> (a) "[a]n entity offering the transmission, routing, or providing of connections for digital online communications between or among points specified by a user, or material of the user's choosing, without modification as to the content of the material as sent or received;"[8] and
>
> (b) "[a] provider of online services or network access, or the operator of facilities therefor."[9]

All entities whose services fit these descriptions—and the definition in (b) is intended to be broad—may qualify for the safe harbor with regard to those activities.

However, it is critical to the limitation that the definitions only involve the passive activities of the OSP. To the extent the OSP's actions involve creation and posting of content, choosing recipients of messages or controlling users, the limitation does not apply, and regular copyright rules respecting proper clearance, as well as fair use and other defenses, are applicable.

Conditions for Qualifying for the Limitation.

To qualify fully for the limitation with regard to all covered OSP activities, a set of conditions for each specific function must be met. If an institution performs all the OSP functions, as most do, then all requirements must be met. The following summary breaks down the requirements into three pertinent categories.

1. *Material.*

   i. The material must be made available online by someone other than the OSP.[10]

   ii. The OSP cannot modify the material.[11]

   iii. No copy of the material during intermediate storage shall be maintained longer than "reasonably necessary."[12]

   iv. The OSP does not have "actual knowledge" that the material or the activity is infringing; more specifically,[13]

      a. it is not aware of facts or circumstances from which infringing activity is apparent; or

      b. upon receiving such awareness, the OSP acts expeditiously to remove or disable access to the site.

2. *Parties to the Transmissions.*

   i. The transmissions must be initiated by or at the direction of another person and sent to another.[14]

   ii. No copy of the material during intermediate storage shall be made accessible to another person.[15]

   iii. The OSP must not select recipients.[16]

   iv. The OSP does not receive a financial benefit directly attributable to the infringing activity, in a case in which the OSP has the right and ability to control the activity.[17]

3. *Procedures.*

   i. The transmission, routing, provision of connections, or storage must be carried out through an automatic, technical process.[18]

   ii. The OSP must follow rules relating to refreshing, reloading, or other updating of the material.[19]

   iii. The OSP cannot interfere with technology associated with the material, such as access requirements or preconditions for use, such as passcodes or fees.[20]

   iv. The OSP must comply with:

      a. "notice and takedown" procedures, *i.e.*, upon "proper notification," expeditiously remove or disable access to the offending material,[21] and

      b. "counter-notice and put back" procedures, i.e., upon "proper *counter notice*," promptly notify copyright owner of the dispute and replace material within two weeks, unless the matter is referred to court.[22]

Obligations of Copyright Owners

The limitation has countervailing obligations for copyright owners. Among the most relevant are the following:

1. When the owner makes material available online, it must adhere to "a generally accepted industry standard data communications protocol for the system or network through which that person makes the material available."[23]
2. As to the OSP's obligation not to interfere with technology controlling access to the material (e.g., passcodes and fees), the owner's technology must
    i. "not *significantly* interfere with the performance of the [OSP's] system or network or with the intermediate storage of the material,"[24]
    ii. be "consistent with generally accepted industry communications protocols,"[25] and
    iii. "not extract information from the [OSP's] system or network about the person initiating the transmission that it could not have acquired through direct access to that person."[26]
3. Comply with notification requirements in connection with "notice and take down" procedures.[27]

Notice and Take Down

"Notice and take down" is an essential part of the protections sought by the content community and forms a regulatory regime for both OSPs and copyright owners. If a content owner reasonably believes that a site misuses copyrighted matter and it notifies the OSP according to statutory procedures, or if the OSP independently becomes aware of the facts and circumstances of infringement, then the OSP must expeditiously remove the material or disable public access to the site, or face loss of the safe harbors.

Among the elements of the notice and takedown process are the following:

1. The OSP must have a designated agent to receive notices and it must use a public portion of its Web site for receipt of notices.[28]
2. The OSP must notify the U.S. Copyright Office of the agent's identity.[29] The Copyright Office maintains electronic and hard copy registries of Web site agents.[30] In November, 1998, the Copyright Office published interim rules and procedures for registering Web site agents as service providers.[31] As of 2005, thousands of agents have registered. They are listed on the Copyright Office's Web site at http://www.copyright.gov/onlinesp/list/index.html.
3. Proper written notification from a copyright owner to an OSP must "substantially" include the following information:
    i. information, such as name and address, that is reasonably sufficient to permit the OSP to contact the complaining party;[32]
    ii. the written or electronic signature of the complaining party;[33]
    iii. sufficient information to identify the copyrighted work or works;[34]
    iv. the infringing matter and its Internet location;[35]
    v. a statement by the owner that it has a good faith belief that there is no legal basis for the use of the materials complained of;[36] and

    vi. a statement of the accuracy of the notice and, under penalty of perjury, that the complaining party is authorized to act on behalf of the owner.[37]

4. Any misrepresentation of material facts will subject the offending party to claims for damages and attorneys fees.[38]

Good Samaritan Immunity and "Notice and Put Back"

If the OSP complies in good faith with the statutory requirements, the new law immunizes it from liability to subscribers and third parties; however, this immunity is conditioned upon affording the affected subscriber notice of the action. If a subscriber files a proper "counter notice," attesting to its lawful use of the material, then the OSP must "promptly" notify the copyright owner and within 14 business days restore the material, unless the matter has been referred to a court. The counter notice must contain these elements:

1. The subscriber's name, address, phone number, and physical or electronic signature.[39]

2. Identification of the material and its location before removal and a statement under penalty of perjury that the material was removed by mistake or misidentification.[40]

3. Subscriber consent to local federal court jurisdiction, or if overseas, to an appropriate judicial body.[41]

Special Rule Regarding Teaching and Research Employees of Public and Nonprofit Higher Educational Institutions

The OSP regime also makes one special exception to the general rule that an institution is responsible for the acts of its employees.[42] In recognition of the principles of academic freedom and scholarly research and the practice of administrators of higher educational institutions of not interfering with classroom work, the statute provides that faculty and graduate students employed to teach or research shall not be considered "the institution" for OSP purposes. Thus, if, for example, a member of the faculty posts infringing content, selects recipient of infringing matter, or knows of an infringement, the institution would not automatically lose its right to the limitation.

The exception has three important qualifications:

1. The faculty or graduate student's activities do not involve online access (including e-mail) to materials that were "required or recommended" within the preceding three years for a course taught by the employee at the institution.[43]

2. The institution has not received more than *two* notices of actionable infringement by the faculty or graduate student.[44]

3. The institution provides all users of its system or network informational materials on compliance with U.S. copyright laws.[45]

If properly followed, the higher educational institution is not tainted by the actions of its teaching and research employees. As an institution, it would qualify for protection against money damage claims and could not be required to block access or terminate a subscriber. It could still be subject to other injunctive remedies, such as those involving preserving evidence.

PRIVACY AND SUBPOENA RULES

The statute also recognizes the importance of protecting the privacy of a user's identity on the Internet. Because many infringers are only known by an IP address that is meaningful only to the OSP, procedures are set forth in the DMCA by which a complaining copyright owner may subpoena information from the OSP about the identity of individual subscribers.[46] The principal safeguard involves the content owner's compliance with a formal court request that may be acted on by the clerk of a federal court. The request must contain the following information:

1. a copy of a notification required to be served on the OSP and described in the section dealing with notice and take down;[47]
2. "[a] proposed subpoena;"[48] and
3. "[a] sworn declaration to the effect that the purpose for which the subpoena is sought is to obtain the identity of an alleged infringer and that such information will only be used for the purpose of protecting rights under this title."[49]

If issued, the subpoena authorizes and orders the service provider to "expeditiously disclose to the copyright owner or person authorized by the copyright owner information sufficient to identify the alleged infringer of the material described in the notification to the extent such information is available to the service provider."[50] "If the notification filed satisfies the provisions of [Section 512(c)(3)(A)], the proposed subpoena is in proper form, and the accompanying declaration is properly executed, the [district court] clerk [must] expeditiously issue and sign the proposed subpoena and return it to the requester for delivery to the service provider."[51] If the copyright owner follows this process, the OSP is not only obligated to comply and disclose identifying information, but it will be protected from liability under federal or state prohibitions respecting release of information regarding individual subscribers. All this noted, if the subscriber who is the target of the investigation or the OSP wishes to challenge the subpoena, a district judge will entertain objections.

Other Key Requirements

In addition to all these rules, the OSP will not qualify for the limitation if it does not do two necessary things: (1) develop and post a policy for termination of repeat offenders; and (2) "accommodate and not interfere with standard technical measures"[52] used by copyright owners to identify and protect their works, such as digital watermarking and access codes. The Act makes clear that the OSP is *not required* to monitor its services for potential infringements. It does not have to seek out information about copyright misuse; however, it cannot ignore obvious facts.

Summary

In sum, the new rules that took effect in 1998 grant qualifying OSPs protection from financial liability for services that may contribute to copyright infringements. The key requirements are that the OSP's activities are passive and technically automatic, and the OSPs lack knowledge sufficient to stop the infringing activity. The limitations are not presumed, but are granted only to OSPs who can prove that they meet the requirements of the law. In other words, all OSPs wishing to be covered by the limitation regime must not be direct copyright infringers and must proactively comply with the section 512 rules. For example, failure to register with the Copyright Office, to post policies, or to cancel repeat offenders can be fatal to the claim of financial immunity.[53] Similarly, knowledge of infringing activities requires the OSP to take specific actions to disable access to its system or otherwise contain the opportunity for unauthorized digital copying or distribution.[54] Loss of the limitation can result in exposure to full liability for copyright infringement by anyone using the OSP's system.

For educational institutions that question whether they qualify as a service provider, the answer in almost all cases is "yes, they do." The statutory definition is very expansive, encompassing any provider of Internet access or online network services.[55] Broadly interpreted, most educational institutions qualify. However, with the safe harbors come clear burdens, including creating a Web site agent, registering that individual with the Copyright Office, satisfying the other conditions of the OSP rules, and responding rapidly to notifications of infringement. Because the Copyright Office registry may make notification by concerned copyright owners fast and effective, registered OSPs may find themselves embroiled in online copyright disputes over everything from songs to motion pictures to individual photographs and poems, digitally exploited by students, faculty, and visitors.

DEVELOPMENTS SINCE PASSAGE OF THE DMCA

The Case Law

Since 1998, several court battles have clarified the OSP Limitation on Liability. From the early cases, several points can be stated.

1. The Definition of Service Provider Will Be Broadly Construed. Courts are willing to define broadly who qualifies as a service provider for purposes of the limitation. In

In re Aimster Copyright Litig., 252 F. Supp. 2d 634 (N.D. Ill. 2002), *aff'd*, 334 F.3d 643 (7th Cir. 2003), *cert. denied*, 124 S. Ct. 1069 (2004), the Illinois courts determined that a service that connected digital signals from one user to another so that they could be identified as "buddies" qualified as a service provider.[56] The material sent was chosen by the users, and the service provided the means for digital connections by subscribers.[57] Moreover, the safe harbors apply not only to the service provider, but also to employees acting within the scope of their employment. *Hendrickson v. eBay, Inc.*, 165 F. Supp. 2d 1082, 1094–95 (C.D. Cal. 2001). For educational institutions, this latter point means that persons working in a school's technology departments are exempt from financial exposure.

2. *The Conditions of the Limitations Will Be Strictly Construed.* One theme that has been consistently repeated in litigation is that courts will strictly construe the terms and conditions of the limitation. When the statute requires that several conditions be met, compliance with less than all the conditions can be fatal to a defense against infringement. Thus, in *ALS Scan v. RemarQ Cmtys., Inc.*, 239 F.3d 619 (4th Cir. 2001), the court focused on the requirements in section 512 (c) that grant OSPs safe harbor from liability when storing material at the direction of the user, as long as three conditions are met: "(1) it has neither actual knowledge that its system contains infringing materials nor an awareness of facts or circumstances from which infringement is apparent, or has expeditiously removed or disabled access to infringing material upon obtaining actual knowledge of infringement; (2) it receives no financial benefit directly attributable to infringing activity; and (3) it has responded expeditiously to remove or disable access to material claimed to be infringing after receiving"[58] statutory notice from a copyright owner. To satisfy the limitation, an OSP must establish all three elements. In *ALS Scan*, the allegation that the OSP had knowledge of the infringements created a "triable issue" of fact.[59] Even though the copyright owner provided a flawed notification of infringement, it may have been adequate to place the OSP on notice and void the limitation.[60]

Two other cases underscore this point. In *Ellison v. Robertson*, 357 F.3d 1072 (9th Cir. 2004), the Court concluded that the failure of AOL to arrange for the forwarding of e-mail messages sent to an old e-mail address also raised a "triable issue" as to whether the OSP had "reason to know" about an infringement.[61] In the fall of 1999, AOL changed its e-mail address from copyright@aol.com to aolcopyright@aol.com, but it waited until April 2000 to register the change with the Copyright Office.[62] It also failed to configure the new address so it could receive notifications sent to the old address.[63] Finding that this failure was unreasonable, the Court concluded AOL may be deprived of any claim to innocence about infringing activities on its user network.[64]

In *Perfect 10, Inc. v. Cybernet Ventures, Inc.*, 213 F. Supp. 2d 1146 (C.D. Cal. 2002), the Court concluded that the failure reasonably to implement a policy to terminate repeat offenders was itself a basis for the loss of the limitation.[65] Because the statute requires, as a condition for eligibility, that OSPs must adopt and "reasonably implement" a policy that provides for the termination of subscribers "who are repeat infringers," failure to take such steps is fatal to the claim of safe harbor.[66]

3. *The Elements of the Notification Need Only Be "Substantially" Satisfied.* ALS Scan also stands for the proposition that less than perfect notification may still be sufficient. In that case, the OSP complained that the copyright owner neither identified the works infringed, nor the material that needed to be removed, with sufficient specificity.[67] Assuming that to be the case, the Court still found that the copyright owner met the statutory requirement, because the limitation only requires that the notice "substantially" include enumerated information.[68] Strictly reading the statute, the Court concluded ALS Scan's notice satisfied the statutory obligation.[69]

4. *The Subpoena Process Is a Key Battleground for Definition of Rights.* Many of the current DMCA legal disputes involve the practice of file sharing. Starting with Napster, *A & M Records, Inc. v. Napster, Inc.* 284 F.3d 1091 (9th Cir. 2002), which held that the innovator of Internet file sharing services was responsible for infringements caused by its subscribers, and continuing with the *MGM v. Grokster,* 380 F.3d 1154 (9th Cir. 2004), *cert. granted,* 543 U.S. 1032 (2004), *vacated and remanded* by 125 S. Ct. 2764 (2005), file-sharing technology has been the precipitating cause of many disputes. With file-sharing software is ubiquitous on college campuses, universities have needed to stay vigilant with respect to how their students and faculty use the technology available to them, lest the schools be pulled into the fray with legal exposure. Elsewhere in this book, file-sharing developments are discussed in depth. For OSPs, the file-sharing disputes have focused primarily on the need of content owners to find the infringers when they are only identified by a private Web address. Utilizing the mechanism of the subpoena process spelled out in section 512(h) of the safe harbor for OSPs, representatives of music and film owners have sought the full identity of subscribers. The cases have followed two particular paths.

First, content owners have notified OSPs, including schools, of the infringements they believe are rampant on their networks. When institutions indicate that privacy concerns prevent their divulging the student's or subscriber's identity, the copyright proprietors have filed for subpoenas with local courts. In *Elektra Entertainment Group, Inc., v. Does 1-9,* 2004 U.S. Dist. LEXIS 23560 (S.D.N.Y. 2004), copyright owners learned that students at colleges were sharing music without authority, but they could not identify the users sufficiently to sue them.[70] So the publishers filed subpoenas with the New York court to force the colleges to disclose the students' identities.[71] After receiving the subpoenas, the colleges told the students they were being forced to disclose their names.[72] On behalf of the students, the schools challenged the subpoenas (moving to quash them), arguing among other things that students had a First Amendment right to anonymity on the Internet.[73] Finding that the subpoenas were sufficiently specific to satisfy the statutory requirements, the Court rejected the defenses, concluding that there was only a minimal expectation of privacy on the Internet and the need to disclose the names to prevent copyright infringement outweighed the First Amendment interest.[74]

Second, in a closely watched case, *RIAA v. Verizon Internet Services, Inc.*, 351 F.3d 1229 (D.C. Cir. 2003), the Court held that the Section 512(h) subpoena may only be issued to an OSP that engaged in storing on its servers material that is infringing or the subject of an infringing activity.[75] A subpoena is not enforceable, the Court found, if the OSP did not store the content but only routed infringing material to or from a personal computer owned and used by a subscriber.[76] In 2005, this ruling was followed by a North Carolina court that quashed subpoenas issued to the University of North Carolina seeking the identity of students that used peer-to-peer programs to obtain music files.[77] The judge was persuaded that, as long as the university merely transmitted the content and did not store the songs on its server, the subpoena process in the DMCA was inapplicable.[78]

5. MGM v. Grokster: Inducing Infringement in a Digital Age. Whenever a case makes it onto the Supreme Court's calendar, it generates interest. Sometimes, the news of the case is so widespread, that the case's reputation precedes it. That was the situation with *MGM v. Grokster*, the Supreme Court case involving peer-to-peer (P2P) file-sharing software. Few copyright cases in the last generation have evoked more interest and debate, pitting parts of the copyright owning community against the technology creating and user communities.

The details of the ruling are well known. Grokster and other successors to Napster, the maverick file-sharing entity shut down by copyright litigation in 2002, developed file-sharing software that eliminated the legal flaw of its predecessor: rather than serving as a hub for sharing purposes, Grokster distributed software that, once loaded on a user's computer, facilitated file sharing directly between all similarly situated users without direct involvement of Grokster. The popularity of P2P software, marketed to enable downloading of music files, created enormous consternation on the part of the music and movie industry. Music, in particular, claimed a precipitous decline in sales of CDs with the rise of downloaded files.

Grokster had successfully argued in the U.S. Court of Appeals for the Ninth Circuit, 380 F.3d 1154 (9th Cir. 2004), that its software facilitated user access to public domain and freely available files (including many sponsored by under-appreciated musicians who favored P2P's informal distribution system to get their works out). Even though the P2P software companies claimed ignorance of what users were doing—indeed, how could they know what bits of data were in or out of copyright?—the District Court record suggested that 90 percent of the downloaded files were illegal copies. The P2P software companies urged that technology was the digital equivalent of the VCR, technology validated in the 1984 Sony Betamax case that held recording television programs off the air to be a fair use (legitimate time-shifting) and the technology that facilitated the fair use was thus capable of substantial noninfringing uses. *Sony Corp. of America v. Universal City Studios, 464 U.S. 417 (1984).*

The stage was set when the Supreme Court accepted MGM's petition for certiorari. Despite the *Sony* underpinning of the Ninth Circuit ruling, the Supreme Court declined to revisit or refine that important decision. Rather, the Court reversed the 9th Circuit and concluded the case should not be resolved on the basis of fair use. Instead, the case needed to be analyzed under the principles of contributory infringement. According to the Supreme Court, the marketers of P2P software, actively encouraged or induced infringing behavior by the hordes of P2P users, and took no steps to minimize infringing behavior by users. Finding such activity actionable infringement, it held: "[O]ne who distributes a device with the object of promoting its use to infringe copyright, as shown by clear expression or other affirmative steps taken to foster infringement, is liable for the resulting acts of infringement by third parties."[79] In essence, the Court determined that when unmistakable evidence establishes that someone is promoting the distribution of a product on the basis of encouraging infringing activities of users, and there is evidence of infringement on a gigantic scale, the law will not allow the fact that the product may be capable of substantial noninfringing uses to exculpate its distributors.

Legislative Developments

1. The Responsibility of Universities and Peer-to-Peer (P2P) File Sharing. In the past five years, Congress has held numerous hearings regarding peer-to-peer file sharing. The role of universities was the focal point of a February 2003 House Judiciary Committee hearing attended by representatives of the Joint Committee of the Higher Education and Entertainment Communities, which was formed in December 2002 to facilitate collaborative efforts to address the problem of unauthorized file sharing. File sharing has vexed both universities and their students, as sites and software enable both legitimate and illegal transfer of digital files. The role of universities has been spotlighted, because computer-savvy students have the machines and talent to effect massive transfer of files, and schools have provided high-speed Internet access, which makes the process fast and easy. Even as commercial digital networks grow, the university community has been the prime focus of enforcement efforts by the entertainment industry. In particular, the Recording Industry Association of America has launched high-profile litigation against students who have downloaded music files without permission. The universities have been drawn into the litigation, primarily based on their role as OSPs. Even though the OSP limitation on liability does not require the university to monitor content, the Joint Committee representatives indicated that some schools were indeed tracking the size of files downloaded by students in dorm rooms. While not reviewing the content per se, by identifying large file download activity, university administrators have been able to anticipate problems associated with the misuse of P2P software and the schools' Internet facilities.

In April 2004, a committee of universities published a paper entitled "University Policies and Practices Addressing Improper Peer-to-Peer File Sharing," www.educause.edu/ir/library/pdf/CSD3092.pdf (last viewed April 29, 2005).[80] The paper outlined a range of responses that different educational institutions have employed to address the problem of unauthorized P2P file sharing. The responses include educating students regarding legal and ethical issues, employing technological procedures to manage computer networks, institutionalizing policies covering copyright, and punishing those who abuse the resources of the schools.

These steps go beyond what is required under the OSP limitation, since no active monitoring is mandated to qualify. However, once institutions undertake voluntary activities, the statute will impose a higher duty on them to take corrective action when questionable practices are discovered. Failure to act may jeopardize the safe harbor because the universities could be charged with knowledge of infringing behavior. Thus, the commendable steps taken to establish ethical rules on campus raise the catch-22 that failure to enforce the rules may leave the institution more vulnerable to financial liability.

2. *The INDUCE Act*.[81] A corollary of the P2P debate has been the goal of content owners to extend copyright doctrine to cover not only direct, contributory, and vicarious infringing actions, but also to provide that anyone who "intentionally induces" a violation by selling a product or service shall be deemed an infringer.[82] The concept of intentional inducement has been recognized in other areas of law, most notably patent law. As argued by the content owners, the business plan of publishers of P2P software is to market their products by encouraging users to download copyrighted music and films without permission of the copyright owners. They claim that the overwhelming purpose of the software is to violate third party rights, and its use results in widespread violations of copyrights. The legislation sparked controversy in the 108th Congress but was sympathetically received by most legislators. Even though the Supreme Court's *Grokster* ruling mooted the urgency of acting on the INDUCE Act, because it was popularly received by many legislators, it may be anticipated that the legislation will be on the agenda of the congressional committees in the 109th Congress. If the INDUCE Act reemerges in 2006, a new version of the bill will likely propose tighter constraints on certain new technologies that could limit libraries in their ability to serve the research needs of their patrons.

The induce theory was also the subject of some discussion during oral argument before the U.S. Supreme Court in the file-sharing case of *MGM v. Grokster*. Even though the record of the case was incomplete and could require a further trial at the district court level, several Supreme Court Justices seemed troubled that the P2P software companies built their businesses around the plan that consumers would use their products to obtain copyrighted works without consent of the owners.[83] The ramifications of this inducement argument evoked strong concern in the tech community, which fears that certain popular technological advancements may be similarly criticized because they arguably encourage infringing behavior. For example, Apple's wildly popular iPod can copy and store up to 10,000 songs. Even with Apple's iTunes licensing system, how many people own rights to copy 10,000 songs? In its defense, Apple markets the iPod as a product that can store songs consumers bought online, through iTunes or another service, or previously acquired with a CD, not illegally downloaded off the Net. However, for a different enterprise to build its consumer base primarily, if not substantially, upon a foundation of inducing infringement, that is a different story. If not the courts, then more likely the Congress appears prepared to outlaw expressly such behavior.

Looking Forward

In the seven years since its adoption, the DMCA has become familiar to millions of people in education, and administrators, faculty, and students expend a lot of time thinking about and addressing the statutory requirements. Provided that the critical procedures outlined in this chapter are rigorously followed, the limitation on liability for service providers has served educational institutions by relieving them of potentially huge financial liability,

However, the DMCA has raised a number of fundamental and complex problems for educators. These include:

1. What is the relationship of privacy and freedom of speech to the DMCA and educational use of the OSP limitation? To secure the protection of the OSP limitation, universities may be required to disclose the identity of and personal information about students or faculty. Courts have determined that the expectation of privacy on the Internet is not as great as one might expect, and certainly nothing like that which exists for private letters. Thus, the DMCA regime intrudes into areas that many believe are the domain of academic freedom. Yet, because the DMCA enforces a complementary societal value—protection of the intellectual property rights of copyright owners—there is no easy answer. When important values conflict in an unyielding way, one esteemed value will suffer.

2. Is there a role for individual due process in the DMCA regime? As the discussion of the OSP limitation underscores, many of the DMCA procedures are designed to ensure expeditious action and reaction: subpoenas obtained by filing a declaration with the clerk of a court, notice and take down, counter notice and put-back, all occurring with limited oversight. The concern that digital piracy can wreck havoc with ownership of works in a relatively short time obligates the law to make its reactive times short. However, many questions that arise in copyright are complex and not susceptible to speedy responses. Have all the requirements of the OSP limitation been met by the owners, as well as the OSP? Do any copyright law exceptions apply to the infringing use? For example, is a download permitted

under the doctrine of fair use, and, more particularly, how is that determination to be made when the copyright owner is pressing for a quick take down? Are we asking universities, in their capacities as OSPs, to turn into copyright police, monitoring the workings of their technological networks and in the process reviewing the habits of students and faculty? It is important that university administrators take the initiative to ensure that their reaction properly balances the pressures of copyright owners and legislators and the needs of their communities.

3. Are there simpler or better alternatives? At its core, copyright is a set of rules to ensure the economic benefits of creativity. The DMCA goes to certain extremes to enable copyright owners to stop unauthorized downloading of digital works. A viable alternative to the DMCA approach can be seen in various licensing regimes. Composers and authors have long prospered by a regulated licensing regime that ensures that the public performance of their works is compensated. Cable and satellite television operations, public broadcasters, digital music services, and jukebox operators pay compulsory royalties to the Copyright Office, which redistributes the funds to copyright owners on a periodic basis. Some educational institutions are experimenting with acquiring campus-wide licenses for downloading music. A voluntary or compulsory scheme could be an answer to many of the legitimate complaints of the various sides of these disputes.

These questions illuminate a fundamental tension in the DMCA for educators. While the DMCA anticipates some of the issues involved in the use of digital works, technology continues to pose challenges that drain the safe harbor and leave it a murky place.

NEXT STEPS

▶ Manage your risks by: (1) establishing internal mechanisms within the library/institution functioning as an OSP in order to ensure compliance with DMCA Safe Harbor provisions; and (2) monitoring your efforts regularly.

▶ Develop and post a policy for termination of repeat offenders; accommodate and do not interfere with "standard" technical measures used by copyright owners to identify and protect their works, such as digital watermarking and access codes.

▶ Develop a compliance policy as an OSP to qualify for limitation.

▶ Formulate a response to address the problem of illegal peer-to-peer file sharing.

▶ Formulate a policy on privacy and freedom of speech where DMCA is concerned.

▶ As administrators, take initiative to ensure that reactions properly balance the pressures of copyright owners and legislators and the needs of educational communities.

▶ Keep an eye on proposed new legislation and get involved.

ENDNOTES

[1] *Playboy Enters., Inc. v. Frena,* 839 F. Supp. 1552 (M.D. Fla. 1993); *Sega Enters. Ltd. v. Maphia,* 857 F. Supp. 679 (N.D. Cal. 1994). In both cases, the BBS operation was held to be directly liable. A more rigorous analysis should have found the BBS operator not directly liable, but only liable (if that were appropriate) as a contributory or vicarious infringer.

[2] For example, when The Copyright Act of 1976 established rules for the cable compulsory license, telephone companies were held to be exempt in their passive activity of transmitting broadcast signals from television transmitters to cable system operators. 17 U.S.C. §111(a)(3) (2000).

[3] 17 U.S.C. §512 (2000).

[4] 17 U.S.C. § 512(a).

[5] 17 U.S.C. § 512(b).

[6] 17 U.S.C. § 512(c).

[7] 17 U.S.C. § 512(d).

[8] 17 U.S.C. § 512(k)(1).

[9] 17 U.S.C. § 512(k)(1).

[10] 17 U.S.C. § 512(a)(1), (b)(1)(A).

[11] 17 U.S.C. § 512(a)(5), (b)(2)(A).

[12] 17 U.S.C. § 512(a)(4).

[13] 17 U.S.C. § 512(c)(1)(A).

[14] 17 U.S.C. § 512(a)(1), (b)(1)(B).

[15] 17 U.S.C. § 512(a)(4).

[16] 17 U.S.C. § 512(a)(3).

[17] 17 U.S.C. § 512(c)(1)(B).

[18] 17 U.S.C. § 512(a)(2).

[19] 17 U.S.C. § 512(b)(2)(B).

[20] 17 U.S.C. § 512(b)(2)(C).

[21] 17 U.S.C. § 512(d)(3).

[22] 17 U.S.C. § 512(g).

[23] 17 U.S.C. § 512(b)(2)(B).

[24] 17 U.S.C. § 512(b)(2)(C)(i).

[25] 17 U.S.C. § 512(b)(2)(C)(ii).

[26] 17 U.S.C. § 512(b)(2)(C)(iii).

[27] 17 U.S.C. § 512(b)(2)(E).

[28] 17 U.S.C. § 512(c)(2).

[29] 17 U.S.C. § 512(c)(2)(A).

[30] 17 U.S.C. § 512(c)(2).

[31] 17 C.F.R. § 201.38(c) (2005).

[32] 17 U.S.C. § 512(c)(3)(A)(iv) (2000).

[33] 17 U.S.C. § 512(c)(3)(A)(i).

[34] 17 U.S.C. § 512(c)(3)(A)(ii).

[35] 17 U.S.C. § 512(c)(3)(A)(iii).

[36] 17 U.S.C. § 512(c)(3)(A)(v).

[37] 17 U.S.C. § 512(c)(3)(A)(vi).

[38] 17 U.S.C. § 512(f).

[39] 17 U.S.C. § 512(g)(3)(A), (g)(3)(D).

[40] 17 U.S.C. § 512(g)(3)(B), (g)(3)(C).

[41] 17 U.S.C. § 512(g)(3)(D).

[42] 17 U.S.C. § 512(e)(1).

[43] 17 U.S.C. § 512(e)(1)(A).

[44] 17 U.S.C. § 512(e)(1)(B).

[45] 17 U.S.C. § 512(e)(1)(C).

[46] 17 U.S.C. § 512(h)(1).

[47] 17 U.S.C. § 512(h)(2)(A).

[48] 17 U.S.C. § 512(h)(2)(B).

[49] 17 U.S.C. § 512(h)(2)(C).

[50] 17 U.S.C. § 512(h)(3).

[51] 17 U.S.C. § 512(h)(4).

[52] 17 U.S.C. § 512(i)(1).

[53] 17 U.S.C. § 512(i)(1)(A).

[54] 17 U.S.C. § 512(c)(1)(A), (d)(1).

[55] 17 U.S.C. § 512(k)(1).

[56] *See In re* Aimster Copyright Litig., 334 F.3d 643, 645-47 (7th Cir. 2003).

[57] *See id.*

[58] *ALS Scan v. RemarQ Cmtys., Inc.*, 239 F.3d 619, 623 (4th Cir. 2001).

[59] *Id.* at 623-25.

[60] *Id.* at 625-26.

[61] *Ellison v. Robertson*, 357 F.3d 1072, 1077 (9th Cir. 2004).

[62] *Id.*

[63] *Id.*

[64] *Id.*

[65] *Perfect 10, Inc. v. Cybernet Ventures, Inc.*, 213 F. Supp. 2d 1146, 1179 (C.D. Cal. 2002).

[66] *Id.* at 1174.

[67] *ALS Scan*, 239 F.3d at 621-22.

[68] *Id.* at 625.

[69] *Id.*

[70] *Elektra Entm't Group, Inc. v. Does 1-9*, 2004 U.S. Dist LEXIS 23560, at *4 (S.D.N.Y. 2004).

[71] *Id.* at *2-*4.

[72] *Id.*

[73] *Id.* at *5-*13.

[74] *Id.* at *9-*13.

[75] *RIAA v. Verizon Internet Servs., Inc.*, 351 F.3d 1229, 1233 (D.C. Cir. 2003).

[76] *Id.* at 1234-35.

[77] *See* Recording Indus. Ass'n of Am. v. Univ. of N.C. at Chapel Hill, 367 F. Supp. 2d 945 (M.D. N.C. 2005).

[78] *Id.* at 952-56.

[79] 125 S. Ct. 2764, 2770.

[80] *Educ. Task Force of the Joint Comm. of the Higher Educ. Entm't Communities, Am. Council on Educ., University Policies and Practices Addressing Improper Peer-to-Peer File Sharing* (2003), www.educause.edu/ir/library/pdf/CSD3092.pdf.

[81] S. 2560, 108th Cong. (2004).

[82] S. 2560, 108th Cong. § 2 (2004).

[83] *See MGM v. Grokster*, 125 S. Ct. 2764, 2780-83 (2005).

►7

DIGITAL RIGHTS MANAGEMENT (DRM) AND HIGHER EDUCATION:
OPPORTUNITIES AND CHALLENGES

KIMBERLY B. KELLEY
KIMBERLY M. BONNER
CLIFFORD A. LYNCH
JAEHONG PARK

This chapter discusses the following topics:
- ► Defining digital rights management
- ► Overview of the study on the use of digital rights management systems in higher education
- ► Results and conclusions of survey research

INTRODUCTION

Higher education institutions struggle to balance two, equally meritorious, aspects of creating and using copyrighted works: the need to protect the rights of the copyright owner and the need to ensure that copyrighted works can be disseminated widely in support of scholarship, teaching, and learning. The technologies used to control access to digital works often create barriers for access or discourage or eliminate uses that are authorized by law. Within the digital domain, the development of technologies that protect copyrighted works has outpaced the development of technologies that both protect and permit legal uses of copyrighted works.

Online and traditional universities that provide online learning materials use a variety of digital learning objects, courseware, and digital materials to teach and conduct research. Higher education institutions are also using third-party copyrighted materials to support the educational enterprise. As these patterns of use continue to grow, so too do the concerns from publishers about the possible risks of piracy.[1] In response to the potential abuses for piracy, commercial vendors of copyrighted works, such as record companies, movie studios, and publishers, have developed technical mechanisms to enforce their copyrights and receive payment for copyrighted works. These technical mechanisms have been labeled Digital Rights Management or DRM systems.[2]

Although the higher education community has similar concerns regarding the protection of copyrighted works, attribution and usage tracking are primary concerns. Payment is a goal, but sharing and reuse of copyrighted works are also goals. In other words, universities are often most interested in facilitating the fullest possible legal use of copyrighted materials in the pursuit of good scholarship.

Recently passed legislation, such as the Technology, Education, and Copyright Harmonization (TEACH) Act of 2002, requires that technological controls be in place that reasonably prevent retention of copyrighted work and unauthorized dissemination of the work in accessible form.[3] The TEACH Act technological measures, similar in function to the types of DRM systems presently in place, would limit the ability of a user to distribute and copy works. Given the high degree of institutional and legal pressure brought to bear on academics today, it becomes all the more essential that we know what we are talking about when we talk about DRM.

DEFINING DIGITAL RIGHTS MANAGEMENT

Settling on an adequate definition for DRM is more difficult than might be expected. In the simplest possible terms, DRM describes technologies that place limits on the transmission and reproduction of copyrighted digital materials. To fully encompass all the possible connotations of the term, such a definition would need to address both systems that included DRM components but were not defined specifically as DRM systems and systems that were primarily or exclusively DRM systems. Variations of two definitions have emerged in the literature:

(1) management of digital rights—the responsibility of expressing and managing the rights to content in electronic or digital form—and,

(2) the ability to physically manage intellectual property and proprietary rights in content by way of an electronic system or process, associated with copyright management systems.[4]

Some of the literature from the higher education community further notes that there is a difference between the conventional definitions of DRM and broader academic uses of the term. The former focuses on protection of the interests of copyright owners, while the latter also embraces end-user rights, such as fair use, first sale, and the use of the public domain.[5]

Unable to cut through the morass of contradictory definitions, the CIP researchers who worked on the study described later in this chapter settled on an alternate term: digital content control systems (DCCS). For the purposes of this study, DCC systems are defined as: *any technological system that controls access, retention, redistribution, and reuse of digital content such as documents, images, video, or audio.* Significantly, this definition focuses on content management, as opposed to rights management, allowing it to encompass the concerns of both users and owners of copyrighted works. It is, however, important to remember that the more common term DRM can be used to describe either or both of these interests, depending on the circumstances.

USES OF DRM AND DCC SYSTEMS

DRM or DCC systems have many potential uses, but they tend to entail the placement of limitations on the dissemination of works. Professor Julie Cohen describes a possible DRM system through which if one purchases a collection of essays online, the copyright owner can charge for the file, generate a record of the reader's identity, what was purchased, and insert pieces of code into the file that will notify the copyright owner every time the reader opens one of the essays.[6] In other circumstances DRM systems can prevent users from opening or printing the information until they have paid.[7] One capability of a DCC system that is rare is the ability of a technical system to completely prevent the user's ability to retain, redistribute, or reuse copyrighted digital content.

Indeed, the survey we conducted revealed that there is little true DRM or DCCS technology in place on college campuses. While access management technology is basically universally deployed to control who can use copyrighted materials, as we expected there is almost no true DRM—in the traditional sense of comprehensive and strong downstream control of continued use, reuse, or redistribution of content—deployed on the campuses. Certainly, the study findings did not demonstrate that there are ubiquitous DRM technologies being developed as an integral part of campus information technology and networked information infrastructure among the respondents. In the cases where campuses reported the presence of such technology in the initial survey, and we followed up to verify and clarify through telephone interviews, the reported systems higher level of controls tended to evaporate under close examination, at least in terms of widely deployed infrastructure.

Even so, the implementation of DRM must be approached with great care. Professor Lawrence Lessig has observed that DRM systems have the ability to enforce copyright law in cyberspace even as they can enhance copyright beyond its actual legal scope.

> As privatized law, trusted systems regulate in the same domain where copyright law regulates, but unlike copyright law, they do not guarantee the same public use protection. Trusted systems give the producer maximum control . . . Code displaces the balance in copyright law and doctrines such as fair use.[8]

Our survey of numerous campuses revealed that the main constraints of DCC systems are limited control over content and a lack of flexibility, which generally means that these systems overly constrain access and reuse of content or preclude legal fair uses of the content. Other problems include impaired or limited access to the content, cumbersome controls that make delivering the content on various platforms very difficult, and a level of complexity that further hampers the delivery and use of content.

More sophisticated DCC systems would allow the user to lend, resell, or permanently archive third-party digital content, an ideal technological realization of the traditional "first sale doctrine" from the Copyright Act. The definition of first sale is described within section 109(a) of the Copyright Act. The copyright owner's exclusive right of "distribution" is limited by section 109(a) because the exception limits the copyright owner's control over copies of the work to their first sale or transfer. After the initial sale or transfer, the copyright owner no longer has exclusive rights. According to section 109:

> § 109. Limitations on exclusive rights: Effect of transfer of particular copy or phonorecord:
> (a) Notwithstanding the provisions of section 106(3), the owner of a particular copy or phonorecord lawfully made under this title, or any person authorized by such owner, is entitled, without the authority of the copyright owner, to sell or otherwise dispose of the possession of that copy or phonorecord.[9]

According to Marshall Leaffer in *Understanding Copyright Law*, once a work is lawfully sold or transferred gratuitously pursuant to 109(a), the copyright owner's interest in the material object, the copy or phonorecord, is exhausted. The owner of the copy can dispose of the work as he or she desires.[10]

STUDYING DRM PRACTICES

In an effort to better understand current applications of DCC technologies on college campuses, the Center for Intellectual Property recently conducted a thorough survey of DCC implementation on college campuses. To better facilitate the understanding and reflection of those attempting to evaluate the role of DCC systems in their own contexts, our results are reproduced in abridged form below.

Research Design

The overarching purpose of the study was to determine what DCC systems are in use at Research I (RI) institutions and liberal arts colleges (LACs), as designated by Carnegie Foundation for the Advancement of Teaching,[11] to control access, distribution, and downstream reuse of copyrighted digital content. Copyrighted digital content was defined as including both digital content created on-campus and third-party copyrighted materials.

Two methods of data collection were employed to answer the research questions and hypotheses developed for the study. The first data collection method was a survey questionnaire. The second data collection mechanism was a follow-up telephone interview with respondents who met certain criteria based on their response to several questions on the survey. The survey questionnaire was distributed to the chief information officer, the dean of continuing, professional or distance education, and the dean or director of the library. These individuals were chosen as they were considered the most likely to have both knowledge of and control over the implementation and creation of such systems.

In total, 709 institutions met the various criteria established in this survey and 1437 individuals in some version of one of the three roles described above received the survey. A total of 227 submissions were received in paper format and 166 were completed via the Web for a total of 393 submissions. After reviewing the submissions, the researchers found 46 that were incomplete, and therefore unusable, and 14 were duplicates. This reduced the total valid submissions to 333 for a total response rate of 23.17%. Of those individuals who responded to the survey, 17.4% (N=58) were the dean or director of continuing, professional, or distance education. Of the survey sample, 45.6% (N=152), were the dean or director of the library and 26.7% of the sample (N=89) were the chief information officers (CIO) for the institution. Thirty-two respondents gave their position as "other," and two individuals left the question blank. Respondents indicated slightly greater knowledge concerning copyright law than their familiarity with DCC systems.

A total of 13 of the institutions in the study were found to meet the criteria defined by the researchers for further inquiry about adoption and advanced implementation of DCCS and were included for the telephone follow-up interviews. Further, the researchers identified 25 institutions that met the criteria to be contacted by phone about compliance with the TEACH Act. In some instances, the same institution was included in both category one (early adopter institution) and category two (TEACH Act–compliant institution). In all, 36 telephone interviews were conducted.

Knowledge of Digital Content Control Systems (DCCS)

Within the survey population, 65.7% (N=216) indicated they offered online courses or programs. Of those who offered online courses, 94.3% (N=198) reported that they have a DCC system in place that controls access to the online course or program material. Similarly, when respondents were asked about the prevalence of Web-enhanced courses that included some type of technological controls restricting access to the content (SQ5), 91.3% (N=304), indicated they had a technological control in place restricting access to the course content online.

Of respondents , 88.3% (N=294) indicated they were aware of at least one digital content control system in use on their campus that controlled access to content. If a respondent answered affirmatively to this question, s/he was then asked to indicate whether s/he knew whether there were any DCC systems on campus that controlled the user's ability to retain, redistribute, and reuse the copyrighted material. On this account, a mere 37.3% (N=109) of respondents indicated their system had additional controls beyond restricting access. For SQ13, only a small minority of respondents indicated their DCC systems had the ability to completely prevent retention, redistribution, or reuse of copyrighted material. Of the respondents, 6.9% (N=20) indicated their systems completely prevented reuse of copyrighted material; 94.6% (N=278) indicated that their systems did not have this level of functionality.

Another purpose of the study was to determine what types of DCC systems or technologies were in use across RI institutions and LACs. Accordingly, respondents were asked to "check off" any of the types of DCC systems or technologies in use on their campus. Of the choices offered, the respondents selected course management systems (92.2%), digital library systems (70.1%), streaming media servers (62.9%), and client-side digital viewers or players (68.4%), as being most prevalent. The other choices of digital watermarking techniques (4.8%), physical copy protection mechanisms (4.8%) and server-side digital viewers or players (26.2%) were deployed at the minority of respondents' campuses.

FIGURE 7.1: Top Four DCC Technologies

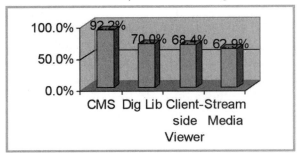

A minority of respondents indicated their system had sophisticated downstream capabilities. On deeper investigation, the researchers found that none of the systems in place had the technical capability to completely prevent reuse of the copyrighted materials.

The Capabilities of the Digital Content Control Systems

The majority of respondents (97.6%) indicated their DCC system controlled access to the copyrighted digital content. However, only a small minority of respondents indicated their DCC systems could prevent retention (39.6%), prevent or limit redistribution (19.4%), limit the number of times or duration (19.6%), or limit reuse (16.5%).

The RI institutions were significantly more likely to report their DCC system had the ability to control reuse of digital content than the respondents from LACs. Otherwise, there were no further differences in the capabilities by type of institution.

A relatively small percentage (21.1%) of institutions reported that they had developed their own DCCS technologies, though it should be noted that this was higher than expected. Relying on home-grown or noncommercial systems requires more expertise and development time on the part of the institution. Therefore, fewer institutions would be able to afford the expense and/or time to invest in developing these systems for their local use. However, it is also the case that these systems might offer greater flexibility for the local campus and potentially offer more choice in how the local campus manages its copyrighted digital content.

A few locally developed systems were mentioned, however. Three systems were mentioned most by those using a home-grown or noncommercially obtained system: SAKAI (http://sakaiproject.org), Moodle (http://moodle.org), and Segue (http://segue.middle bury.edu). These three products are all open-source course management systems. However, they are not systems designed to manage digital rights. Instead, they are systems that contain some digital rights management capabilities but their purpose is to support teaching and learning. Unexpectedly, course management systems figured prominently in many of the open-ended questions and more respondents mentioned these types of systems more often as their primary DCC system on campus.

Use of Digital Content Control Systems on Campus

The third section of the survey sought to learn about the unmet needs of respondents for additional features for their DCC system and to learn more about the institutional purposes and goals for DCC systems in use on campus. Of respondents, 61.3% thought their DCC systems would benefit from having more features and greater control than was currently available. The majority of respondents indicated that there was a need for greater controls for three primary reasons: (1) to permit wider dissemination of digital content, particularly images, while ensuring copyright compliance and maintaining privacy; (2) to reduce institutional liability; and (3) to use the technology to allow portions of works to be used more flexibly. Respondents indicated that they believed more works are being digitized.

Respondents also expressed a desire to have a DCC system that had the ability to control reuse of copyrighted works, something unavailable with current systems. The other most frequently mentioned features that were missing were: (1) the ability to integrate DCC systems across platforms; (2) the ability to permit selective copying; and (3) providing an educational component within the system that informs users of the copyright law and thereby helps prevent infringing uses.

Respondents provided their perception of the three main benefits of DCC systems: their protections guarantee that more digital content is made available; they reduce liability for the institution; and they limit access to authorized users, reducing the potential for copyright infringement.

Institutional Policies and License Agreements for DCC Systems

The first reason cited by survey respondents for implementing DCC systems was "to comply with license agreement requirements" (81.3%), followed by "to comply with copyright law" (76.5%), "to protect sensitive information" (67.3%), and last, "to protect copyright owner's rights" (49%). This arrangement of priorities makes sense when one takes into account that 82.9% of respondents indicated that their license agreements did require that they have technical controls in place. Of those respondents familiar with licensing agreements, 36.2% indicated that their license agreements restricted or prohibited reuse of the digital content after a certain period of time. As for fair use, 20.7% indicated that their license agreements "frequently" or "occasionally" prohibited fair uses of the licensed digital content. Carnegie classification was found to be significantly correlated with knowledge of whether a license agreement restricted fair uses. RI institutions were significantly more likely to have a license agreement restricting fair uses than LACs.

FIGURE 7.2: DCCS Goals

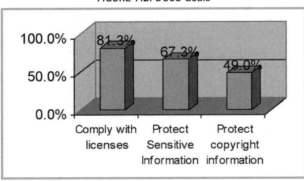

The majority of respondents in the study (78.9%, N=282) indicated they had acceptable use policies for copyrighted works.

The Technology, Education, and Copyright Harmonization (TEACH) Act

There were nine questions on the survey requesting information on the respondent's perception of his/her campus's ability to meet the technological measures to be eligible for the TEACH Act exemption. First, the respondent was asked to give a self-assessment of his/her knowledge of the requirements of the TEACH Act. Respondents were almost evenly split on their self-reported knowledge of the TEACH Act requirements: Only 8.7% indicated they were very knowledgeable about the TEACH Act. A larger percentage (44.8%) indicated they were somewhat knowledgeable. A smaller percentage (29.6%) indicated they were slightly knowledgeable and 12.3% indicated they were not knowledgeable at all.

Additional questions asked respondents to indicate the extent to which their institutions had the needed technological controls in place to comply with the TEACH Act, and if they had taken reasonable measures, as required by the TEACH Act, to prevent further copying of the digital content. Of respondents, 70.2% indicated they had "to a great extent" (27.6%) or "to some extent" (42.6%) ensured they had the necessary technological controls in place to comply with the TEACH Act requirements. However, the majority of respondents did not indicate they had reasonable measures in place to prevent further copying of the digital content (i.e., "downstream" copying). Some 49% of respondents indicated they had instituted the required controls to "a great extent" (15.3%) or "to some extent" (32.7%), while 47.4% of respondents indicated they did not know if such measures were in place (33.3%), did not think they had these controls in place to a great extent (9.6%), or did not think their campus had these controls at all (4.6%).

Other questions asked respondents about their educational materials, policies, and guidelines and intention to seek exemption under the TEACH Act. A minority of respondents (32.4%) indicated they had educational materials available concerning the TEACH Act. A similarly high percentage of respondents indicated they did not know whether materials were available concerning the TEACH Act (38.3%). It is interesting that a higher percentage of respondents did not know than those who were aware of whether such material existed. A total of 29.3% of respondents indicated that their campus did not have educational materials concerning the TEACH Act available on their campus. Similarly, respondents were not knowledgeable about their campus policies concerning the TEACH Act (i.e., a policy or guideline that included something about the application of the TEACH Act on campus). The majority of respondents indicated they did not know if their campus had such a policy (43.6%). Only a few respondents indicated they did have a policy or guideline; 8.7% indicated they had a policy and 7.5% reported having a guideline concerning the TEACH Act.

The majority of respondents were also unaware as to whether their campus would seek exemption under the TEACH Act. A full 82.8% of respondents indicated they did not know whether their campus would seek exemption. A small percentage, 7.8%, indicated their campus intended to seek exemption, and 8.1% of respondents indicated that their campus had decided against seeking exemption.

Digital Content Control System Balancing Rights Are Rare

Our study confirmed there are no systems in use that can provide a balanced approach that allows both control and legitimate uses of digital content such as fair use simultaneously. One system, which was developed in-house from an open-source product, had the ability to scramble digital content such that a user could not download the entirety of a Web page. While this was a creative solution, and certainly protected the digital material better than many DRM technologies, it would be equally likely to prevent a legitimate use.

The inability of the DCC systems to discern legitimate from illegitimate uses was the fundamental problem respondents had with these systems. While DCC systems can be made more secure, and are likely to continue to evolve to include tighter controls, they cannot balance the rights of society and the copyright holder as expressed in the Copyright Act. The balancing of rights in the Copyright Act is essential to the free flow of information and the creation of new works. Therefore, more technological protections are not the solution. The telephone interview participants were clear in their concern about the growing emphasis on DCCS, the inclusion of technology control requirements in recent amendments to the Copyright Act, and the potential of DCC systems to further erode a fragile balance that plays an important role in society.

DCC Systems are Adequate. Although no DCC system had perfect controls, respondents relayed that the systems were adequate and performed their functions well. In the view of the respondents for this survey, the systems protected the copyright owner's rights while still permitting the use of the materials by the campus community.

Few Taking Advantage of the TEACH Act. Few institutions have proactively addressed the complex institutional requirements presented in the TEACH Act that must precede any consideration of an exemption for the use of copyrighted materials as described in the TEACH Act. Quite a few respondents indicated that fair use was sufficient for their purposes and there was not a pressing need to become versed in the TEACH Act requirements. Or, it was often the case that respondents would indicate that because the TEACH Act provides an exemption, they would consider whether to invoke the TEACH exemption if and when the need arose. They indicated that there was not a pressing need at this juncture in time.

DISCUSSION OF RESULTS AND CONCLUSIONS

The results of this study contribute significantly to a greater understanding of the state of deployment and use of digital rights management and other related access control systems in higher education, particularly within Carnegie Research I universities. The study findings also offer insight into the ways in which the higher education community views these technologies and the state of their deployment. While the base of survey data prior to our work has been, as far as we can determine, highly limited, at least some of the researchers have considerable general familiarity with the state of deployment.

Vendors and License Agreements Do not Call for Sophisticated Technology Controls

There seemed to be little or no requirement by organizations that licensed scholarly content to universities for sophisticated DRM systems. The license agreements call for access control, and the campuses have deployed access control that meets the requirements of these licenses. While it's not clear from the study whether scholarly publishers are not calling for DRM systems because the DRM systems are not deployed (and thus it would severely limit their potential marketplace) or whether DRM systems are not deployed because publishers are not calling for them, we certainly have other anecdotal evidence that draconian downstream DRM controls are of little interest to the major scholarly publishers. Within the survey results and comments one finds interesting hints about DRM and consumer-marketplace content (movies, popular music, etc.) that might serve as raw material for instruction and research. However, much of this material is effectively unavailable for use in instruction, research, and scholarly communication today, and some respondents expressed the hope that in an environment with stronger DRM controls the owners of such material might make it more available (under reasonable and affordable terms) for these purposes. But, there is no real reason to believe this; we suspect it is a spillover from the threatening lobbying positions taken by groups like the RIAA and the MPAA that like to suggest that they will withhold content from the marketplace unless there are strong, ubiquitous DRM controls (and draconian legal penalties backing up these technical controls) in place, and that they will only make content available if these criteria are satisfied.

At best, there was lukewarm interest within the survey sample for the greater deployment of DRM systems within higher education, with two main drivers for this interest. The first is the (unsubstantiated) belief that it would mean that more content was available to support teaching and research already discussed. The other is fear and concern about litigation and liability; many respondents suggested that by deploying more elaborate DRM systems as part of the institutional infrastructure, higher education institutions might be able protect themselves and limit their liability for copyright infringement. The actual evidence to substantiate these assumptions is again unclear. Among other things, it seems likely that deploying DRM systems would provide much more detailed logs of the use of copyright material, which might well be exploited as evidence in potential litigation. We cannot help but wonder about the extent to which the recent flood of litigation and threatened litigation about copyright infringement is reflected in the atmosphere of fear emerging from the responses here. The other problematic aspect of more elaborate DRM systems is the potential for inadvertently violating the privacy of the user with potentially negative, unintended consequences resulting.

Fair Use Is of Central Importance to Higher Education

The responses to the survey provided a powerful reaffirmation of the central importance of fair use as an enabler for teaching and research in our institutions of higher education. The most common concern expressed about possible future deployment of more extensive and ubiquitous DRM systems was that they would constrain the ability of faculty and students to exercise fair use rights that are an essential part of teaching, learning, and scholarly discourse. There was a fairly widespread assumption—which we believe is entirely justified—that DRM technologies and fair use are intrinsically incompatible at a very fundamental level because the judgments and contextual considerations such as the *intent and purpose* in using copyrighted materials, which are an integral part of fair use, cannot be accommodated by algorithmic decision-making. Further, it is clear that the complex calculus of technology-enabled exemptions and protections offered by the TEACH Act were unattractive—or at least unpersuasive—to many institutions and faculty when compared to the simpler, though perhaps more subjective, defenses offered by traditional fair use.

Policy, Not Technology, Protects Intellectual Property Rights

Related to this reaffirmation of the role of fair use, the survey results also remind us that our higher education institutions have—appropriately, in our view—chosen to emphasize education, policies, and the development and respect of community values as key tools in addressing concerns about the use of intellectual property in higher education. Our universities want members of their communities to make thoughtful, conscious, informed decisions, and also want to provide them with the understanding and knowledge to make these decisions, rather than have actions, choices, and opportunities constrained and shaped by mechanistic DRM technologies.

A Few Surprises

Finally, a few comments on the three surprises in the survey data are in order. The first is the reported lack of knowledge by respondents about the implications of the terms of license agreements for access to copyrighted materials. We deliberately reached out to those institutional leaders that we expected would be most knowledgeable about these agreements, yet it seems clear that beyond library leadership, understanding of these terms and conditions is not widespread. A more precise and nuanced understanding of this problem would be very valuable. One question that the survey did not explore is the extent to which faculty are aware of these constraints. Certainly, we uncovered evidence that academic leadership in the information technology and distance education areas are unfamiliar with these issues, and this is disturbing. But front-line faculty members also play a key role in shaping institutional decisions. A better understanding of why knowledge of license agreements is not more widespread might also shed light on the lack of interest in TEACH Act provisions.

Another surprise—and one that has very important near-term implications given developments such as the momentum that is developing around the SAKAI project, on the one hand, and the recent announcement of the Blackboard-WebCT consolidation, on the other—is the identification of course management systems (CMS) as a key environment for the management of digital content resources. Learning management systems (LMS) are not designed as DRM environments, yet the respondents in our survey identified them as a central component in the landscape of institutional content management. They offer features that make it inconvenient to export content, and features that control the use, sharing, and reuse of content as long as it remains within the learning management system. We were, frankly, amazed to see CMS/LMS platforms identified as a key component of a content management infrastructure within higher education, and these responses raise an intriguing and important set of questions. How often, for example, do institutional libraries hold *copies* of materials held in the learning management system that do not have technical encumbrances that might block fair use as a safety net? What do these survey responses suggest in terms of development priorities for systems such as Moodle or SAKAI? How strong is the DRM perimeter established by a LMS? How practical is it to bypass the DRM capabilities offered within the constrained environment of such a system by simply exporting content from it? These are issues that demand more detailed near-term exploration, and, given the involvement of the Andrew W. Mellon Foundation with SAKAI, seem to be particularly fruitful venues for follow-on work.

A third surprise, related to the finding on the importance of course management systems, is the number of respondents who mentioned their involvement with open-source software deployment. Although the numbers were relatively small, the study results suggest that open source is of great interest to higher education institutions. Further, these systems may offer an avenue for managing digital rights where higher education has more input into the parameters of the system to ensure greater compatibility with the needs within higher education. None of the commercial systems mentioned by respondents generated the level of interest as the open-source solutions. These findings suggest another area for additional study to determine what role open source might play beyond providing a course management system and whether the open-source model has implications for the next generation of digital rights in higher education.

The study results confirm that institutions of higher learning are actively engaged in deploying digital rights technologies and formulating policies and educational materials to ensure the proper use and dissemination of copyrighted works for teaching and learning. While the systems deployed are not sophisticated, the community of respondents demonstrated that they are competently managing digital content and continually examining new systems to do it better or more consistently across platforms.

Further, the study results do not suggest there is a need for a "better mousetrap" or that higher education is not fulfilling its obligation to protect the rights of the copyright owner. On the contrary, the respondents demonstrated a level of thoughtfulness about these issues that was enlightening. What was clear from the results is that technology cannot provide a level of sophistication that will balance the rights of the owner and the user. Instead, the technology performs one role and is unlikely to ever evolve to become the across-the-board answer for balancing a complex set of rights.

This study suggests that the combination of policy, technology, and education is key for managing copyrights and a singular focus on developing any one of these areas over another, has the potential to create an imbalance between the rights of the owner and user. When examining the use and control of digital content for teaching and learning, no burning piracy or misuse issues arose. Instead, what becomes clear is that other, peripheral issues such as music sharing, can cloud the discussion and create a sense of concern when there is no real basis for such concern. Instead, there continues to be a need for debate, exploration, and confirmation of the importance of technology but also the equal importance of concepts such as fair use and first sale that are essential for the teaching and learning process and contribute, as they were intended to do, toward the creation of new knowledge for the betterment of society.

NEXT STEPS

► Determine whether or not your institution is legally obligated to implement DRM technologies, i.e., TEACH Act compliance, or license agreements.

► If so, evaluate DRM systems to determine which systems permit compliance with legal obligations and also fit institutional needs.

► Approach digital content management with a strategy that includes, but is not limited to, technological approaches.

► Continue to evaluate best practices developed by other colleges and universities.

ENDNOTES

[1] Bill Rosenblatt, *Major Publishers Pilot EBooks on College Campuses*, DRM Watch, Aug. 10, 2005, http://www.drmwatch.com/ocr/article.php/3526566 [hereinafter Rosenblatt, DRM Watch]; F. Hill Slowinski, *What Consumers Want in Digital Rights Management (DRM): Making Content as Widely Available as Possible in Ways That Satisfy Consumer Preferences* 3-5 (Association of American Publishers, Inc. and American Library Association, White Paper, March 2003), *available at* http://www.publishers.org/press/pdf/DRMWhitePaper.pdf [hereinafter Slowinski].

[2] Slowinski, *supra* note 1, at 23.

[3] 17 U.S.C. § 110(2)(D)(ii) (Supp. II 2003).

[4] Slowinski, *supra* note 1, at 23.

[5] Mairead Martin et al., *Federated Digital Rights Management: A Proposed DRM Solution for Research and Education*, D-Lib Mag., July/Aug. 2002, http://www.dlib.org/dlib/july02/martin/07martin.html.

[6] Julie E. Cohen, *A Right to Read Anonymously: A Closer Look at "Copyright Management" in Cyberspace*, 28 Conn. L. Rev. 981, 983 (1996).

[7] *Id.* at 984.

[8] Lawrence Lessig, *Code and Other Laws of Cyberspace* 135 (1999).

[9] 17 U.S.C. § 109(a) (2000).

[10] Marshall Leafer, *Understanding Copyright* 310 (3d ed. 1999).

[11] The Carnegie Foundation for the Advancement of Teaching, *The Carnegie Classification of Institutions of Higher Education: 2000 Edition* 10-19, 195 (2001), *available at* http://www.carnegiefoundation.org/dynamic/downloads/file_1_341.pdf (Note that the Carnegie Classification system was changed for the 2000 edition and Research I institutions are now included as Doctoral/Research—Extensive and Liberal Arts Colleges are now labeled Baccalaureate Colleges.)

▶8

COPYRIGHT EDUCATION PROGRAMS

OLGA FRANÇOIS

This chapter discusses the following topics:
- ▶ Purpose of teaching copyright
- ▶ Steps for developing an effective © literacy program
- ▶ Best practices of established © programs
- ▶ Methods for teaching and assessing copyright knowledge

INTRODUCTION: LOOKING BACK AT ©ED, MOVING FORWARD TO ©LITERACY

The legal framework of copyright has been discussed in the other chapters of this text. However, often little attention is given to how to increase the knowledge instructors, students, and general users have about the proper use of copyrighted materials. Education is a special and distinct copyright environment. This chapter provides an overview of the components of copyright education programs and reviews the goals of these educational efforts hoping to lay a foundation for basic best practices that can be used in establishing copyright education programs. This chapter will not address the instruction of copyright in law schools for the legal profession; it will, however, look at the application of copyright and its impact on scholars in academic disciplines other than law.

Historically, copyright education developed from copyright management and has been mostly delivered by entities and offices that were charged with reducing the abuse of copyrighted materials, often to lessen institutional impact and liability. Many scholars advocate for a broader discussion of copyright, that includes its social and ethical implications, to be incorporated into the broader academic curriculum.[1] Additionally, the introduction and application of information literacy curriculum, to be discussed later in this chapter, has highlighted the need for faculty and students to broaden their knowledge of how information is produced and consumed inside and outside of the academy. Copyright sits squarely in the center of the academic enterprise: from the teaching and course materials purchased, licensed, or borrowed; to the ownership and authorship of faculty research, etc. Who has the responsibility of teaching this broader understanding of copyright issues? What do faculty need to know about copyright for their own scholarship and publications? What do they need to know to direct the work product of their students? What do students need to know to become responsible researchers, creators, and authors?

THE SHIFTING EDUCATIONAL LANDSCAPE: WHY TEACH COPYRIGHT?

©Ed and the Law

Heightening the awareness of your students and faculty regarding the definition and impact of copyright not only reduces the legal liability of academic institutions, it encourages students and faculty to be more responsible scholars and to think critically about the resources they use.

With the increase in online access to resources and services, many academic institutions become default Internet service providers for staff and faculty in their offices, students in their dorms, homes, and on campus libraries. Congress addressed the challenges of universities becoming Internet service providers by limiting the liability of academic institutions from the unknown infringing acts of its users if certain conditions are met. In 1998, the Digital Millennium Copyright Act was adopted. Section 512 (3) (e) (c) requires that:

> the institution provides to all users of its system or network informational materials that accurately describe, and promote compliance with, the laws of the United States relating to copyright.[2]

In addition, on November 2, 2002, Congress amended Title 17 by passing the Technology Education and Copyright Harmonization (TEACH) Act. The TEACH Act addresses the needs of online educators regarding the performance of multimedia works and in doing so also provides a limit to the liability of academic institutions if infringing acts were discovered. To claim some harbor in this amendment, the new section 110(2) (D) (i) requires that an institution:

> institutes policies regarding copyright, provides informational materials to faculty, students, and relevant staff members that accurately describe, and promote compliance with, the laws of the United States relating to copyright, and provides notice to students that materials used in connection with the course may be subject to copyright protection.[3]

It can be argued that the TEACH Act moves a bit further than the DMCA regarding stated requirements concerning copyright and the promotion of copyright in higher education institutions. You will notice that these clauses do not use the language of "copyright education." The DMCA simply requires that academic institutions provide accurate information resources regarding copyright and vaguely asks that compliance is advocated. The TEACH Act adds to this the requirement of articulated policies and clearly requires that electronic transmissions include a notice to students of the copyright status of works used. Some institutions meet these minimal legal guidelines to minimize legal liability.

The 108th Congress attempted to enhance general copyright knowledge with the introduction of H.R.2517, the Piracy Deterrence and Education Act of 2003. This act was "to enhance criminal enforcement of the copyright laws, educate the public about the application of copyright law to the Internet, and clarify the authority to seize unauthorized copyrighted works."[4] The bill did not make it out of the House of Representatives. It was reintroduced as H.R. 4077, Piracy Deterrence and Education Act of 2004. In this reiteration the subtitle was changed to read:

> To enhance criminal enforcement of the copyright laws, to educate the public about the application of copyright law to the Internet, and for other purposes.[5]

The bill proposes to spend $500,000 annually to establish/institute a national Internet Use Education Program that would simply increase awareness of infringement issues."[6] It passed in the House and was received in the Senate in September of 2005 and is still pending as of the date of this writing. Because of the rapid growth in digital technologies, it is possible that future bills will continue to highlight the need to educate the general public about copyright.

Beyond the Law: Ethics of Information Use and Responsibility

The articulation of a set of skills defined as "information literacy" usually includes a component that requires that a student use information and information resources ethically and legally (see Figure 8.1 and Figure 8.2); this places copyright in the center of student learning and faculty teaching. A focus on developing student skills in these areas not only supports the legal requirements for the limitation of institutional liability; it opens the door to a broader discussion of copyright and the assessment of student knowledge of copyright. For example, the information literacy standards articulated and adopted by the Association for College and Research Librarians (ACRL) in 2000, and subsequently adopted by many U.S. colleges and universities, address the subject of copyright through its fifth standard—*"The information literate student understands many of the economic, legal, and social issues surrounding the use of information and accesses and uses information ethically and legally."*[7] Figure 8.1 illustrates the outcomes directly related to the issue of copyright. For a more detailed discussion of information literacy standards see this chapter's section titled "Foundations for ©Literacy."

▶ **FIGURE 8.1: ACRL Information Literacy Standard Five with Highlighted Copyright Related Outcomes[8]**

Performance Indicators:

1. *The information literate student understands many of the ethical, legal and socio-economic issues surrounding information and information technology*
   Outcomes Include:
   a. Identifies and discusses issues related to privacy and security in both the print and electronic environments
   b. Identifies and discusses issues related to free vs. fee-based access to information
   c. Identifies and discusses issues related to censorship and freedom of speech
   d. Demonstrates an understanding of intellectual property, copyright, and fair use of copyrighted material

2. *The information literate student follows laws, regulations, institutional policies, and etiquette related to the access and use of information resources.*
   Outcomes Include:
   a. Participates in electronic discussions following accepted practices (e.g., "Netiquette")
   b. Uses approved passwords and other forms of ID for access to information resources
   c. Complies with institutional policies on access to information resources
   d. Preserves the integrity of information resources, equipment, systems and facilities
   e. Legally obtains, stores, and disseminates text, data, images, or sounds
   f. Demonstrates an understanding of what constitutes plagiarism and does not represent work attributable to others as his/her own
   g. Demonstrates an understanding of institutional policies related to human subjects research

3. *The information literate student acknowledges the use of information sources in communicating the product or performance.*
   Outcomes Include:
   a. Selects an appropriate documentation style and uses it consistently to cite sources
   b. Posts permission granted notices, as needed, for copyrighted material

The social impact of copyright law is no longer just an interest of the librarian or the lawyer. Scholars and students are impacted by copyright daily, and this impact is being made more clear because of fundamental changes in the structure and infrastructure of how data is moved and used. We are now aware of bytes, bits, file formats, digitally parsed and digitally managed rights of access, etc. Scholars debate the possible chilling of scientific research because of the DMCA anti-circumvention clauses. Libraries develop institutional repositories in the name of "knowledge management" or to combat the rising costs of providing periodical literature to their community. The research environment has become increasingly complicated, and students need to acquire the skills and knowledge to best navigate this environment within their chosen discipline.

> The ethics of the law must be grounded in fundamental notions of justice and fairness, for without this, the rules devolve into conveniences which will be obeyed only when punishment is close at hand. If the only reason to respect copyright is to avoid being caught, it has outlived its purpose.[9]—Jon M. Garon, Dean and Professor of Law

Compliance with the "do's" and "don'ts" mandated by U.S. copyright law is ultimately a question of individual choice. What choice one would make is based upon multiple factors, including but not limited to personal ethics. A student's inability to appropriately comply with the copyright law or scholarly conventions of attribution is often due to a lack of modeling from faculty and peers and the lack of guidance from institutional policies. As more and more students find themselves subject to litigation brought by rights owners because of claims of copyright infringement due to the alleged illegal file sharing of copyrighted songs and films, academic institutions must take on the responsibility of creating an informed citizenry among their students.

The online universe provides students with access to a plethora of scholarly, functional, and popular resources. This somewhat anonymous hyperlinked landscape can leave students feeling cavalier about their ability to "use" what they encounter. There can be a perceived absence of an author or ownership—when, of course, the concept of ownership is complex—whether reading a scholarly article that was originally published in a print journal but is now being viewed from a database that has been subscribed to by the student's college or university or whether viewing a film clip from a recent independent film provided by a reviewing Web site. Downloading, saving, and using a logo from a large corporation's Web site to illustrate a point made in a term paper is not the same as placing that logo on an open Web site because it's "just your favorite thing in the world!"

While a student is expected to understand whether a use is legal or proper, we also want them to give attribution to the original author of the works they are using. We cannot expect that students will know by osmosis how to best manage their use of third party copyrighted works. Faculty must model and teach proper citation and the benefits of scholarly attribution. The rise (and perceived rise) in cases of plagiarism is well documented.[10] Donald McCabe's studies also document a student's inability to understand the impact of purposeful plagiarism.[11] These infractions may be seen as minor by students, while others feel that they undercut the foundation of academic scholarship.

Garon asserts that "the future development of copyright will flow from technological innovation, legal constraints, and social norms."[12] As institutions work to decide which technological solutions they will use to manage the use of copyrighted materials, the classroom can work with students to begin discussions about the social norms that impact a student's decisions and the policies students must work within.

What Students and Faculty Know about ©-Attitudes and Knowledge

While some faculty manage the need for a sophisticated understanding of copyright by not using any third party course content, many instructors will, at some point in their teaching careers, find that they need to make third party developed course content available to their students. Research also shows that faculty may avoid discussing copyright because they feel they lack the expertise to address the topic.[13] Several doctoral studies have assessed what teaching faculty and librarians currently know about copyright. These studies help to plan and set the framework for future copyright programming. Because of the growth of online instruction many of the more recent studies have focused on the application of intellectual property laws in distance education, particularly regarding the ownership of course materials.

Phillis C. Sweeney investigated faculty knowledge of the application of U.S. copyright law and fair use when designing online course materials.[14] Of the 24 instructors who participated in Sweeney's focus groups, 72% rated themselves as having a low level of comprehension of the university's copyright policies.[15] Faculty reported feeling "uncertain about fair use rules in general, including who to contact at the university about them . . ."[16] Overall, the conclusions of the Sweeney study did not show a statistical difference in knowledge from the broad spectrum of disciplines.

Renner studied educators in the state of Ohio and tested their knowledge of basic copyright concepts, contracts, authorship, work for hire, etc. rather than focus on the use of third party copyrighted works.[17] Of the 62 individuals tested, 12% achieved a proficiency score of 75% or higher.[18]

A larger study looked at how faculty and administrators self-reported their knowledge levels. This study looked more at the ownership of course materials and campus policies. Mary Pogue reported that the majority of the participants (96.3%, N=400) were familiar with the broader concept of intellectual property (in addition to copyright, trademark, and patents); however almost 20% fewer (N=259) reported knowing that their institutions had intellectual property policies.[19] Of those that were aware that their institution had an IP policy, very few had read their policies firsthand (N=85).[20] From there the picture gets a bit more grim: many faculty did not understand how the policy allocated rights to course materials. However, Pogue notes that many faculty and administrators feel that their policy provisions pose little problem for them.[21] Active copyright programs can empower teaching faculty.

In 1994, before the passing of the DMCA, Mark E. Chase surveyed media professionals in higher education to analyze their knowledge of specific areas of the copyright law: exclusive rights (sec. 106), fair use (sec. 107), exemption of certain public performances (sec. 110), and selected guidelines for materials used in teaching.[22] A copyright knowledge proficiency level was determined to have been achieved at or above a score of 75%.[23] Only 18% of the survey respondents scored 75% or higher.[24] The author noted that the mean performance was only slightly higher than previous studies of its type. The highest level of proficiency was demonstrated when the respondents were queried on the *Guidelines For Off-Air Taping*, with 62%, suggesting that educators tend to focus on the requirements for the job at hand.[25] How does this impact what we attempt to teach to faculty or students?

While Pogue and Sweeney illustrated that faculty are aware of intellectual property and specifically copyright, the study by Chase allows us to see more closely the need for professional development opportunities for faculty, administrators, and academic staff.

Through recent research in information literacy, the preparation, implementation, and assessment of information literacy curricula, and a significant interest in the users of peer-to-peer file-sharing networks, we have been able to get a snapshot of students' current knowledge of the copyright law and surrounding issues. For example, in the 2003 assessment series by the University of Maryland Baltimore County, students in the Biology and English departments were unfamiliar with the concepts of copyright and fair use and were not able to assess under what circumstances they could or could not appropriately use third-party copyrighted works.[26]

The sharing of copyrighted media (music and video) files across the Internet by individuals is a copyright issue naturally forced into the educational landscape by changes in technology and the very nature of how information is produced, stored, and accessed by students and faculty. The 2005 survey of 1,421 adult Internet users by the Pew Internet and American Life Project shows that:

> 49% of all Americans and 53% of Internet users believe that the firms that own and operate file-sharing networks should be deemed responsible for the pirating of music and movie files. Some 18% of all Americans think individual file traders should be held responsible and 12% say both companies and individuals should shoulder responsibility . . . Young adults' skepticism rivals that of always-on broadband users; 55% believe illegal file-sharing is beyond government control, while 36% think the activity can be controlled.[27]

These attitudes, when compared to the actions and attitudes reported in the 2005 IPSOS Public Affairs/Business Software Alliance Survey of over 1000 university and college students, leaves a huge gap for educational initiatives to fill.[28] This survey revealed that campus networks and systems are used by 45% of students for downloading of copyrighted media files. Additionally, it reports that this is an acceptable practice to 52% of the students polled. In comparing the 2005 study to the 2003 study conducted by the BSA, IPSOS reports that students' awareness of their campus policies has increased. While the connection between faculty modeling and student action is well documented,[29] it is interestingly noted that:

> Among the college and university professors and administrators surveyed, few believe it is acceptable to encourage swapping or downloading illegally, yet no more than one quarter of students report that professors and administrators actively discourage these behaviors.[30]

The challenges faced by today's researcher and research environment can only be met by developing an arsenal of definitions, skills, questions, perceptions, guidelines, and a framework for making the best decision possible when a need arises. Copyright management needs to be replaced with a *copyright literacy* that actively addresses the social, political, and technical world in which information use takes place. The needs of students as lifelong learners will only be met by developing in them the ability to evaluate and question the tools and services they use to deliver information to their desktops, PDAs, iPods, etc. All disciplinary instructors play an important role in this process. This means that the instructors need a basic understanding of copyright law and its provisions as well as guidance on how to appropriately embed these issues in their departmental curricula, their syllabi, and their instruction.

DEVELOPING PROGRAMS

Here are some basic steps for developing a successful copyright education program at the institutional level:

- ▶ begin to discuss concerns and issues with individuals around campus;
- ▶ set meetings of vested parties (departmental representatives, student services, information technology offices, librarians, administrators, university counsel, etc.);
- ▶ assess institutional needs, goals, and concerns;
- ▶ outline the approach, establish the process, plan for the assessment of programming;
- ▶ work for buy-in of additional parties if necessary (deans, etc.);
- ▶ develop policies;
- ▶ advertise and outreach to constituents (students, faculty, staff, etc.)
- ▶ teach and deliver programming; and
- ▶ assess programming.

A small informal survey of several directors of university and college copyright offices looked at some of the best practices of institutions with well-established copyright programs.[31] These programs were managed by university counsel, librarians, and faculty who held dual appointments as teaching faculty and center directors. Overwhelmingly, these individuals worked with a staff of not more than two staff members (including themselves) who worked on the issue of copyright or copyright education. Less than a quarter of the respondents reported to have seven or more staff members doing this work. Several directors expressed a need for more staff to accomplish their work. As many as 67% reported their primary audience as classroom faculty, with only one reporting "students" as their primary audience. Most often, students were seen as their secondary audience over librarians, staff, or administrators. Even given this fact, 88% report that they regularly offered workshops and classes for students and 100% offer them for faculty. Teaching the teacher is the common paradigm.

Most of these programs were developed as the result of working groups established by university administration or library administration. Currently, administrators of these programs see their work as a function of "copyright management" but report a growing concern about how to more directly address these issues with students. Suggested barriers to the delivery of quality copyright education on campuses are: (1) outreach to students and faculty and how to simply notify their constituents of upcoming programming; (2) perceptions by faculty of the importance of the issue. It is believed that a positive impact could be accomplished by offering incentives to faculty for further professional development in this area, and (3) the lack of necessary staff to run these departments and offices. Half of the surveyed programs (56%) have standing copyright or research advisory committees. The duties of these committees range from overseeing the publication and distribution of materials on copyright, conducting workshops, policy development, assisting with faculty publications and patents to making recommendations on copyright ownership questions.

Foundations for ©Literacy

To set the foundation for copyright literacy, colleges and universities should develop solid policies for all constituents (staff, students, and faculty), cover these issues in student and faculty handbooks, advocate for faculty to discuss these issues in their individual course syllabi, and write information literacy standards for their programs and departments. The foundational awareness achieved by these tasks should not be overlooked or undervalued. Awareness achieved at the point of need is an important part of teaching about the impact of copyright on society.

Policies, Handbooks, and Course Syllabi

Copyright and academic integrity are often mentioned in legal discussions for academic administrators.[32] Administrators are charged with setting the parameters or policies that guide, and sometimes govern, individual academic communities. These policies serve as reference points to manage problem situations when they arise. They are preventive measures that not only provide guidance to readers but can give procedures for adjudication. Often, the process to establish academic policies is open and gives opportunity for faculty, librarians, staff, and students to have input and to work to encourage others to take those opportunities to participate in policy development when they present themselves.

Copyright is embedded in many academic policies. Typical areas addressed by policies are:

▶ faculty ownership of course materials and research (work for hire, etc.);

▶ student ownership of course materials and research;

► institutional ownership of scholarship, course materials, products, or research results;

► Internet and campus network use;

► fair use guidelines;

► software piracy;

► TEACH Act guidelines;

► reserves for print and electronic library and research materials;

► downloading and technology use; and

► academic integrity and plagiarism.

The provisions of those policies are varied and fluctuate depending on the target population and institutional need. For example, David Alan Makin in 2002 undertook a study which looked at college students' behavior and attitudes toward uploading material to file-sharing networks. The survey results suggested that students felt a social pressure to upload files to sharing networks and questioned if they had a feeling of "share and share alike."[33] Although he does not feel that institutions can stop students' file-sharing activities he does feel that the suggestions below may temper student activities:

1. Implement better technological controls into the hardware and software. (Limit port ranges).

2. Implement training to inform students about the financial and social impact of their behavior.

3. Develop and require students to sign a "computer and Internet use" policy prior to receiving access to the Internet.

4. Illustrate through policies that not everyone engages in the behavior.

5. Include statements informing individuals of the social and economic impact of the behavior in hardware and software systems that facilitate file sharing of copy-protected media.

6. Advocate that Internet service providers implement policy that includes copyright warnings and additional appropriate legal warnings.[34]

As illustrated above, one campus issue has many components, including but not limited to the implementation of a policy to govern student actions. Makin also illustrates that a policy can be drafted to work toward shaping the community's perspective on a particular issue.

Final policies should define the relevant issues and also they should include examples of proper compliance and outline the consequences of violating policies. Policies do not, and should not, live in a closed book or rarely accessed Web site. Institutional policies should be living documents that are printed in student and faculty handbooks and included in print and online syllabi for constant reference. It is unfair to students to hold them accountable for policies that they do not understand and or do not know exist. As suggested by Makin, having students sign to acknowledge that they have read and understand policies such as a computer use policy to manage files sharing over campus networks or academic integrity policies heightens their awareness and possibly lessens cases of violations.

Copyright Management and Guidelines

Intellectual property policies vary; no two look alike. You may find that many are very brief, while others may give minute details or include guidelines for managing particular procedures. At the same time, you may find these guidelines exist as separate documents throughout campus communities—for example, guidelines for using and requesting interlibrary loans or reserves, guidelines for computer use, guidelines for making copies for classroom use, guidelines for using video in course instruction, etc. Institutions and most especially, libraries, also adapt, use and promote guidelines written by professional associations. These documents can, and often do, give very specific recommendations to users; for example they may specify a number of pages that are acceptable to photocopy from a text owned by a library; See Figure 8.2 for some of the most common copyright guidelines.

Guidelines are believed to be written to provide the least amount of risk to users and content owners alike, most especially the guidelines resulting from actions mandated by the U.S. Copyright Office. Some copyright scholars feel that guidelines should be used cautiously because they may overly restrict the legal uses of copyrighted works; while others feel that users should be cautious and make sure that they adhere to established guidelines because without them, the general researcher or writer may find themselves in a wealth of trouble.

Historically, "copyright management" has included suggesting methods, setting limits, and standards for using third-party copyrighted works. Examples of these activities are: providing guides and guidelines to users, providing postings near photocopy machines that remind users that the material they are using may be copyrighted, setting limits on interlibrary loan and reserve materials, and advising users on how to get permission to use the work of others. While some of these activities are voluntary, some are mandated by law. These activities are important for the daily use of third-party copyrighted material.

IL Standards, Outcomes, and Objectives

The 1987 Boyer Report on undergraduate education places libraries and librarians in the center of the educational enterprise.[35] The 1998 Boyer Commission Report, *Reinventing Undergraduate Education*, helped to create an environment for the adoption of the Association of College and Research Libraries (ACRL) Information Literacy Standards. The Commission envisions the university as an "intellectual ecosystem," acknowledging an organic and natural connection between disciplines and student development and makes a plea for inquiry and research-based learning as standard educational practice.[36] In 2001, a three-year follow-up survey found that 64% of campus administrators from Research I & II institutions reported their

▶ FIGURE 8.2: Common Copyright Guidelines

AALL Guidelines on the Fair Use of Copyrighted Works by Law Libraries, May 1997, Revised January 2001
American Association of Law Librarians
http://www.aallnet.org/about/policy_fair.asp

ACM Copyright Policy, Version 4, 2002
Association for Computing Machinery
http://www.acm.org/pubs/copyright_policy/

Agreement on Guidelines for Classroom Copying in Not-For-Profit Educational Institutions with Respect to Books and Periodicals, 1976
http://www.lib.jmu.edu/org/mla/guidelines/accepted%20guidelines/Educational%20Photocopying.asp

Best Practices for Permissions Processing, n.d.
Association of American Publishers
http://www.publishers.org/about/copyeducation.cfm

Checklist for Fair Use, 2002
Copyright Management Center, Indiana University-Purdue University Indianapolis
http://copyright.iupui.edu/checklist.htm

Circular 22—How to Investigate the Copyright Status of a Work,
U.S. Copyright Office
http://palimpsest.stanford.edu/bytopic/intprop/circ22.html

Conference on Fair Use ("CONFU") Guidelines for Educational Uses of Digital Works, 1997
  Multimedia Development
  ▶ Software Uses
  ▶ Electronic Reserves
  ▶ Interlibrary Loans
http://www.uspto.gov/web/offices/dcom/olia/confu/conclu1.html

Copyright Management Guidelines, Revised July 2001
Medical Library Association
http://www.mlanet.org/government/positions/copyright_mgmt.html

Federal Guidelines for Off-Air Recording of Broadcast Programming for Educational Purposes, 1981

Guide to Good Practice in the Digital Representation and Management of Cultural Heritage Materials, 2002
National Initiative for a Networked Cultural Heritage
http://www.nyu.edu/its/humanities/ninchguide/

Image Collection Guidelines: The Acquisition and Use of Images in Non-Profit Educational Visual Resources, n.d.
Visual Resources Association
http://www.vraweb.org/copyright/guidelines.html

Library and Classroom Use of Copyrighted Videotapes and Computer Software, 1986
American Library Association
http://library.cmsu.edu/circulation/Model_Policy.pdf

Model Policy Concerning College and University Photocopying for Classroom, Research and Library Reserve Use, 1982
American Library Association
http://www.ifla.org/documents/infopol/copyright/ala-1.txt

Statement on the Copyright Law and Fair Use in Music, 1996
Music Library Association
http://www.lib.jmu.edu/org/mla/

Statement on Fair Use and Electronic Reserves, November 2003
American Library Association
http://www.ala.org/ala/acrl/acrlpubs/whitepapers/statementfair.htm

campuses encouraged faculty development for this type of student learning; though the implementation still seems limited.[37] The ACRL Information Literacy Standards also advocate the implementation of a curriculum that fosters student development and is based in critical inquiry, research and investigation.

Barbara Ludlow argues that higher education institutions are just beginning to contemplate student ownership of intellectual property beyond collaborative work of graduate students and doctoral dissertations.[38] David Bawden traces the first mention of the phrase "information literacy" back to Paul Zurkowski in 1974.[39] This definition included the phrase "transformation of traditional library services into more innovative private sector provision, and the policy issues associated." This early incarnation included components of Standard 5, in particular the policy issues surrounding the use and production of information. In 1996, Shapiro and Hughes argued that the contemporary librarian's view of "information literacy" only encompassed "resource literacy," and rarely covered other literacies they believed necessary to serve the needs of an information society.[40] Shapiro and Hughes proposed an information literacy curriculum that included Tool Literacy, Social-Structure Literacy, Research Literacy, Publishing Literacy, and Emerging Technology Literacy. Together these additional literacies address the broader concept and implications of copyright in our society. ACRL embraced many of these proposed literacies in drafting Standard 5, its performance indicators, and outcomes. However, in the 2001 document titled "Objectives for Information Literacy Instruction: A Model Statement for Academic Librarians," the Instruction Section Task Force did not write objectives for many Standard 5 performance indicators that were designated beyond what could be addressed by librarians alone or collaboratively with course faculty (see "Responsibility Tags for Competency Standards").[41] The new *ACRL Standards Toolkit* moves beyond that 2001 document. ACRL through the Information Literacy Competency Standards and Toolkit has broadened the definition and application of information literacy, inviting academics, librarians and course faculty, to wrestle with finding appropriate ways to incorporate Standard 5 into their curriculum.[42]

Consensus within librarianship on the issues raised by Boyer and by Shapiro and Hughes has been slowly forming, especially around the thorny issues of inquiry-based curriculum and social-structure literacy. Even still, these problem-based and resource-based curricular changes require students to think and act critically as they interact with copyrighted material and become creators themselves.

The ACRL Information Literacy Standards were endorsed by the American Association for Higher Education in 1999 and the Council of Independent Colleges in 2004. Accompanying the ACRL information literacy standards are similar sets of standards and performance indicators from related bodies and constituencies that also address the subject of copyright. See Figure 8.3 for additional examples of instructional standards.

▶ **FIGURE 8.3: Copyright and Learning Standards**

American Association of School Librarians (AASL) (K-12)
Information Literacy Standards for Student Learning: Social Responsibility Standards[43]

> **Standard 7:** The student who contributes positively to the learning community and to society is information literate and recognizes the importance of information to a democratic society.

> **Standard 8:** The student who contributes positively to the learning community and to society is information literate and practices ethical behavior in regard to information and information technology.

Australian and New Zealand Institute for Information Literacy (ANZIL) and Council of Australian University Librarians (CAUL) (Higher Ed)
Australian and New Zealand Information Literacy Framework[44]

> **Standard 6:** The information literate person uses information with understanding and acknowledges cultural, ethical, economic, legal, and social issues surrounding the use of information

International Society for Technology in Education (ISTE) (preK-12)
Technology Foundation Standards for Students[45]

Standard 2: Social, ethical, and human issues
▶ Students understand the ethical, cultural, and societal issues related to technology.
▶ Students practice responsible use of technology systems, information, and software.
▶ Students develop positive attitudes toward technology uses that support lifelong learning, collaboration, personal pursuits, and productivity.

International Society for Technology in Education (ISTE) (preK-12)
The National Educational Technology Standards (NETS) for Teachers[46]

Standard 6: SOCIAL, ETHICAL, LEGAL, AND HUMAN ISSUES.
Teachers understand the social, ethical, legal, and human issues surrounding the use of technology in PK-12 schools and apply those principles in practice. Teachers:

A. model and teach legal and ethical practice related to technology use.
B. apply technology resources to enable and empower learners with diverse backgrounds, characteristics, and abilities.
C. identify and use technology resources that affirm diversity
D. promote safe and healthy use of technology resources.
E. facilitate equitable access to technology resources for all students.

With the focus on copyright in the standards of professional associations for the K-12 sector, one could ask, "Why does the higher education community still need to address these issues?" Because suggested curricular standards are building blocks. A student moves through multiple levels of proficiency and sophistication as she or he moves through her/his education and experiences. The standards and any accompanying objectives and learning outcomes allow for clear articulation of what faculty will teach, what is expected of students, and what will be assessed.

Passive and Active ©Education

Many of the tasks typically associated with copyright management on college campuses are also forms of copyright education. By conducting these tasks, you raise user awareness of the issues surrounding copyright and begin to teach them proper use of copyrighted material and media.

▶FIGURE 8.4: Copyright Education

Management	→	Awareness	→	Knowledge/Education
(Foundations)		(Passive)		(Active)

Passive copyright education provides users with tools that, when combined with self-study and application, can lead to a deeper understanding of copyright. Some of these tools are:

▶ Web sites,
▶ guides,
▶ guidelines,
▶ postings and notices, and
▶ flyers, table-tents, brochures, posters, etc.

Seen most often are Web sites developed by individual libraries or associations that provide basic definitions and referrals to a small selection of frequently cited outside information or educational resources (e.g. association Web sites, copyright centers, association pages, etc.). It is also not uncommon for a library or organization to develop resources that they feel more directly meet the needs of their target audience. When developing a Web site, think about the audience.

▶ How will they find the Web resource? From what other pages will this page be linked?
▶ What is the entry point for faculty or students?
▶ Will it cover all subjects (i.e., permissions, ownership and self-authorship, copy limits, etc.)?
▶ Does it need to serve all disciplines?

Think about its design and layout.

▶ Should it be one long page?
▶ Are a collection of short linked pages more appropriate for the subject matter?
▶ Is it best to keep resources on citation styles separate from resources on student ownership?

Successful resources come from well-thought-out development and design stages. Washburn University took a unique method of engaging its students by creating a portal specific to the needs of its students and their perspectives. This portal is separated into three sections: Headlines, Bylines, and Guidelines. "Headlines" highlights news stories where college students have been charged with infringing the copyrights of someone else. "Bylines" highlights students from the institution who had created copyrighted original works. And, as expected, the "Guidelines" section provides students with information on copyright in research.[47]

While some passive educational tools are developed out of need (i.e., notices near photocopiers and Web sites), many passive tools like flyers, posters, and brochures can be viewed as advertisements or fluff. Though passive in nature, these types of outreach tools are proactive and can greatly heighten community awareness of an issue. For brick and mortar campuses, think about the power in copyright posters that speak directly to issues that impact the sciences posted through out departmental hallways. A commercial example of this is posters produced by the Motion Picture Association to deter the file sharing of Hollywood movies placed in theaters and video stores. The issue of copyright becomes personal to your everyday actions. Distance educators can collaborate with course faculty and course developers to program pop-up ads that would appear at several select times during a semester or term. They would force students to engage with the subject matter before they could move on to a research assignment or paper. Unlike the latter suggestion, many of these methods can be overlooked or purposefully neglected by users, thereby negating their educational benefits.

Active forms of copyright education are also a road to copyright literacy. Directly addressing the social, ethical, and political issues that surround information use and information policies within the formal confines of professional development for faculty or the disciplinary curriculum for students can better meet the standards and objectives articulated by information literacy. The challenge is to empower faculty to make decisions for their own scholarship, teaching, and publishing and to prepare them to teach copyright issues (that they may have missed) to students. This challenge is present for many teaching library faculty as well. Active copyright education can come in many forms:

▶ workshops (stand-alone and academic program integrated);

▶ face-to-face classroom instruction, library instruction, and collaboration;

▶ online course modules; and

▶ learning objects (stand-alone tutorials and course embedded, etc.).

Stand-alone workshops for faculty and students are often offered by libraries or information technology departments. In addition, academic counsel and copyright offices provide stand-alone workshops for faculty and graduate students. Established copyright programs find that they offer face-to-face workshops for faculty once or twice a semester. These workshop offerings can sometimes be lightly attended depending on the climate of the institution, the outreach to potential attendees, or whether attendance is mandated by institutional governance. Undergraduate students can be introduced to information policy and its impact through freshmen seminars and freshmen orientations. This is becoming more common in face-to-face settings when students are introduced to the expected etiquette accompanying access to the campus network.

However, education at the point of need, or course-integrated copyright education as a component of information literacy, has a more lasting impact. This is not a suggestion that all courses become information policy courses—that would be absurd; however this is a suggestion that some subjects can foster a natural discussion of information policies while other courses may require that instructors be more detailed when assigning students to assemble a multimedia group project on nineteenth-century workhouse songs of the Mississippi Delta. These suggestions sometimes mean that an instructor may need to change what or how they teach particular subjects in their face-to-face or online courses. While undergraduate faculty teaching outside the English department would like to rely on their students' previous experience with authorship and attribution, by not covering this material with students faculty miss an opportunity to raise students' knowledge about the rights associated with authoring scholarship or research in their discipline. Concluding a 1998 study of 411 journalism and mass-communication program administrators, Smethers advocates for integrating the topics of the legal and ethical use of information into broader course material across the curriculum rather than establish stand-alone courses to address this subject. In this field the topic could be covered in introductory and survey courses, courses on ethics and communication law, and communication technology courses.[48] Course faculty would benefit from workshops aimed at assisting them to rearticulate their class assignments and course syllabi.

English departments, technology departments, and libraries are developing digital learning objects to supplement course instruction in these areas. Online copyright tutorials can do two things: introduce and teach a concept and then test a student's knowledge of the material introduced. While the developments of tutorials is time-consuming, and can be very costly depending on the level of programming needed, it is believed that they lessen the instructional burden on course faculty and can reach a broader spectrum of students. This is only true if there is a programmatic distribution of these tutorials with departmental buy-in. Tutorials can sit unused if they are not assigned by course faculty or embedded in other widely attended workshops or library instruction sessions. If you are undertaking the development of a tutorial be sure to:

- ▶ outline your educational goals;
- ▶ articulate what specific standards and outcomes will be addressed;
- ▶ clearly define and research the audience;
- ▶ research potential production platforms and technologies;
- ▶ seek buy-in from faculty and administrators;
- ▶ pay attention to graphics, style, and function;
- ▶ be conscious of the technological skill of the potential users; and
- ▶ make it engaging.

Together, active and passive methods of teaching the subject of copyright make up the components of successful institutional copy education programs. It is most likely that one method alone will not truly meet the needs of your user population. Evaluate their needs carefully.

MEETING THE INSTRUCTIONAL NEED

Who Should Teach ©

If you look around you will find a wealth of agencies, large and small non-profit organizations, professional associations, and corporations with a stated position or interest in the issue of copyright. From the educational sector you may find copyright information and instructional materials and courses being offered by:

- ▶ libraries and librarians,
- ▶ multimedia staff,
- ▶ information technology departments,
- ▶ course faculty,
- ▶ academic counsel,
- ▶ campus rights clearance offices,
- ▶ peer guidance,
- ▶ K-12 district and regional offices, and
- ▶ administration at the university system level.

Copyright law is fundamental to the function of all libraries, including academic libraries that have traditionally served as clearinghouses for copyrighted works. By nature they collect copyrighted books, journals, magazines, pamphlets, film, videos, learning objects, personal papers, etc. Once these materials are collected, they are made available in accordance with the U.S. copyright law and managed by developed policies. To ensure that they are carrying out their missions, libraries often need to make their users aware of the laws, including copyright, which shape their policies. This is true of all types of libraries: academic, public, private, commercial, government, association, and organizational, etc. Depending on the size of the institutions, the staff available and or the perceived importance to the mission, individual departments charged with dealing with issues of ownership, rights clearance, and/or technology transfer are established as subdivisions of libraries or academic counsel offices.

There is an almost daily growth in the technological platforms and technologies provided by institutions to students. Because institutional liability increases with the support of these technologies, the decision to provide a comprehensive copyright education program is often supported by academic administrators.[49] Information technology departments are partly charged with developing "tech fluency" in the student population. The 2000 report *The Digital Dilemma: Intellectual Property in the Information Age*, issued by a committee of national scholars through the National Research Council, calls for broader copyright education.[50] Although it seems that the committee was unresolved on some points. "The committee could not decide on how extensive copyright education should be, who should conduct this education, or who should pay for it."[51] In speaking of the importance of copyright education the committee issued this conclusion:

> A better understanding of the basic principles of copyright law would lead to a greater respect for this law and greater willingness to abide by it, as well as produce a more informed public better able to engage in discussions about intellectual property and public policy.[52]

In addition to information technology departments that manage campus-wide computer networks, other offices that may address the subject of copyright can be technology transfer offices, and offices set up to strictly address copyright permission for the use of copyrighted works. While these are often internal to library services they can also be external departments. Faculty from several disciplines address copyright and copyright related topics within their curricula—for example, communications, computer science, disciplinary ethics courses, as well as general research methods courses for undergraduates and graduate students.

Examples of guidance from higher levels in the institutional structure (district, regional, or system offices) provide internal constituents with basic copyright resources that they can easily deliver to other campus users. A noteworthy program would be the University of Texas (UT) System Office of General Counsel. This program has developed resources that directly address the needs of the individual campuses (and faculty) within the UT system and provide resources that are frequently referenced and used by many institutions and individuals outside the UT system. This model has been adopted by many university systems; another example would be the California State University System. Diane Barbour, chief information officer at the Rochester Institute of Technology advocates for copyright education and instruction on cyber ethics to begin at the K-12 level.[53] Many K-12 systems, schools, and individual faculty concur with this sentiment and have developed individual course assignments, copyright tutorials, and guidelines for K-12 teachers and students.

Other agencies and organizations with a vested interest in copyright are the professional associations such as the library associations (American Library Association, Special Library Association, etc.), the National Association of College and University Attorneys (NACUA), EDUCAUSE, American Society of Journalists and Authors, and the American Society of Media Photographers, to name a small select few. Truthfully, the list is too expansive for this publication. These associations provide for their membership guidance on the proper use of information within their professions through policy and position statements, conference presentations, and published journal articles.

Other great resources not to be overlooked are the recommendations and copyright initiatives of rights holders' agencies. For example, associations representing book publishers, composers, software developers, corporate filmmakers, musicians, and music publishers work to protect their copyrights by providing suggested guidelines and procedures for users of their content and products. With the proliferation of copyrighted content publicly made available through the Internet, it stands to reason that these agencies would work to provide guidance on the use of works that they own and manage. Adding to the guidelines and recommendations offered up by the above agencies are third-party organizations and advocacy groups such as the Electronic Frontier Foundation, the Copyright Clearance Center, Creative Commons, the Center for Academic Integrity, the Center for the Public Domain, and the Center for Intellectual Property. The perspectives of these advocacy groups and organizations can be quite different from that of rights holders' agencies and associations previously mentioned. If looking to them as a resource be critical and evaluate their missions along with your needs carefully.

Skills and Experience Necessary to Teach ©

To meet the (c)Literacy instructional demand, faculty, librarians, academic counsel, and administrators must all seek the professional development necessary to become conversant in the law and institutional policies. While many attorneys specialize in intellectual property law, others are generalists, such as academic counsel, and look for professional opportunities to further develop their expertise in intellectual property law. Similarly, there are librarians who hold law degrees, but they lack the expertise in copyright and look to professional associations for programs and courses on the subject. Just over half (56%) of the program directors surveyed[54] were not degreed lawyers. While the majority of the survey respondents did not feel that a law degree is necessary to teach basic copyright principles to faculty, staff, and students, they feel that the law degree would benefit someone doing the instruction. As one could imagine, a disciplinary faculty member may feel that she/he does not have the expertise to address this topic. As previously discussed in this chapter, institutional copyright offices typically offer workshops and classes for disciplinary faculty. Another way to teach or learn about copyright in online courses is to have a visiting instructor moderate this portion of the content. This is sometimes more difficult in face-to-face instruction, but visiting lecturers are a standing practice in academic instruction. Evidence of a successful program is a campus where multiple entities, people, and offices can be pointed to as champions of copyright awareness and education.

What to Teach, What Do They Need to Know?

Topics typically covered in faculty professional development include:
- ▶ copyright basics, including the DMCA;
- ▶ copyright policies;
- ▶ fair use;

▶ exemptions;

▶ permissions for use;

▶ faculty ownership of course materials and scholarship; and

▶ the TEACH Act and online use of copyright material.

No less important, but not as frequently covered, are the subjects of copyright and the Internet, e-reserves, file sharing, piracy, and plagiarism and proper citation. Paradigm shifts in scholarly publishing and the information landscape have introduced new material into many disciplinary curricula. Because of the ease with which we can now manipulate electronic data, students crave a seamless electronic universe; this can only be successfully accomplished with a developed understanding of the copyright law. Some of the subject areas classroom faculty could address with their students as appropriate to their course material:

▶ basic copyright law;

▶ personal intellectual property rights;

▶ responsibilities and compliance;

▶ public domain;

▶ first sale doctrine;

▶ fair use;

▶ cyber law;

▶ cyber ethics;

▶ plagiarism, citation, and attribution;

▶ proper use of copyrighted media and multimedia works; and

▶ the consequences of improper use of copyrighted works.

Other subject areas for instruction mentioned by the surveyed directors of copyright programs were the need for reform of the copyright law to better protect the rights of users, shortening of the copyright period for protected works, the possible concentration of IP rights among fewer and fewer corporations, and the impact of this on policy and access to copyrighted materials. The University of Maryland University College Information Literacy and Writing Assessment (ILWA) Project offers several assignment examples that would help to teach students about some of the details of copyright and copyright provisions.[55] See Figure 8.5 for these and other examples.

Laura Kaemming developed a four-day copyright lesson for eighth graders that allows students to learn the meaning of copyright, explore the meaning of originality and ownership, and explore questions of infringement. In this assignment on day one, students are introduced to copyright through a worksheet and read an article on intellectual property in music and songs. On day two, students share their answers from the first day's worksheet and are then introduced to the concept of fair use. Day three, they listen to several songs where one or more songs *sample* an original recording. On day four students discuss the concept of fair use and review all worksheets. *See Appendix A* for the assignment details.

► **FIGURE. 8.5: Sample Classroom Assignments**

An Assignment Integrated into a Project	ACRL Information Literacy Standard Five ► Adapted by ILWA from Anne C. Coon, "Using ethical questions to develop autonomy in student researchers," College Composition and Communication, 40, February, 1989, 85-92.[56]

Students are asked to write papers on an activity in which an individual knowingly breaks a societal, religious, or *institutional law*; possible actions such as: copyright abuse, plagiarism, or piracy. As a first step, students conduct a literature search for information on prevalence, arguments for and against, and consequences of the action they have chosen to study. With this preparation, students plan and carry out a piece of original research—a survey, interview, observation, etc. The results must be included in their final paper. Make it clear to students that although their research is not strictly scientific, their findings do have a valuable place in their papers. In a brainstorming activity, students are encouraged to consider their topics from different perspectives by writing in-class profiles titled "I am a ___," in which they pretend they are the law-breaker, the law-enforcer, the victim, and so on.

Information in Society	ACRL Information Literacy Standard Five ► By ILWA[57]

Have students examine the role of information in a democratic society. What are the issues? How is information relevant or important to them?

Website Development	ACRL Information Literacy performance indicators: 5.1.d, 5.2.c, 5.2.e and 5.3.b (*See Table 1*)

This common assignment is very flexible and can be connected to almost any area of study. It requires that students work independently or in small groups to create a web site including text, images, and any other form of multimedia. During this process students learn about the proper use of multiple formats, seeking permissions, and attribution.

Archaeological Field Study	ACRL Information Literacy performance indicators: 5.1.d and 5.2.f (*See Table 1*) ► By Kyzyl Fenno-Smith, CSU Libraries and Olga Francois

Archaeologist search with an understanding that what they find originates from someplace, and sometime; there is a possible owner of what was found and there is a definite creator. This assignment asks students to approach their use of research in a similar manner. In this assignment students create a Field Research Journal. Select a solid article or piece of research to be fact-checked. Students will then locate all referenced scholarship and discuss if each item is appropriately used: are the arguments properly represented? Is the item properly cited? Etc.

Linking to Protected Works	ACRL Information Literacy performance indicators: 5.1.b, 5.1.d and 5.2.e (*See Table 1*) ► By The Copyright Site[58]

The authors of this assignment suggest that it would work well for an upper level marketing course as well a general research class. Students are put into groups and are given a list of URLs that lead to various web pages. They are to evaluate each web page for the following:
► How many links (or levels) are there between the given link and the home page?
► How many advertisements are missed by using the deep link?
► Is there critical information on the skipped links?
► Which sites are likely protected under copyright law?
► Which are not likely protected? *See Appendix A*

For faculty and college-level students, practical assignments that put copyright in context with their own scholarship work well, along with case studies and scenarios. Kimberly Kelley of the Center for Intellectual Property developed the following scenario to help faculty begin to think about what material can be used in their online courses after the passing of the TEACH Act:

DR. NO (FACULTY MEMBER):

I'd like to create a password protected Web site for my course, "The History of Rock and Roll", and I need your help.

I'd also like for you to load 10 songs that I'm using in my course to the site so my students will be able to retrieve them off the Internet.

I know I couldn't do this previously, but now, with the new TEACH Act, I think I can. I'm really excited about this new flexibility in using music for teaching. Now, my students don't have to visit the library. Instead, they can listen to the tunes from their dorm room or wherever they want.

No more complaints about back ups in getting to an available listening room in the library.

I used a new de-encryption program to get two of the songs, and without it, I wouldn't have been able to include them.

It's probably also fair use, so, getting the songs, whatever way we can, should not be a problem. I have this tech-savvy student, who retrieved several of the songs for me from the Internet, a site she called "freshnoise.com". I'm glad, because she saved me hours of searching to compile this set of songs!

I might be able to include an opera on the site next semester when I teach my "History of Opera" course.

IT CONSULTANT:

I'd be glad to help. And it's very helpful to hear that you know the ins and outs of the TEACH Act.

I can do this tomorrow. No problem. See you later, Dr. No.

(*Pauses, looking at CD.*) Wait a second . . . is everything that Dr. No did okay?

From this scenario, the Center for Intellectual Property and Dr. Kelley created a video clip that is now used in online workshops and classes. [59] The *Copyright Site* also uses scenarios as a method for instruction; it offers six scenarios with a special section dedicated to issues in higher education. In addition, this site gives several copyright assignment suggestions dedicated to K-6 and 7-12, as well as higher education. This comprehensive teaching site was initially developed by Information Technology doctoral students to fulfill a perceived need in the teacher education program at the University of Alabama. Author Hall Davidson offers 20 fair use scenarios in his Copyright Quiz that have been used for classroom discussions with students.[60]

A wealth of resource lists are available online on the subject of copyright. Often you will find a short list, including items like the main Web site for U.S. Copyright

Office, reproduced from one Web site to another. *See the Appendix* for a resource list of copyright learning objects that can be assigned to faculty or students or used for self-education.

©Ed Assessment

Copyright offices, libraries, and departmental programs can employ a variety of assessment measures to evaluate student information competency and copyright knowledge; these include:

▶ Program level pre-post tests and surveys, which can provide an overview of student skill across a department, institution, or system program. Constraints of instrument design to assess copyright knowledge make it difficult to assess higher-level skills and knowledge through this method;

▶ Course level pre-post tests and surveys, which can be quantitative or qualitative, and are usually delivered at the beginning of a course or after the instruction has taken place. Analysis of survey data can inform instructional planning and enhance future instructional experiences of students. It can also be difficult to assess higher-level skills through this method;

▶ Qualitative assignment evaluation, which can employ criteria or a rubric to evaluate a student's performance of the defined outcomes. Methods of assessing applied knowledge require more time and effort to grade;

▶ Self-assessment and perception surveys solicit qualitative responses when students reflect on their own learning and abilities;

▶ Peer-assessment processes provide an important opportunity for students to practice applying assessment criteria to their peer's work (usually during the drafting process). It is most important to discuss student outcomes when employing this method.

To design effective learning experiences, assignments, and formative assessments for classroom instruction, it is useful for the instructor to reflect on the following questions: What do I want the student to be able to do (performance indicators, objectives, outcomes)? How will I, and the students, know when they are able to do it well (assessments)? What do the students need to learn or experience to be able to do it well (assignments, classroom activities)?[61] These questions are informed by the purpose of the assessment and where and how the assessment is taking place. When reassessing the ethics and copyright module of their courses, scholars Colleen Swain and Elizabeth Gilmore, asked themselves these questions:

▶ What pre-existing information/misinformation did students have about the topic prior to our instruction?

▶ What areas of the unit were successful and what areas needed improvement?

▶ What steps could we take to better address the misunderstandings or confusion about the topic?

▶ How could we promote a consciousness of thought about computer ethics and copyright that would permeate the teacher education program?

▶ How could we better promote discussion and student reflection about copyright and computer ethics?[62]

In the classroom, students' understanding of the multifaceted issue of copyright and information policy is best assessed with methods that are directly tied to the course material and where the assessment can immediately affect the course instruction. However, surveys and multiple choice questions are sometimes easier to use and more expedient when assessing full programs and some class assignments. To test the effectiveness of your program with surveys, it can be helpful to use the same survey instrument at multiple times over a period of time. For a list of assessment instruments and quizzes see Figure 8.6.

CONCLUSION

Educational institutions play a role in creating both informed information consumers and informed citizens who have a voice in the intellectual property policies that affect their lives. We should work to create educational opportunities not only so people can obey the law, but also so they can question the law when appropriate. As the individual's access to information resources continues to shift and change, so too must the methods used to teach information policy. Students are

▶ FIGURE 8.6: Resources for Copyright Quizzes, Questions, and Assessments

The Copyright Challenge
By Copyright Kids.org
http://www.copyrightkids.org/quizframes.htm

Copyright and You, April 5, 2001
By Gary H. Becker, DCMO BOCES, Support Services Center
http://www.dcmoboces.com/dcmoiss/staffdev/wsflwup/crs/crs.htm

Copyright Test and Answers
Provided by WestEd
http://www.wested.org/techplan/copyright/copyright_answ.pdf

The Educator's Guide to Copyright and Fair Use: Copyright Quiz Assessment and Answers, October 15, 2002
By Hall Davidson. Technology & Learning
http://www.techlearning.com/db_area/archives/TL/2002/10/copyright_answers.html

Fill-in-the-Blank Copyright Cloze Quiz
Provided by Kent School District, Washington
http://www.kent.k12.wa.us/KSD/IT/wwwdev/tests/cloze_test.htm

True/False Copyright Quiz
Provided by Kent School District, Washington
http://www.kent.k12.wa.us/KSD/IT/wwwdev/tests/T_F_Quiz.htm

Survey of College Students Regarding Copyright Law Information
By Angela Congrove, Otterbein College
http://www.otterbein.edu/surveys/copyright/

now online as well as in brick and mortar classrooms. Copyrighted teaching materials can now be accessed in traditional libraries and in the airport. The text of an instructor can now be archived and placed in institutional repositories, as well as filmed or recorded and streamed to students. New publishing formats for data increase the demands on one individual's understanding of how to access, use, and manipulate these formats.

A simple understanding of the definition of copyright is no longer sufficient to navigate today's information landscape. Students and faculty alike need a functional level of copyright literacy. With an ultimate goal of ©literacy for students, all hands must be on deck—from college welcome addresses by campus IT representatives, to the use of copyrighted material for course projects by an individual student or group, to instruction on the proper attribution of works in their own scholarship. Putting copyright in context with disciplinary content keeps it fresh, relevant, and easily digestible. Established and posted guidelines can only address but a few of the possible scenarios that could present itself to a user in a given day. Let's arm information consumers with the tools necessary to make informed and legal decisions when researching, debating, and using the works of another.

NEXT STEPS

▶ Review best practices.
▶ Evaluate current institutional policies and guidelines.
▶ Assess current student and faculty knowledge.
▶ Assemble a task force to study the legitimacy of integrating copyright literacy throughout the curriculum.
▶ Research and review examples to create clear and detailed copyright policies.
▶ Consult with available campus expertise (academic counsel, IT, faculty, librarians).

ENDNOTES

[1] See, e.g., Barbara L. Ludlow, *Understanding Copyright and Intellectual Property in the Digital Age: Guidelines for Teacher Educators and their Students*, 26 Teacher Educ. & Special Educ. 130 (2003); David Alan Makin, Internet File Sharing: A Theory of Planned Behavior Approach (May 2004) (unpublished Masters of Science thesis, University of Louisville) (on file with UMI Microform, UMI Number: 1420235) (thesis approved on April 16, 2004); Jasmine Rita Renner, An Analysis Of The Knowledge Levels Of Post-Secondary Educators In Public/ State, Private And Two-Year Colleges And Universities Regarding Copyright Ownership Of Online/Web-Based Courses (Aug. 2002) (unpublished Ed.D. dissertation, Bowling Green State University) (on file with UMI Microform, UMI Number: 3066409); Phyllis C. Sweeney, What Faculty Know About Designing Online Materials in Compliance With

Current U.S. Copyright and Fair Use Laws (May 25, 2004) (unpublished Ph.D. dissertation, University of South Florida) (on file with UMI Microform, UMI Number: 3140226).

[2] 17 U.S.C. § 513(3)(e)(C) Limitation on Liability of Nonprofit Educational Institutions).

[3] 17 U.S.C. § 110(2)(D)(i)

[4] H.R. 2517, 108th Cong. (as introduced in House of Representatives, June 19, 2003), *available at* http://frwebgate.access.gpo.gov/cgi-bin/useftp.cgi?IPaddress=162.140.64.21&filename=h2517ih.pdf&directory=/diskb/wais/data/108_cong_bills (last visited Jan. 24, 3006).

[5] H.R. 4077, 108th Cong. (as introduced in the House of Representatives, March 31, 2004), *available at* http://frwebgate.access.gpo.gov/cgi-bin/useftp.cgi?IPaddress=162.140.64.88&filename=h4077ih.pdf&directory=/diskb/wais/data/108_cong_bills (last visited Jan. 24, 3006).

[6] H.R. Rep. No. 108-700, at 3, *available at* http://thomas.loc.gov/cgi-bin/cpquery/T?&report=hr700&dbname=cp108& (last visited Jan. 24, 2006).

[7] Association of College and Research Libraries, Information Literacy Competency Standards for Higher Education 14 (2000), *available at* http://www.ala.org/ala/acrl/acrlstandards/standards.pdf (last visited Jan. 24, 2006).

[8] *Id.*

[9] Jon M. Garon, *Normative Copyright: A Conceptual Framework for Copyright Philosophy and Ethics*, 88 Cornell L. Rev. 1278, 1283 (2003).

[10] *See generally* Donald L. McCabe, Linda Klebe Trevino & Kenneth D. Butterfield, *Cheating in Academic Institutions: A Decade of Research*, 11 Ethics & Behav. 219, 220–22 (2001); Patrick M. Scanlon & David R. Neumann, *Internet Plagiarism among College Students*, 43 J. C. Student Dev. 374 (2002).

[11] *See, e.g.*, Donald L. McCabe & Linda Klebe Trevino, *Individual and Contextual Influences an Academic Dishonesty: A Multicampus Investigation*, 38 Res. Higher Educ. 379 (1997); Donald McCabe, Linda Klebe Trevino & Kenneth D. Butterfield, *Dishonesty in Academic Environments: The Influence of Peer Reporting Requirements*, 72 J. Higher Educ. 29 (2001); Donald McCabe & Patrick Drinan, *Toward a Culture of Academic Integrity*, Chron. Higher Educ., Oct. 15, 1999, at B7.

[12] Garon, *supra* note 9, at 1284.

[13] Steven Smethers, *Cyberspace in Curricula: New Legal and Ethical Issues*, Journalism & Mass Comm. Educator, Winter 1998, at 15, 19–21.

[14] Sweeney, *supra* note 1, at viii–ix, 9–10.

[15] *Id.* at 80.

[16] *Id.* at 78.

[17] Renner, *supra* note 1, at iii-iv, 7-8.

[18] *Id.* at 76.

[19] Mary I. Pogue, A Comparison of Administrator and Faculty Self-report and Knowledge of Distance Education, Related Intellectual Property Laws and Policy, and Tenets of Academic Freedom 80–81 (May 2004) (unpublished Ph.D. dissertation, Louisiana State University) (on file with UMI Microform, UMI Number: 3136197).

[20] *Id.* at 82.

[21] *Id.* at 85.

[22] Mark E. Chase, *An Analysis of Knowledge Levels of Media Directors Concerning Relevant Copyright Issues in Higher Education,* 1995 Proc. 1995 Ann. Nat'l Convention Ass'n Educ. Comm. Tech. 55, 59.

[23] *Id.* at 57.

[24] *Id.* at 58.

[25] *Id.*

[26] Teresa Y. Neely, et al., UMBC Information Literacy Survey—2003 Executive Summary 8, 18–20, 21 (November 2003), *available at* http://aok.lib.umbc.edu/reference/information literacy/ESinfolit2003.pdf (last visited Jan. 19, 2006).

[27] Pew Internet Project Data Memo by Research Specialist Mary Madden and PIP Director Lee Raine, Music and video downloading moves beyond P2P (March 2005), at 1,4, *available at* http://www.pewinternet.org/pdfs/PIP_Filesharing_March05.pdf (last visited Jan. 19, 2006).

[28] PR Newswire, *Nationwide Survey Shows Most College Students Believe It's Okay to Download Digital Copyrighted Files at School, in Workplace Educational Efforts Have Spurred Improvements Since 2003 Survey, But Current Attitudes and Behaviors Alarming,* Coldfusion Developer's J., Jun. 29, 2005, http://cfdj.sys-con.com/read/105346.htm (last visited Jan. 19, 2005).

[29] *See, e.g.,* Teresa Y. Neely, Sociological and Psychological Aspects of Information Literacy in Higher Education (2002).

[30] PR Newswire, *supra* note 28.

[31] Olga Francois, Copyright Education: A Survey of Campus Copyright Program Administrators (June, 2005) (unpublished manuscript, on file with the author).

[32] *See, e.g.,* David M. Quinn, *Legal issues in educational technology: Implications for school leaders,* 39 Educ. Admin. Q. 187, 187–88, 199–202 (2003).

[33] *See* Makin, *supra* note 1, at v, 6.

[34] *Id.* at 45–47.

[35] Patricia Davitt Maughan, *Assessing Information Literacy among Undergraduates: A Discussion of the Literature and the University of California-Berkeley Assessment Experience,* 62 C. & Res. Libr. 71, 72 (2001).

[36] Boyer Comm. on Educating. Undergraduates Research Univ., Reinventing Undergraduate Education: A Blueprint for America's Research Universities 9 (1998), *available at* http://naples.cc.sunysb.edu/Pres/boyer.nsf/ (last visited Jan. 23, 2006).

[37] Boyer Comm. on Educating. Undergraduates Research Univ, Reinventing Undergraduate Education: Three Years after the Boyer Report 7 (2001), available at http://www.sunysb.edu/pres/0210066-Boyer%20Report%20Final.pdf (last visited Jan. 23, 2006).

[38] Ludlow, *supra* note 1, at 139–40.

[39] David Bawden, *Information and Digital Literacies: A Review of the Concepts,* 57 J. Documentation 218, 230 (2001).

[40] Jeremy J. Shapiro & Shelley K. Hughes, *Information Technology as a Liberal Art: Enlightenment Proposals for a New Curriculum,* Educom Rev., Mar./Apr. 1996, at 31.

[41] American Library Association, Objectives for Information Literacy Instruction: A Model Statement for Academic Librarians, January 2001, http://www.ala.org/Template.cfm?Section=Information_Literacy&template=/ContentManagement/ContentDisplay.cfm&ContentID=8983 (last visited Jan. 19, 2006).

[42] Association of College and Research Libraries, Standards Toolkit, http://www.ala.org/ala/acrl/acrlissues/acrlinfolit/infolitstandards/standardstoolkit.htm (last visited Jan. 19, 2006).

[43] American Association of School Librarians & Association for Educational Communications and Technology. Information Literacy Standards for Student Learning: Standards and Indicators 5-6 (1998), *available at* http://www.ala.org/ala/aasl/aaslproftools/information power/InformationLiteracyStandards_final.pdf (last visited Jan. 19, 2006).

[44] Australia and New Zealand Information Literacy Framework: Principles, Standards and Practice 22 (Alan Bundy ed., 2004), *available at* http://www.anziil.org/resources/Info %20lit%202nd%20edition.pdf (last visited Jan. 19, 2006).

[45] Int'l Soc'y for Tech. in Educ. (ISTE). ISTE National Educational Technology Standards for Students (NETS*S), http://cnets.iste.org/students/NETS_S_standards.pdf (last visited Jan. 19, 2006).

[46] Int'l Soc'y for Tech. in Educ. (ISTE), Educational Technology Standards and Performance Indicators for all Teachers (2000), *available at* http://cnets.iste.org/teachers/pdf/page09.pdf (last visited Jan. 19, 2006).

[47] Copyright Committee, Washburn University, Student Copyright Information: What Copyright Means to You, http://www.washburn.edu/copyright/students/index.html (last visited Jan. 19, 2006).

[48] Smethers, *supra* note 13, at 21–22.

[49] Kevin Johnson & Nancy Groneman, *Legal and Illegal Use of the Internet: Implications for Educators*, 78 J. Educ. for Bus. 147, 147, 152 (2003).

[50] Computer Sci. and Telecomm. Bd., Nat'l Research Council, The Digital Dilemma: Intellectual Property in the Information Age Appendix F (2000).

[51] *Id.* at 17.

[52] *Id.* at 217.

[53] Diane Barbour, *Technology Ethics Lessons Shouldn't Begin at College*, Rochester Democrat and Chronicle, June 7, 2005, at 13A, *available at*, http://www.democratandchronicle.com/apps/pbcs.dll/article?AID=/20050607/OPINION02/506070319/1039/OPINION (last visited Jan. 19, 2006).

[54] Francois, *supra* note 31.

[55] Information and Library Services, University of Maryland University College, Information Literacy and Writing Assessment Project: Tutorial for Developing and Evaluating Assignments, Section 4: Designing Assignments that Contain Writing and Research, http://www.umuc.edu/library/tutorials/information_literacy/sect4.html (last visited Jan. 19, 2006).

[56] *Id.*

[57] *Id.*

[58] The Copyright Site, Teaching Ideas for Higher Education Faculty, http://www.thecopyright site.org/teaching/highered.html (last visited Jan. 19, 2006).

[59] *See* Appendix # F for the link to the multimedia clip of this scenario.

[60] Colleen Swain & Elizabeth Gilmore, *Repackaging for the 21st Century: Teaching Copyright and Computer Ethics in Teacher Education Courses*, 1 Contemp. Issues Tech. & Teacher Educ. [Online Serial] (2001), http://www.citejournal.org/vol1/iss4/currentpractice/article1.htm (last visited Jan. 19, 2006); Hall Davidson, *The Educator's Guide to Copyright and Fair Use (Cont'd): The Copyright Quiz*, Tech Learning, Oct. 15, 2002, http://www.techlearning.com/ db_area/archives/TL/2002/10/copyright_quiz.html (last visited Jan. 19, 2006).

[61] Debra L. Gilchrist & Kyzyl Fenno-Smith, An Abilities Model of Library Instruction. Presentation at the 25th Annual LOEX Library Instruction Conference.

[62] Swain & Gilmore, *supra* note 60.

▶9

COPYRIGHT LAW, INTELLECTUAL PROPERTY POLICY, AND ACADEMIC CULTURE

CLIFFORD A. LYNCH

This chapter discusses the following topics:
- ▶ Creation of the scholarly record
- ▶ The central role of fair use in academic production
- ▶ Public domain and orphan works
- ▶ University missions as determining policy choices
- ▶ The role of university presses and scholarly societies

INTRODUCTION

This paper, which is based in large part on a keynote address delivered at the University of Maryland University College Symposium *Pirates, Thieves and Innocents* on June 16, 2005, and which retains some of the informal nature of that address, examines the interplay between copyright law and academic values. While it identifies a number of areas in which copyright law as currently shaped presents serious barriers to academic inquiry and the research and teaching missions of our universities, the paper also focuses on policy *choices* that the academic community makes about various rights that are granted under copyright and the very significant ways in which these choices can influence, facilitate, or impede the academic mission within the existing framework. The academy is not simply a victim of current copyright laws and their consequences, however convenient and comforting it may be to fall into that role, and I argue here that it needs to do much more than simply advocate for legislative change and relief; universities can and must take a key leadership role in helping to alleviate many—though certainly not all—of the problems that the current copyright law creates for scholarship by making explicit policy choices that are consistent with fundamental academic values, and they can lead (and, hopefully, help to shape) the broader public thinking about these issues by their example. Some of these choices are difficult, in that they involve renouncing the possibility of enjoying certain (usually in reality nominal) revenue streams in favor of remaining true to fundamental mission imperatives. In this sense, the paper offers an agenda for reflection and self-examination by institutional communities within higher education about intellectual property policy choices and their relationship to fundamental academic values.

This paper is intended as a survey; it covers a great deal of ground at a high level and does not delve exhaustively into the details of any particular topic. It's intended to offer a framework and a sampling of the kinds of questions that need to be raised within the context of that framework. I hope that it will be useful as a starting point for community discussions in a variety of settings.

Finally, I need to include here the disclaimer that I am not an attorney, and nothing here is intended as legal advice.

THE PRACTICE OF SCHOLARSHIP: BUILDING UPON EVIDENCE AND THE PRIOR SCHOLARLY RECORD

The most fundamental part of research, teaching, and scholarly discourse is the ability to *build upon* both evidence and prior scholarship. This word "build" is very important. It's chosen to underscore the need not just for access to evidence and prior scholarship, but the ability to effectively integrate and reintegrate these materials into the ongoing fabric of scholarly discourse. Access to these materials is certainly a necessary prerequisite to the scholarly enterprise, but it is not sufficient. It's important to differentiate the twin problems of building upon prior scholarship and building upon evidence broadly in scholarly inquiry and discourse; while copyright law is a common denominator, the functional frameworks for the control and use of these two classes of material are quite different.

The scholarly process of building-upon goes beyond access; it's about the ability to quote; it's about the ability to analyze, to paraphrase, to talk about, to critique, to point other people to things, to cite sources and make attributions (which is a very important and much overlooked capability); to say, "if you look at this document that I give you a reference to, then ten years later you can find it and have some confidence that you are looking at the same document that I discussed in my work" (that is, to have an expectation of effective and responsible stewardship of the scholarly and broader cultural record). All of those things are fairly fundamental traditional parts of scholarly and academic practice and culture. Let me suggest, though, that the idea of building-upon is getting much richer in the new digital world. Consider all of the activities I've just described, not just in the traditional context of texts, but in the context of movies, software, images, and interactive Web sites.

Recently, Professor Larry Lessig of Stanford University has been giving a wonderful talk on "remix culture," as he calls it—the idea of reusing, repurposing both scholarly and (perhaps, in his view, most importantly) popular culture materials in order to construct new arguments, new creative or scholarly works; his examples draw strongly on the practices that are familiar and compelling to the current generation of students, and on multimedia content that underpins these practices. Clearly, video, music, and imagery completely redefine our ideas about quotation, reuse, and building-upon.

There's another issue, much less discussed, which I think is going to become crucial in the next decade in terms of building-upon. And that's the notion that literature, corpora of literature, corpora of evidence, aren't just things that are engaged by, read by, humans. They are resources that we *compute* on. They are resources that people want to manipulate through algorithms and computational agents. Part of this is the growing emphasis on the rapidly developing technologies of "data mining" and "text mining." These technologies are being applied to all kinds of textual databases very aggressively, fueled by heavy government investment, both in the United States and elsewhere. And the idea of text mining something like the biomedical literature, trying to extract leads and hypotheses that point the way toward planning new scientific investigations is actually becoming quite commonplace. The biomedical literature is a particularly rich source because of the amount of work that has been done on terminology, ontologies, and other kinds of knowledge superstructure; the fact that many papers have a sort of a standard template to them that facilitates algorithmic analysis; and because often the same thing is referred to in different ways in different sectors of the literature. The literature of biomedicine is vast, sprawling, and rapidly growing, yet results in one subspecialty represented in this literature may have significance for another, quite distinct, subspecialty—if only the connection can be made.

The computational analysis of massive corpora within the scholarly record (and indeed, in the broader body of evidence) will, I think, become very crucial to scholarship and research in the next few years. It is worth noting that a number of significant projects are already under way, as I indicated, both in the United States and abroad, and these projects are starting to explore these kinds of activities in serious ways. The life sciences, and also intelligence analysis, and public relations and business competitive intelligence in the commercial sphere, are leading the way. It seems likely that other scientific fields, particularly emerging, interdisciplinary ones like nanotechnology, will also be fruitful, but one can easily imagine these techniques extending rapidly into the social sciences and humanities as appropriate corpora of material become available to support computational analysis; the Perseus project, at Tufts University, is already beginning to explore applications in the humanities, for example.

We need to enable and protect the ability to build-upon, in this very broad sense, for both the scholarly record and for the broader cultural record, if teaching, learning, and research are to continue to flourish.

The essence of scholarly work is building upon the scholarship that has come before: extending it, elucidating it, and critiquing it in an explicit fashion. This is so fundamental that failure to do so properly is recognized in the inherently academic crime of plagiarism, which is related to copyright infringement but goes far beyond the strictly legal questions of infringement to a deeper academic cultural value. With regard to building upon the scholarly record, let me simply state at this point that, to a first approximation, the academy controls the scholarly record: it creates it, it represents the primary market for this record, and despite concerns about the current behaviors of scholarly publishers, at a very fundamental and long-term level, the rules surrounding the disposition and use of the scholarly record can, must, and will be under the control of the academy—though it must exercise the will to reassert this control in some very critical areas—and, ultimately, I believe that the values and practices surrounding the use of this scholarly record will be congruent with academic missions and values. This is a problem of values, of policy, and of will. It is not in essence a legal problem (other than to the extent that overcoming some past policy mistakes is made much more difficult by the legal impediments to undoing these choices). I will have more to say about this later.

The second body of material with which we need to build upon in order to conduct academic inquiry, teaching and learning, and scholarship is what I would call *evidence*. Evidence includes data about the world in which we live, observational data—what has been the weather in various places on the globe for the past few hundred years, genetic sequences, species distribution, astronomical observations, all of the richness of observational science. It also involves the record of human thought, human culture, of societal action, of political choice, of history, all of the things we loosely refer to as the cultural record of our own society and of other societies, of other places and other times. Note that the boundaries between the scholarly record and the broader body of evidence are not always crisp and clear, particularly with regard to cultural materials. Both of those, the observational and the cultural, form a body of evidence that needs to be brought into play to support inquiry, to support teaching and research. It has got to be accessible. It's got to be there to build upon. Some of this evidence is created by the academy; some is part of the broad, public, cultural heritage (and technically in the public domain); much of it is created outside of the academy—popular works of entertainment, the records of commerce and government, news, and a vast array of other materials. Here the overall legal framework that governs intellectual property in our culture is critical in dictating the ability to preserve, obtain access to, and build upon a substantial part of the body of evidence. Policy choices by the academy are important here, but only control the properties of a modest part of this overall body of evidence.

LEGAL BARRIERS TO FUTURE SCHOLARSHIP: COPYRIGHT AND BEYOND

Copyright and related intellectual property regimes are increasingly recognized as major barriers to teaching, learning, and research—especially in the new world of multimedia content, digital scholarship, and extended views of "building-upon" that I have just described. Over the past 18 months I have been serving as an advisor to a commission that was established by the American Council of Learned Societies (ACLS), with some funding from the Andrew W. Mellon Foundation. This commission is looking at the so-called cyberinfrastructure in the humanities and social sciences. Fundamentally, the commission is exploring the issues involved in advancing and facilitating a set of emerging scholarly practices in the humanities that make much greater use of digital content and advanced information technology. The commission has held hearings all over the country. They have heard and gathered testimony from humanists, from social scientists, from librarians and museum curators, and from the media industries. This testimony is available on the ACLS web site (www.acls.org).

One message that is coming through very clearly, when you look at that body of testimony gathered by the ACLS commission, is that copyright is probably one of the most serious impediments to doing work in the digital humanities and allied social sciences. It's really quite striking how widespread this view is. What's the problem? The problem is that you can't get rights to things. You can't find out who to ask for rights for things. When you can find them and can get them, they are often enormously expensive or they come with such complex restrictions that it's very hard to do anything with the material. And often, as a scholar, you simply cannot obtain rights at all; even if the rights holders can be identified, they are under no obligation to grant rights, or indeed even to *respond* to your request for permission. I will address this issue further shortly, but I want to recognize here that copyright, narrowly, is not the only problem: issues involved with privacy, with rights to likeness, and similar legal regimes, some of which operate inconsistently from state to state in the United States rather than being defined entirely in uniform federal legislation in the way copyright law is primarily defined. Institutional review boards, as they extend their purview from traditional areas like medical clinical trials into foreign territories they claim dominion over because of the involvement of human subjects, such as surveys in the social sciences or the collection of oral histories, are also erecting new barriers.

In the sciences, the National Academies have published a landmark series of studies over the past decade, including *Bits of Power* and *The Digital Dilemma*, which map out the issues with scientific access to evidence and the scholarly record, and the reuse of these materials. Here, again, the barriers to science go beyond copyright.

If you look, for example, at some of the noxious provisions in the Digital Millennium Copyright Act (DMCA), you will see that fundamentally they are not about copyright, they are about establishing some sort of new legal sanctity for digital rights management (DRM) technology irrelevant to the use to which it is being put. Under the DMCA, you can protect uncopyrighted material through technical means, and it's a crime to attempt to circumvent these technical protections. The DMCA has also been used to chill, or attempt to chill, research in numerous areas.

We have, in the United States at least, managed up to now to avoid enacting the various database legislation proposals that have repeatedly surfaced in Congress. These proposals would establish new intellectual property rights over compilations of facts, which are not covered under copyright. Some other nations have not been so lucky; consider the notorious European Community database directive and its implementation in various national laws within Europe. These database protection proposals are particularly dangerous in that they provide new ways to privatize and lock up the collections of evidence upon which science, and indeed scholarship, broadly rely (to say nothing of their broader implications for society).

Unlike copyright, these new intellectual property regimes and proposed regimes are so damaging precisely because they are so unbalanced; they lack the safeguards such as the fair use provisions within copyright law. While these are not my primary focus here, it is important to identify them as critical issues for the academy, and to underscore the importance of the academy speaking out publicly about the threats that they represent to academic missions and values.

I will simply note here that patents are a problem all their own, particularly with the emergence of software and business process patents, and the growing capability to use patents to interfere with what would traditionally be thought of as speech and expression in a world where these things are embodied in multimedia, in interactive presentations, and in software. Patents also shift liability and responsibility in ways that are bizarre when approached from a copyright-oriented tradition: you cannot infringe under copyright (or plagiarize) a work *that you have never seen*, yet under patent law you can be guilty of simply failing to realize that you are reinventing something that someone else filed a patent on rather than being the first to invent it. But I will not focus on patents further here.

COPYRIGHTED MATERIALS: THE CENTRAL ROLE OF FAIR USE IN ACADEMIC CULTURE AND SCHOLARSHIP

Fair use is a defense against copyright infringement that allows the use of copyrighted materials for certain specific purposes, such as scholarship, criticism, teaching, and parody, under certain specific conditions. The decision about whether fair use applies in a given situation depends on a complex and somewhat subjective calculus of factors.

Fair use is one of the most vital underpinnings of our ability to do scholarship and to do research—it allows the use of copyrighted materials without the need to ask permission, or to pay to obtain such permissions, if they are available under commercial terms. Fair use has recently come under a great deal of pressure from various directions. It has come under pressure in the sense that various rights-holder groups are interpreting fair use very narrowly, suggesting that various activities (some of which are very traditional parts of scholarly practice) are not fair use and aggressively attempting to advance their position by threatening individuals and institutions with lawsuits. Indeed, some rights holders would argue that fair use is an archaic legal doctrine that has no real place, particularly in a digital world.

Fair use also faces threats because it is sometimes misused within the academy, where we find a very strange set of perceptions around fair use. On the one hand, you run into academics who have, shall we say, a naïve notion of fair use; you can find anecdotal evidence of a reasonably widely held mythology that characterizes fair use in these terms: "I'm an academic. That means that any use I make of it is fair." And that is simply not true.

But, on the other hand, we have some dynamics in the legal precedents around fair use that basically are saying, "use it or lose it," and we are not really using it enough—we are not actively and proudly pushing those uses that are, in my view, clearly within the purview of fair use, in the academy. We are not defending our rights vigorously enough. We are in a world where academics are being strongly encouraged by a risk-averse organizational culture to use material *only* when permissions have been explicitly obtained and, where necessary, paid for, rather than living with the uncertainty of being prepared to legitimately argue a fair use defense against a charge of copyright infringement.

The most basic example of this problem: 30 or 40 years ago someone might reuse, for an example in a scholarly work, a paragraph or two, a stanza, a verse, or something out of some other copyrighted work (attributed appropriately) and not worry about it too much. The author (with the concurrence of his or her publisher) would take the position that, in all reasonable judgment, this reuse, this quotation, is fair use. (Of course, the only way to *prove* this was correct was to be sued, and to win the court case.) Somewhere along the line, the practice grew up of writing away for permissions to quote, and then, even beyond the writing away for permissions, having the rights holder say, "Well, we'll charge you a hundred dollars for that permission," and the author agreeing to pay that price. In an ever more litigious world, it was better to pay for certainty than to accept the risk of being challenged. So now we have this whole traffic in permissions and permission payments for uses which, at least to my innocent eyes, look like they fall pretty squarely under fair use. One of the dangers here, of course, is that, if you look at the factors that are considered into deciding whether something is fair use, one of them is about economic impact of the use. If we were back about 30 or 40 years ago, when there was no market in paying for these kinds of small quotations, there obviously wasn't much of an economic impact. Now, for better or worse, we've created a market, a documentable revenue stream, which raises the specter of rights holders being able to argue that payment is customary and expected, and what was once a fair use is now having a real negative economic impact on the rights holder.

This move toward a complete permissions-based culture of scholarship is an abomination for many reasons. It represents a huge burden and tax on the productivity and intellectual life of scholars, who are being required to clear permissions both to protect themselves, and as a condition of publication. It chills scholarship by causing scholars to avoid certain topics because they cannot clear permissions (and the issues here are not just economic; permission to quote from a work may not be granted for an analysis that is critical of that work, for example). The drafting of agreements and the exchange of large numbers of small payments create a great deal of overhead and friction in the system of scholarly discourse to little real economic gain. And, of course, it makes a travesty of the fundamental constitutional basis of copyright law in advancing the growth of knowledge.

I think we also need to recognize another aspect of fair use and why the ability to invoke fair use is going to be crucial in the future. If you consider the sort of text-dominated culture that has characterized most scholarship for centuries, you will realize that for texts, if you can read a text you can probably make a copy of a portion of that text that's good enough to use as evidence in scholarly discourse— you can read and transcribe by hand if you have to. This is within the capabilities of almost anybody. Virtually any author can do this, and scholars do all the time. You don't *need* to be able to cut and paste; that's just a convenience, an amenity. So, in some sense, being able to read something, being able to view it, which, after all, you have to be able to do if textual material is to be available in any meaningful way, opens up the door for readers to make choices about reuse under fair use; it doesn't make much sense to have content that's locked up so people can't even see it. They certainly won't pay for it if they can't get any access to it.

But moving beyond text, we see the situation is very different for images. It surely is not the case for music that listening implies the ability to quote. It surely is not the case with something like a movie that viewing means you can share what you see with others. Very few of us are good enough as artists that we can look at a picture and draw a copy of it without applying a technological aid, like a camera that you can ban. Very few of us can really reproduce accurately a bit of a musical performance well enough to talk about it, to share a little segment of it with other people. "Quoting" briefly from a film—taking a little clip out of a movie in order to study or critique it—is not likely to be something you can do by transcription with pencil or paper or by transcribing using your keyboard, so the ability to make fair use in a sense of actually taking bits of multimedia works is very crucial, much more crucial and with a very different character than what has come before in the text-oriented world. For multimedia, technical barriers to reuse constitute real barriers to the choice to invoke fair use. So, that is one of the reasons that I think it is especially important that we nurture fair use, going forward.

A final point: much more is published today, in the sense that it is globally visible through the Internet and the worldwide Web. While challenges to the fair use of material in scholarly work was once limited to the fairly small segment of scholarship that was formally published in monographs and journals, now theses, dissertations, term papers, class projects, course materials, and a vast array of other works that are available on the Internet in digital form are all subject to scrutiny and challenge by rights-holders. So the need for fair use is greater than ever, and questions about permission practices are real, not just in the relatively rare case of the works of "published" scholars, but arise for students as well as faculty in an enormous number of settings. Indeed, we have seen the emergence of computational "trolls" that use search engines to scan the Web for documents that quote from copyrighted works or use trademarked phrases and then send frightening letters to the authors of these materials demanding license fees or threatening litigation.

We seem to have a disturbingly well-developed culture in our universities that is very risk-averse about these issues. I don't know quite where it came from, but it's clear when you listen to general counsels that many of them really are taking a very risk-averse position about the issues having to do with copyright and fair use. I'd invite you to explore, in particular, some of the thinking from James Boyle of Duke University, who is especially articulate, passionate, and clear on the endangered state of fair use in the academy. The argument is that fair use is one of the underpinnings of free speech and free inquiry and that if there are any touchstone academic values, they are around free speech and free inquiry. These values are important enough that our universities have, over the years, stepped up and come to their defense in other contexts. Boyle makes the compelling argument that one of the things we need to do is help university general counsels to understand the connections here, and why it is important to take principled stances rather than expedient risk-reducing stances about fair use. This is about academic freedom and free speech.

While we certainly need to work to prevent legal diminution of our fair use rights through new legislation or shifting norms, the academy's rights under current copyright fair use provisions are very powerful. But we must make the policy choices to stand up for them.

THE IMPORTANCE OF THE PUBLIC DOMAIN AND THE ORPHAN WORKS PROBLEM

The public domain is a crucial component of the ability to do scholarship. Materials in the public domain are clearly unencumbered and allow the most transformative reuse and building-upon. A large, healthy, vibrant, and continually growing body of public domain works will fuel scholarship, teaching, and learning.

I think that one problem that has been observed over and over again about much of the intellectual property legislation activity is that there is a well-organized, wealthy commercial sector that clearly benefits from the extension of the term and scope of copyright and the limitation of exemptions to their rights under copyright. This is a profit stream to them; the more extensive the protection they can get for their properties, the greater and longer-lived the revenue stream will be. So it's clear that plenty of organized groups are prepared to speak up in favor of copyright enlargement, in whatever dimensions of time and practice that you want to consider that extension. Who advocates for the interests of the general public, of the consumer, of the cultural memory sector? Fewer people and organizations and a lot less money are speaking up for the public interest and the public domain, which is so vital in supporting and nurturing the values of scholarship and teaching. Higher education and the cultural memory sector almost by default bear a great deal of this responsibility for advocacy, particularly through institutions like the research libraries. We need to make cogent and compelling—indeed, passionate—arguments for the importance of scholarship and the facilitation of scholarship, and I think that one of the things that we need to recognize, perhaps unfortunately but certainly realistically, is that a lot of what has happened in the past decade or so has been about maximizing profit for a miniscule number of works. The higher education, library, and cultural memory sectors have taken a stand opposing this on principle, and lost, rather than being pragmatic about what seems politically possible. Legislation extending the protection of these few works—and everything else—has carried the day. The collateral damage from that has been horrific.

There is no question in my mind that the greatest copyright legislation disaster, in terms of its impact on the general public and on the academy in particular, has been the Sonny Bono Copyright Extension Act. This law extended copyright terms for decades—both prospectively for new works, and also (nonsensically, as I will explain shortly) on a retrospective basis for existing works. It effectively halted the growth of the public domain for two decades. And many people are now expecting that it represents the first step on what will effectively be perpetual copyright, doled out a few decades at a time—a first step in what will be a cynical legislative circumvention of the constitutional principles underpinning copyright.

The motivation for the Bono Copyright Extension Act, as best as I can determine, was a relatively small number of enormously valuable and profitable properties that were in danger of coming out of copyright protection and entering the public domain—notably, certain works belonging to the Walt Disney Corporation, among others. These corporations felt that the loss of these revenue streams would be intolerable, so they went to Congress and sought relief. Now, the unfortunate thing about this situation is that we are talking about a relative handful of works. If Congress had simply said, "Send us a list of these profitable works and we will pass a special bill for you that entitles you to continue raking in the profits of those works for another twenty years," that would have been, in my view, a disturbing capitulation to these corporations and a poor public policy choice, but what Congress actually did was infinitely worse. What Congress did instead was to extend copyright on *everything currently under copyright and all newly created works* for another twenty years. The retrospective component is particularly difficult to rationalize as anything other than a handout: if one proceeds from the constitutional basis that copyright is a limited term monopoly intended to incentivize creators to produce works and make them available to the public, then clearly retrospective term extension is not going to incentivize creators, particularly dead ones. But the effect of the extension act is that all of the out-of-print books, all of the old photographs, films, bits of music, works that are of some interest to scholars, works that, as they enter the public domain, can be reused and remixed and can foster activities to further scholarship and creativity—all of this got locked up for another twenty years.

Over the past year, Marybeth Peters, the U.S. Registrar of Copyrights, has called for and received many hundreds of comments on the problem of what she has termed *orphaned works*. We are still struggling for a precise definition of orphaned works, but fundamentally the idea is that these are works—perhaps a book, perhaps a piece of music, perhaps a photograph or a film—that are relatively old, of no real commercial interest, but still under copyright. Typically, for an orphan work you cannot find, or often even identify, the copyright holder. New copies of the work have long since vanished from the commercial marketplace. Just think about a book that is 50 years out of print; in order to determine who holds the rights, you would have to first find the contract between author and publisher, determine whether the rights reverted to the author or are still held by the publisher, and then, who currently has ownership of those rights—it might be a successor corporation to the publisher, or it might be one of the heirs of the author if he or she is no longer alive. This is a formidable, and prohibitively costly, investigative challenge. Matters are even worse for photographs and films.

The issue that the Copyright Office is trying to grapple with is this: Can we come up with some kind of rational system of allowing the society as a whole, and, specifically, our scholarly and cultural memory organizations, but probably not exclusively those organizations, to be able to reuse, re-disseminate and preserve this kind of material in some kind of economically rational way. I urge you to look at the copyright office Web site for some of the comments and discussion on this issue: http://www.copyright.gov/orphan/. Now, this is enormously important to those of us concerned with scholarship, teaching, and learning, because so much of this is essential scholarship and essential evidence for future scholarship. The hope is that if it is done right, an orphan works provision will not be terribly controversial.

This will be a way of dealing with at least a large number of the works that are not generating any money.

One of the most obvious imperatives for the academy is continuing to speak up on a policy basis about the impact of legislation that has passed and the impact of new legislation under consideration. An enormous coalition of higher education institutions and the societies that serve and support them, ranging from the Association of American Universities (AAU), to the Association of Research Libraries, EDUCAUSE, and many, many others, has been active in those policy debates for the last decades. They need the support of their member institutions and they need their member institutions to continue to work with them on these issues. Of all the many and diverse issues currently on the agenda, I believe that orphan works may be one of the most important. And it may be an area where there is a real possibility of positive progress in the sense that it does not directly set the academy into conflict with very wealthy, politically powerful rights holder interests.

THE MISSION OF THE UNIVERSITY AS A CENTRAL DETERMINANT OF POLICY CHOICES

There is a very interesting debate that is quietly brewing about the mission of higher education. If you ask people, "What's the mission of your university?" "What's the mission of the academy?" They will usually come out with the time-honored trinity of teaching and learning, research, and public service; sometimes they will use a term such as "public engagement," which is somewhat stronger and more aggressive than public service. Those are the classic missions that are invoked for higher education. But do research and teaching and learning, the creation and transfer of knowledge, as fundamental mission components, imply a mission that also encompasses the *dissemination and preservation of scholarship?*

I am aware of several European universities now that are stating quite openly and clearly that they believe that their institutional mission includes, explicitly, the dissemination and preservation of knowledge. In the United States, I hear answers that are certainly more varied, and, at least sometimes, much more equivocal; public institutions, as a gross generality, seem more comfortable with this formulation of mission than some private institutions, though one can also point to certain private institutions such as MIT that have taken a great deal of leadership in this area. While some institutions would point to their investments in network-based dissemination of content, to their institutional repositories, to their research libraries, university presses, and university museums as part of their commitment to the preservation and dissemination of scholarship and its underlying base of evidence, others speak about the role of the university in technology transfer, in monetizing discovery, in using the apparatus of scholarly publishing as a way of dissemination (and complaining that they are paying too much to use this apparatus, or not getting enough return from it).

I also want to make one further note here, which is important in shaping the public policies that universities may choose to advocate: the extent to which the mission of universities, primarily embodied in their embedded cultural memory institutions—research libraries, archives, museums, and perhaps public broadcasting units—encompasses not only the dissemination and preservation of the scholarly record, but also, more broadly, the stewardship and preservation of the overall cultural record as essential evidence to support future scholarship. This is a mission that is typically shared with other, non-university-based cultural memory organizations, most notably public and private museums and national libraries and archives, to some extent through scholarly societies, and scientific and scholarly data archives funded on a national basis through governmental science and scholarly research funding bodies operating at a national and international level; the distribution of responsibility varies greatly from one nation to another, but at least in the United States, as I read the trends, a good deal of the responsibility for these activities is going to fall to higher education institutions by default. To the extent that universities honor and embrace this as part of their fundamental mission, it will certainly shape their advocacy of public policy changes and their institutional investment strategies.

I think the time has come for every academic institution to revisit and consider thoughtfully these questions of mission. It is perhaps *the* most fundamental policy choice that a university can make with regard to institutional mission as it relates to scholarly communication and the practice of scholarship. Institutions must be very clear about their positions here, as this will provide a foundation for making a whole series of much more practical choices about policies and culture regarding the scholarly and cultural record. It also provides a foundation of principles for advocacy about legal and public policy issues. Universities and members of the academic community are increasingly vulnerable in their advocacy when they try to simultaneously argue that they should be able to maximize profit streams for intellectual property that they produce and simultaneously, because of the social importance of their missions, they should have special privileges in the ways that they can make use of the intellectual properties of others. The time has come to openly confront and explore the contradictions and compromises implicit in these positions.

SETTING THE ACADEMY'S HOUSE IN ORDER: POLICY CHOICES AND ACADEMIC VALUES

In the remainder of this paper I want to turn to strategies which are not so much outward looking and engaged with law and public policy, but inward looking and deal with policy and culture at individual academic institutions and across the academy as a whole. Here, unlike the world of legislation and public policy, which sets the ground rules for the broader society, we find a constrained and protected sphere within which universities can largely make their own choices and control their own destinies, if they have the will, if they have the energy and the commitment to build consensus within this sphere. Law and public policy defines the existence of rights and ownership of these rights, but the choices about how to dispose of these rights, about when to choose to enforce them, are part of academic policy and culture. Appropriate policy choices are critical in shaping the future of academic culture and the enterprise of scholarship.

Faculty Works

One of the most fundamental questions in shaping tomorrow's academic culture is the way that faculty think about their own work. It's a commonplace observation that faculty exist in a conflicted, schizophrenic situation where they want to act as aggressive and omnivorous consumers of the works of others, yet at the same time want to exercise tight control over their own works. We are seeing a very healthy debate about this contradiction and conflict.

This discussion began in a series of issues raised by the library community about the unsustainable economics of the scholarly publishing system, and particularly scientific, technical, and medical journals; the Association of Research Libraries played a central role in documenting and publicizing these developments. At first, in response to these developments, faculty were encouraged to retain more of their rights to their own works rather than signing them over wholesale to journal publishers. But more recently, the open access movement, developments like Open Courseware at MIT (and later elsewhere) and the Creative Commons program have reshaped the landscape of discourse—the focus now is more about making scholarship *public* under modest constraints, such as appropriate attribution and limitations on commercial reuse without permission.

Today we have reached a watershed where faculty are beginning to explicitly consider the way in which their work—be it journal articles, monographs, or instructional materials—is being made available to the academic community and the broader public. Institutional and disciplinary norms are being re-established around questions like these:

- ▶ Should faculty work be freely available (with appropriate attribution) for reuse in teaching and research?
- ▶ Should there be an obligation to deposit copies of faculty work in institutional or disciplinary repositories to enable public access?
- ▶ Should faculty work be published in open-access venues?
- ▶ Is the objective of publication commercial gain or outreach to the largest possible audience?

These are questions that people are thinking about now, and talking about now. I think we need to nurture that change in academic culture, and we need to ensure it reaches not just into faculty discussions, but also into questions that students think about and will ultimately take beyond the walls of the university into other segments of their lives. I think that those culture shifts are absolutely critical and I think that the set of issues, not just about respect for intellectual property rights, but about making explicit choices about what one does with one's own intellectual property are among the most critical academic cultural values and questions that we can frame today. It is enormously exciting to see faculty coming together and engaging these issues and, indeed, passing resolutions in the academic senates of our higher education institutions, which really are resolutions about the kind of cultural and academic values they want to see on the campuses. We see this, not just in scholarly work, but also in teaching.

I have not explicitly discussed student works here; the situation surrounding these works is more complex because current policy about the ownership and rights to use the works is often poorly defined at our higher education institutions, in comparison to the status of faculty work. Also, one can think of faculty work in the context of an employment relationship with the institution; linking expectations about student works to conditions of enrollment or graduation involves more complex issues. But the way in which student works are treated by their authors, the way in which they are made available for sharing and for building-upon, needs to be part of any comprehensive debate about the shaping of a campus culture for the coming century. Students will surely be strongly influenced by the examples set by the faculty.

The Role and Behavior of University Presses

University presses are organizations that scholars, and particularly scholars in the humanities, will claim to play an absolutely crucial role in the system of scholarly communication. Their traditional mission, the reason that they were established, is to create a vehicle for the publication of scholarly works that would not otherwise be published because they aren't commercially viable. ("Commercially viable" is a tricky term here—it might range from works not providing as good a return on investment as other works that a purely commercial publisher might choose to publish, and hence yield a smaller profit margin, all the way through works that will definitely lose money and thus can only be published if they are subsidized outright.)

University presses are organizations which, frankly, have suffered from contradictory signals over the past few decades. The host universities alternate between complaining that the presses are running deficits and exhorting them to run more like commercial businesses on one hand, and complaining that the presses are publishing overly commercial and popular-market works rather than specialized, small-market scholarly materials mandated by their missions. The presses have also suffered from criticism that they are not doing enough to move into the digital world, that they are becoming increasingly irrelevant, that they are not keeping up with commercial competitors in the scholarly publishing market-place, while at the same time they have been denied access to sources of capital that would allow them to make investments to facilitate the movement into digital products.

I have a lot of sympathy for university presses and the abuse they are taking, but I also think that we need to decide whether these presses are going to be instruments of university missions and university policies, or if we are going to spin them off as commercial operations. Right now a number of them are behaving, in my view, in ways that are indistinguishable from commercial entities. They are busy, for example, making life miserable for scholars by indulging in the permissions culture and chasing after the small amounts of money they can capture through charging for these permissions. They are not doing all that they can to maximize access to scholarship, and to ensure the preservation of the part of the scholarly record they have helped to create.

One might reasonably think that a university press, behaving in a way that is consistent with the overall values and mission of the academy, would very seriously think about making and putting into effect the same kind of policies that we see some of our scholarly societies making and reflecting in the copyright statements on every publication that state: "This may be freely reproduced for classroom teaching in nonprofit settings or for other noncommercial scholarly work. Feel free to quote reasonable amounts from this or other scholarly work as long as your publisher extends the same courtesy to our authors." We need to, I think, be setting an example in these areas, not having a race to see who can behave most badly.

Most recently, we saw a group of four universities—Oxford, Harvard, the University of Michigan, and Stanford University (along with the New York Public Library)—enter into agreements with Google to digitize part or all of their library collections. We do not have access to all the details of these agreements, except for the one at the University of Michigan, but based on accounts by the leadership of these libraries, and public statements by these institutions, these agreements with Google are clearly and thoughtfully designed to further the agenda of building up digital resources that will be shared by the participating universities. Among the first to protest these agreements and threaten legal challenges was the American Association of University Presses. All four of the higher education institutions participating in the Google program have major university presses. This is a stunning example of the kinds of policy disconnects that we currently face between university presses and their host universities, and it underscores the need to resolve the role of university presses within the academy.

Scholarly Societies

Scholarly and professional societies provide another important case study of the need to either take responsibility for the policies of organizations that might reasonably be considered to be instrumentalities of the academy and to ensure that these policies are consistent with the overall goals of the academy, or to reposition and reconceptualize these organizations as outside the sphere of the academy—to treat them as something akin to commercial players in the overall scholarly publishing system. Again, part of the question here is whether to take continued responsibility for the support and financial health of these scholarly societies as part of the price of demanding and ensuring policy congruence.

Once again, as with university presses, there is enormous diversity. There are scholarly societies that have shown truly visionary leadership in not just what can be done with digital technology, but in supporting and ensuring that their material is readily available for teaching and research purposes. There are others, though, that, frankly, seem to be behaving much more like commercial publishers. To cite just one recent example, we have the spectacle of the American Chemical Society opposing the development of a public access database (PubChem) by the U.S. National Institutes of Health, which seems clearly to support the interests of researchers. We also have several scholarly societies taking the position that publicly accessible electronic theses and dissertations produced at our universities represent prior publication and thus disqualify the authors of these theses and dissertations from publishing their research in the journals of the societies in question. These are serious policy disconnects which raise questions about the extent to which the academy should support the societies in question, and the relationship between these societies and the academy as a whole. They raise questions about how faculty should relate to these professional societies as trustees, as authors, as editors, and as referees.

In the case of scholarly societies, we also have some really interesting financial issues. I will give you just one example: Many scholarly societies view part of their mission, and legitimately so, not just as facilitating scholarly communication by publishing, but also as advancing advocacy for their discipline, advocacy for research funding for their discipline, public outreach, and education about their discipline. They address pipeline issues, trying to do things to ensure, for example, that high school students get interested in careers in biology or astronomy or whatever the subject is. These are all meritorious activities. But right now we are seeing some evidence that these activities are being cross-subsidized from library budgets which are intended to support the dissemination and preservation of scholarship. And it's not clear, at least to me, that that's the right framework for funding these generally meritorious activities. So I think we need to think carefully about what our scholarly societies are doing, how their activities reflect the values around copyright and intellectual property of the academy and how the necessary funding stream is going to reach them if they are going to continue to support these values.

The Role and Policies of Cultural Memory
Organizations within Universities

A wealth of cultural memory organizations are embedded within our universities: museums (some large campuses have dozens of these); archives; libraries; public broadcasting units with rich archives; herbaria and botanical collections; and other organizations. All of these groups are sitting on enormous masses of academically significant content, which is either out of copyright or to which the institution holds the rights. They have some interesting choices to make as they digitize this material. Arguably, what these cultural memory organizations need to be doing, as rapidly as funding permits, is to digitize this material and make it very broadly available on the Net for building-upon, marking it as out of copyright or attaching broad standardized use permissions such as those developed by the Creative Commons. There are many reasons for this: to make the materials more widely available, to advance scholarship, and to protect the material from unnecessary physical wear and even to provide some level of insurance against physical disasters. Many institutions are in fact doing just this.

Unfortunately, one of the things that happened in the broader museum communities (not just, and not primarily, university museums) in the early 1990s as part of the run-up to the great "dot com" bubble and burst, was that various entrepreneurs made the rounds of the museum directors whispering that, "In a digital world, if you licensed all of your stuff to us, preferably exclusively, we can monetize your collection. We'll fund the digitization, or at least help, and we can take care of getting it done if you don't want to manage it in-house. We can provide your museum with revenue streams beyond your wildest dreams of avarice. It will be great. You can expand. You can buy more stuff. You can do all the things that you can't afford to do today." And some organizations signed these agreements. Others did not. But even the ones that did not got very cautious about opening up their materials for public access on the net because there was the perception that, if you put your material up digitally and opened it up, you are writing off a huge revenue stream. Now, to the best of my knowledge, this huge revenue stream has not materialized; tens or hundreds of thousands of people simply aren't going to license the right to browse images from your collection on the Web for $30/person/month for eternity; scholarly authors aren't going to license these images for inclusion in their monographs in vast numbers at $1000 per image (and they shouldn't have to!). And I don't think it's going to show up for most archives, and for most library special collections, and for most museums. Yes, there are some small modest revenue streams that you are going to miss, some royalties from mouse pads, posters, and T-shirts, perhaps, and even here for the materials that are still under copyright, it's possible to attach license terms that entitle the institution to a cut of these kinds of revenue streams.

The loss of the revenue stream is usually going to be insignificant when weighted against the contribution to advancing the academy's mission that will be made as these digital resources become available to the academy and to the public at large. And the cost of collecting the revenue stream, in terms of friction and barriers in the system of scholarship and scholarly communication is very large, just as it is with the permissions culture discussed earlier.

One person who has been wonderfully articulate on this recently is Ken Hamma, from the J. Paul Getty Museum, who did a lovely talk on this issue at the Spring 2005 CNI meeting, specifically about museums; an excellent paper of his on this topic appears in the November 2005 issue of *D-Lib Magazine.*

The situation varies from one type of cultural memory organization to another: probably libraries have the strongest bias toward providing the broadest possible access to their digital content, and the best resource base for creating digital resources; museums are more cautious; many of the other players are resource-starved. For public broadcasting, this is really a new idea: it historically hasn't been technically feasible to open up their archives the way it is becoming today.

In terms of institutional policy, the first priority is to make sure that each embedded cultural memory organization understands the broad policy goals of their parent institution—particularly in terms of facilitating scholarship, teaching, and learning and scholarly communication. Cultural memory organizations need to understand how they can contribute to these goals by setting the right policies and making the right investments. Their parent institutions, in turn, need to think through how to ensure that these cultural memory organizations get enough resources, and enough support from other units within the university (particularly on technical and infrastructure issues) to take advantage of the opportunities. And, perhaps more contentiously, they need to carefully consider how much autonomy they are willing to give these embedded organizations to choose behaviors, policies, and investments that actually run counter to the overarching policy goals of the university as a whole.

Technology Transfer and Licensing Policies

A final area that I want to discuss very briefly is university technology transfer operations (sometimes called technology licensing operations). While these operations typically deal with inventions that are protected by patents rather than copyrights, they deserve mention in this discussion because of the implied policy position that they suggest by their existence and their activities. This position requires scrutiny and careful thought.

Now, tech transfer operations became very fashionable in the 1980s following passage of the Bayh-Dole legislation; they were established to ensure that inventions developed by faculty got patented, and that an effort was then made to license those patents to industry in such a way as to maximize the revenue stream back to the university (which is typically shared with the faculty inventors). The result was that universities established offices with people who basically wandered around the university looking for stuff to patent and for entrepreneurial faculty; this then extended to trying to persuade faculty to look at their work through the lenses of patentable discoveries and entrepreneurship. There are a few cases where universities have really won big on this, and have enjoyed hundreds of millions of dollars of revenue stream from a discovery or cluster of discoveries. A lot of the big successes have been around biotechnology-related areas. But for each winner, it seems, there may be quite a few losers. In January 2005, the U.S. National Academies, in partnership with the Organisation for Economic Cooperation and Development (OECD), hosted a conference on the knowledge economy, at which several scholars suggested that only a very small number of the technology transfer offices in place in higher education in the U.S. are even covering their own overhead. Part of the problem is that current experience suggests a jackpot effect in the economics of technology licensing, and the jackpot is large enough to really make a difference. But looking too hard for the long-shot jackpot, creating barriers to the dissemination of knowledge and unhealthy changes to the academic culture in order to obtain more opportunities to play for the jackpot, can be much worse than not winning the jackpot. The issue is one of balance.

Computer science is a discipline where I think we have seen some fascinating conflicts between the tech transfer organizations, whose mission is to generate cash for the university, and computer science faculty, who are interested in getting their work used, recognized, and built-upon, as well as cash (which they often have other ways of getting, through consulting or participation in start-up companies). As not just freely available software, but fully open source software, has increasingly become the standard model of distributing research software widely and to building communities of interest around such software, we have seen a clear collision of values. To the credit of the academy, my impression is that the values and preferences of the computer science faculty have generally triumphed.

Another way to think about technology transfer offices is to recognize that there is indeed nothing inherently wrong with them, and that they can help advance several useful goals: providing income streams to the university, and helping to build the economy by transferring university knowledge into the commercial sector. The potential problems that arise, in my view, are that they can tie up patents and other works in ways that impede research and teaching, that impede the dissemination of knowledge, and that give rise to a culture of ownership, secrecy, and greed. Perhaps what we need to do is counter-balance the technology transfer operations on our campuses with new offices of knowledge dissemination, which argue that patents be filed only when it makes sense to do so defensively and, if so, then dedicated to the public domain, or at least made freely available for any research or educational use; that advocates nonexclusive terms and standing research exemptions when licenses for university patents *are* issued; and that generally promotes a culture of sharing and circles of gifts, at least within the research and education worlds. This would make it much easier for technology transfer operations to co-exist comfortably with the overall missions of the academy. It may also be helpful as universities recognize more and more that patents issued to organizations outside the academy are becoming barriers to academic research, and that they may ultimately need to argue for some public policy relief in this area.

CONCLUSIONS: WHAT THE ACADEMIC COMMUNITY MUST DO NOW

Advocacy and engagement in legal and public policy debates about intellectual property is necessary, indeed essential, but it is not enough.

As faculty, students, and administrators—collectively, the current stewards of the academic enterprise—we need to question and examine institutional policies and institutional culture with respect to the use of the scholarly and cultural record. We need to recognize that the choices we make here will largely shape the ability of academics to continue to do scholarly work in the future. Behaviors consistent with academic values and mission within the broad academic community need to be encouraged, supported, and rewarded for those within the academic sphere; if necessary, a calculus of mutual deterrence will need to be incorporated in policies toward commercial actors outside of the academy as a way of encouraging them to recognize and honor academic values and missions in their dealings with the academy. There will be hard choices about whether to exclude organizations that have traditionally been viewed as part of the academy but that are no longer behaving in a way that advances the academic values we need to support.

I believe that we need to make policy choices that show the way forward, toward a desirable future, rather than to simply match the most problematic and destructive practices being promoted by the commercial sectors (though there are, as already discussed, some real questions about when strategies of reciprocity are appropriate as tools for trying to change commercial sector behavior). We must also recognize that the choices we make, institution by institution, will play a key role in defining the unique character and culture of each of our academic institutions (and also our disciplines, to the extent that disciplinary norms rather than institutional norms dominate in some practices, such as data sharing) in the new century. Collectively, these choices about institutional culture will shape the future of overall academic culture and the practice of scholarship to come.

NEXT STEPS

▶ Evaluate how copyright law and policy impacts the ability of scholars to build upon previous scholarships at your institution.

▶ Make an institutional choice to defend and support the fair use of copyrighted materials when appropriate.

▶ Support organizations such as Educause, AAU, ARL and others that are advocating on behalf of issues important to higher education relative to intellectual property law and policy.

▶ Institutions should evaluate their missions and determine whether or not those missions should include a commitment to the dissemination and preservation of scholarship.

▶ Institutions should determine whether organizations historically associated with universities, but presently antagonistic to university missions and values, should continue to have university support.

►Appendices

ELDRED, ET AL. V. ASHCROFT, 537 U.S. 186 (2003)

Parties

The petitioners, Eric Eldred, et al., appealed the decision of the United States District Court and the United States Court of Appeals which found the Copyright Term Extension Act ("CTEA") a valid exercise of Congress' authority.

Facts

CTEA is the fourth copyright term extension enacted by Congress. *Id.* at 195. CTEA extended existing and future copyright terms by 20 years but, otherwise, "retained the general structure of the 1976 [Copyright] Act. . . ." *Id.*

The petitioners challenged CTEA as a violation of the Copyright Clause of the United States Constitution as well as a violation of the First Amendment. *Id.* at 196. The District Court "held that the CTEA does not violate the 'limited times' restriction of the Copyright Clause because CTEA's terms, though longer . . . are still limited, not perpetual. *Id.* at 196–96 (citing Eldred v. Reno, 74 F. Supp. 2d 1, 3 (D.C. 1999)). Additionally, the District Court "held that 'there are no First Amendment rights to use the copyrighted works of others.'" *Id.* at 197 (quoting Eldred v. Reno, 74 F. Supp. 2d 1, 3 (D.C. 1999)).

The Court of Appeals for the District of Columbia Circuit affirmed the District Court's holding. *Id.* In its opinion the District of Columbia Circuit "found nothing in the constitutional text or its history to suggest that 'a term of years for a copyright is not a 'limited time' if it may later be extended for another 'limited time.'"" *Id.* (quoting Eldred v. Reno, 293 F.3d 372, 379 (2001)).

Questions Presented

Was the Copyright Term Extension Act, Pub. L. 105-298, § 102(b) and (d), 112 Stat, 2827–2828, a valid exercise of Congress' authority under the Copyright Clauses' "limited times" prescription? *Id.* at 193. May Congress extend the length of existing copyrights? *Id.*

Is the extension of the term of copyright a violation of the First Amendment as a "content-neutral regulation of speech that fails inspection under the heightened judicial scrutiny appropriate for regulating such regulations?" *Id.* at 193–94.

Discussion

CTEA and Congress' Authority to Extend the Copyright Term Under the Copyright Clause

The petitioners argued that even though the copyright term set by the CTEA is fixed and not perpetual, extending existing copyrights, in essence, makes copyright terms unlimited by permitting the evasion of the Constitution's "limited times" constraint. *Id.* at 199, 208. The Court disagreed with this assessment and explained that "a time span appropriately 'limited' as applied to future copyrights does not automatically cease to be 'limited' when applied to existing copyrights." *Id.* The Court pointed to history to underline this assertion highlighting that Congress has extended the copyright term for existing and future copyrights a number of times since the original 1790 Copyright Act. *Id.* at 200–01 (indicating that extensions were granted in 1831, 1909, and 1976). Additionally, these extensions were upheld by the courts when they were enacted and even retroactive applications of extensions were found permissible. *Id.* at 202–03.

After determining that "the CTEA complie[d] with the 'limited times' prescription," the court turned its attention to whether the extension was a rational use of Congress' authority. *Id.* at 204. The Court determined that the extension was a rational exercise of Congress' authority due to Congress' interest in harmonizing United States copyright terms with the Berne Convention. *Id.* at 205–06. Furthermore, the Court found that the extension was designed to address "demographic, economic, and technological changes" in society and that Congress "rationally credited projections that longer terms would encourage copyright holders to invest in the restoration and public distribution of their works." *Id.* at 206–07.

Examining the petitioners' claims, the Court dismissed each. As mentioned above, the Court found it unpersuasive that the extension creates a perpetual copyright. *Id.* at 208–10. In addition, the Court determined that the elements for the original granting of copyright do not apply when considering the term of the copyright that is granted. Therefore, the concepts of originality, promoting the progress of science, and the "quid pro quo" of protection for production are not relevant. *Id.* at 210–12, 214–15. To underscore this, the Court indicated "that it is generally for Congress, not the courts, to decide how best to pursue the Copyright Clause's objectives." *Id.* at 212.

Lastly, the Court found that unlike copyright where the goal is the disclosure of the work, in the case of patent, the disclosure is "exacted" for the grant of exclusive rights. *Id.* at 216. Therefore, since copyright and patent are sufficiently different, the reference to quid pro quo, which is usually used in a patent context, is not relevant. *Id.* at 215–18.

CTEA and the First Amendment

The petitioners argued that "the CTEA is a content-neutral regulation of speech that fails heightened judicial review under the First Amendment." *Id.* at 218. The Court rejected the petitioner's argument citing not only that the framers adopted the Copyright Clause and the First Amendment close in time and therefore intended for the limited restriction on speech, but that the idea and expression dichotomy of copyright law leaves the ideas free for use and only restricts the author's particular expression. *Id.* at 219.

The Court indicated that the principle of fair use as well as specific safeguards included in the CTEA provide for the use of the copyrighted material under certain circumstances making the restriction less than entire. *Id.* at 219–20.

Holding

The Court held that the enactment of the CTEA was not an invalid use of Congress' authority under the Copyright Clause and does not violate the "limited times" constraint. The Court held that the extension of copyright term for both existing and future copyrights does not violate the "limited times" constraint of the Copyright Clause.

Additionally, the Court held that the CTEA is not an impermissible restriction on speech due to the nature of copyright, fair use, and specific exceptions carved out in the CTEA. The Court held that a copyright term extension is not a violation of free speech due to "copyright's built-in free speech safeguards. . . ." *Id.* at 221.

Justice Stevens, Dissenting

Justice Stevens dissented from the opinion on the theory that copyright terms cannot be extended for existing copyrights because patents cannot be extended beyond the patent expiration date. *Id.* at 222–23. Justice Stevens argued that Congress "may not over-reach the restraints imposed by the stated constitutional purpose." *Id.* at 223 (citing Graham v. John Deere Co. of Kansas City, 383 U.S. 1, 5–6 (1966)). Justice Stevens argued that the purpose of copyright, similar to the purpose to patent, was to encourage the creation of new works and the addition to the public domain. *Id.* at 26–28. Under this theory, the quid pro quo disclosure for protection would be necessary for the extension of copyright as well as patent and, therefore, Congress does not have the authority to extend existing copyrights. *Id.* Lastly, Justice Stevens opined that to permit the retroactive extension of copyrights would permit Congress to extend copyrights into perpetuity. *Id.* at 241–42.

Justice Breyer, Dissenting

Justice Breyer dissented for two main reasons. First, the extension of the copyright does not serve the purposes for which the Copyright Clause intended copyright to serve. *Id.* at 243. The CTEA, according to Justice Breyer, does not "serve public . . . ends" and prevents the dissemination of information by increasing the cost of the work in both monetary terms and in terms of time. *Id.* at 247–48. Justice Breyer found this increase in cost to be particularly onerous due to the lack of commercial value of the majority of the works affected as well as the exceptional difficulty or impossibility of complying with the law in some instances. *Id.* at 248–51. Justice Breyer found the protections afford by the CTEA as well as fair use to be little comfort because of their very limited scope. *Id.* at 252–53. Additionally, Justice Breyer found that the economic incentive to create, which copyright is designed to encourage, is not achieved by the CTEA because it benefits individuals other than the original author. *Id.* at 254–55.

Second, Justice Breyer argued that the CTEA will "restrict traditional dissemination of copyrighted works . . . and inhibit new forms of dissemination through the use of new technology." *Id.* at 166.

▶Chapter 2

APPENDIX B

VANDERHURST V. COLORADO MOUNTAIN COLLEGE DISTRICT, 16 F. SUPP. 2D 1297 (D.COLO. 1998)

Parties

The plaintiff of this case is Mr. Stuart R. Vanderhurst, a former Professor and Clinician in Veterinary Technology at Colorado Mountain College. The plaintiff sued the defendant (Colorado Mountain College District and the Colorado Mountain College Board of Trustees) for copyright infringement.

Facts

After twenty-two years as a Professor and Clinician in Veterinary Technology, Mr. Vanderhurst was terminated. *Id.* at 1298. After termination, Mr. Vanderhurst sought damages for copyright infringement of an outline of veterinary technology he produced. *Id.* at 1307.

Question Presented

Does Colorado Mountain College District or Mr. Vanderhurst own the copyright to the documents that Mr. Vanderhurst produced while employed by Colorado Mountain College District?

Discussion

In this case, the situation rests on whether Mr. Vanderhurst produced the "Veterinary Technology Outline" as a "work for hire" or individually. If the work was produced individually, then Mr. Vanderhurst is the proper owner of the copyright. *Id.* at 1307. However, if the work was produced as a work for hire then the employer is the proper holder of the copyright. *Id.*

The court defines a "work for hire" as being:

(1) a work [that] is prepared by an employee within the scope of his or her employment; or

(2) a work [that] is specially ordered or commissioned for use as . . . an instructional test or . . . as answer material for a test . . . if the parties expressly agree in a written instrument signed by them that the work shall be considered a work made for hire. *Id.* (citing 17 U.S.C. § 101).

The question then shifts to whether Mr. Vanderhurst was an employee when the work was produced and whether it was within the scope of his employment. *Id.* (citing 17 U.S.C. § 101(1)). A number of factors are to be considered when determining whether a work is within the scope of employment including "whether: (1) it is the kind of work the person is employed to perform; (2) the work occurs substantially within work hours; and (3) the work is actuated, at least in part, by a purpose to serve the employer." *Id.* (citing RESTATEMENT (SECOND) AGENCY § 228; Nimmer on Copyright 5–33 (1997)).

Applying these factors, the court determined that although Mr. Vanderhurst produced the outline on his own time and with his own materials, he was motivated to do so and it was directly connected with his employment. *Id.*

Holding

Colorado Mountain College District holds the copyright to the "Veterinary Technology Outline" because Mr. Vanderhurst produced the outline as a "work for hire."

COMMUNITY FOR CREATIVE NON-VIOLENCE ET AL. V. REID, 490 U.S. 730 (1989)

Parties

Community for Creative Non-Violence ("CCNV") sued James Earl Reid, a Baltimore, Maryland, a sculptor, for determination of the proper ownership to the copyright of the sculpture "Third World America." *Id.* at 732–35.

Facts

In the fall of 1985 CCNV decided to commission a sculpture of a nontraditional nativity scene which pictured homeless individuals. *Id.* at 733. CCNV decided to contract Mr. Reid to sculpt the work of art and after negotiation, the work was to be made out of a synthetic material with a similar look to bronze and $15,000 would be paid to Mr. Reid for expenses. *Id.* at 733–34.

Mr. Reid produced the first series of sketches of the figures to be included in the sculpture; however, at the suggestion of the trustee of CCNV, the figures in the sculpture were sketched as reclining on steam grates rather than Mr. Reid's original seated design. *Id.* at 734.

At the completion of the sculpture, both CCNV, by way of its trustee, and Mr. Reid filed for copyright registration. *Id.* at 735.

Question Presented

How is the term employee defined in the context of the "work made for hire" doctrine set forth in 17 U.S.C. § 101?

Who owns the copyright to the sculpture "Third World America"?

Discussion

The Court determined that the outcome of this case rested upon the doctrine of "work made for hire" and therefore turned on whether Mr. Reid was an employee of CCNV for the purpose of producing the sculpture. *Id.* at 735–36.

While copyright ownership generally "vests initially in the author or authors of the work" an exception is made for an employer then, absent a written agreement to the contrary, the employer is the holder of the copyright. *Id.* at 737 (citing and quoting 17 U.S.C. §§ 201(a), 201(b)). A work may qualify as "for hire" if it is either "specially ordered or commissioned" or "prepared by an employee within the scope of his or her employment." *Id.* at 738 (citing and quoting 17 U.S.C. § 101). In the current case, the sculpture does not qualify as a work "specially ordered or commissioned" because it falls outside of the acceptable nine types of work for which the statute provides and no written agreement exists regarding the copyright ownership. *Id.*

In the absence of a written agreement, "four interpretations have emerged" regarding who holds the copyright. *Id.* First, the copyright is held by whomever "retains the right to control the product." *Id.* Second, "that a work is prepared by an employee under [17 U.S.C.] § 101(1) when the hiring party has actually wielded control with respect to the creation of a particular work." *Id.* at 739. Third, courts have interpreted "employee" to carry the same meaning as under agency law. *Id.* Fourth, an employee may be interpreted to mean "formal, salaried" employees. *Id.* The Court concluded that the term employee should be "understood in light of agency law." *Id.* at 740–41. Additionally, the Court concluded that the legislative history associated with the Copyright Act of 1976 indicates that Congress only intended for there to be two ways for a work to be deemed a work for hire. *Id.* at 745–51.

In determining whether Mr. Reid was an employee of CCNV, the Court considered:

> . . . the hiring party's right to control the manner and means by which the product is accomplished . . . the skill required; the source of the instumentalities and tools; the location of the work; the duration of the relationship between the parties; whether the hiring party has the right to assign additional projects to the hired party; the extent of

the hired party's discretion over when and how long to work; the method of payment; the hired party's role in hiring and paying assistants; whether the work is party of the regular business of the hiring party; whether the hiring party is in business; the provision of employee benefits; and the tax treatment of the hired party. *Id.* at 751 (internal citations omitted).

After evaluating the situation in light of these factors, the Court concluded that Mr. Reid "was not an employee of CCNV but an independent contractor." *Id.* at 752. Since CCNV conceded that the situation cannot meet the requirements of a specially contracted work under 17 U.S.C. § 101(2), Mr. Reid is the author and therefore copyright holder of the work "Third World America." However, the Court indicated that CCNV's contributions to the project may entitle it to be a co-author and therefore co-owner of the copyright to the sculpture. *Id.* at 753.

Holding

The Court held that the term "employee" should be "understood in light of agency law." *Id.* at 740–41. Furthermore, the Court provided the basic factors that should be considered in determining whether an individual is an employee under the common law of agency.

In this case, the Court determined that Mr. Reid was not an employee of CCNV and since the sculpture does not fit within one of the statutorily prescribed categories of a "specially ordered or commissioned" work, Mr. Reid is the author and holder of the copyright. *Id.* at 752–53.

FORASTÉ V. BROWN UNIVERSITY, 290 F. SUPP. 2D 234 (2003)

Parties

The plaintiff, Mr. John Forasté, sued the defendant, Brown University and Ms. Laura Freid, for copyright infringement of photographs he took while working for Brown University.

Facts

Mr. Forasté was employed by Brown University as a full-time photographer from 1975 to 1998. *Id.* at 236. His duties included taking photographs at the request of other employees of Brown University (editors, art designers, etc.) and at his own discretion that helped "to convey a positive image of Brown to the public." *Id.*

While employed at Brown University copyright policies were adopted in the form of a document named "Policies and Procedures Relating to Copyright." *Id.*

Under this policy the author or originator of a work "result[ing] from . . . one's University duties and activities" was the owner of the copyright. *Id.*

Mr. Forasté was terminated in 1998 due to a staff cut and is asserting that Brown, through the enactment of its copyright policy, transferred the copyrights of the photos to him. *Id.*

Question Presented

Is Mr. Forasté the owner of the copyright to the photographs that he took of Brown University while employed by Brown University?

Discussion

17 U.S.C. §§ 201(b) and 204(a) permit the transfer of copyrights by way of "an instrument of conveyance, or a note or memorandum of the transfer." *Id.* at 237–38. However, the Court circumscribes this by stating that the intent of Congress was to "protect employers' proprietary rights in works made for hire." *Id.* at 238 (citing H.R. Rep. No. 94–1476 at 121 (1976)). Furthermore, the intent of the Copyright Act was for the copyrights of a work made for hire to "vest, as an initial matter, in the employer" and the addition of "unless the parties have expressly agreed otherwise in a written instrument signed by them" underscores that the original owner of the copyright should be Brown University. *Id.* at 237-38 (quoting 17 U.S.C. § 201(b)).

The court continues, assuming that the copyrights could be transferred by Brown University to Mr. Forasté, to discuss whether the copyright policy was sufficient under 17 U.S.C. § 204(a) to transfer the rights. *Id.* at 239. The instrument of transfer must be in writing and must be "signed by the owner of the rights conveyed or such owner's duly authorized agent." *Id.* In this case, the document did not provide any specifics to the transfer of the photograph rights. *Id.* at 239–40. In this case, Mr. Forasté never contemplated the rights to the photographs prior to being terminated and Brown University was too vague in its document to have had an effective transfer of the rights to Mr. Forasté. *Id.* at 239–40.

Holding

Brown University was the original copyright holder of Mr. Forasté's photographs under the work for hire doctrine and the subsequently adopted copyright policy was insufficient to transfer the rights to the copyright from Brown University to Mr. Forasté.

To successfully transfer rights from an employer to an employee a written document must be created which specifically names the materials to which the rights are to be transferred and it must be signed by the party which is transferring the rights.

MANNING V. BOARD OF TRUSTEES OF COMMUNITY COLLEGE DISTRICT NO. 505 (PARKLAND COLLEGE), 109 F. SUPP. 2D 976 (2000)

Parties

The plaintiff, Donald W. Manning, sued the defendant, Board of Trustees of Community College District No. 505 (Parkland College), to prevent the college from using his photographs and the return of the photographs.

Facts

Mr. Manning was employed by Parkland College as a full-time professional photographer from 1979 to 1996. *Id.* at 977–78. While employed by Parkland, the plaintiff asserted that his annual contract and collective bargaining agreements "incorporated the Parkland College Policy Manual" which provided that a staff member who produces materials is the owner of the copyright of those materials unless the staff member and Parkland have contracted otherwise. *Id.* at 978.

In 1996 the position of staff photographer was eliminated by the college and Mr. Manning was subsequently terminated. *Id.* After his termination, relying upon the copyright policy contained in the policy manual, Mr. Manning registered the photographs he took while employed at Parkland College from 1980 to 1996 with the United States Copyright Office as his own works. *Id.*

Mr. Manning sued Parkland College for "(1) an order permanently enjoining Parkland College from using the photographs created or developed by [the] Plaintiff during his employment; (2) an order requiring Parkland College to return to [the] Plaintiff all photographic images created by [the] Plaintiff; and (3) damages, costs and attorney fees." *Id.* at 978. In response, Parkland College, argued that the clause in the policy manual did not apply to Mr. Manning and that the product produced by Mr. Manning was a work made for hire and is therefore the property of Parkland College. *Id.* at 978.

Question Presented

Does a policy manual or employee handbook meet the criteria to overcome the presumption that the copyright to a work made for hire vests in the employer?

Discussion

Generally, "if a work is made for hire, the employer owns the copyright unless there is a written agreement to the contrary." *Id.* at 979 (citing Community for Creative Non-Violence v. Reid, 490 U.S. 730, 737 (1989)). A work made for hire is characterized by the Copyright Act of 1976 as one which is "prepared by an employee within the scope of his or her employment." *Id.* at 979 (citing 17 U.S.C. § 101). In this case, the plaintiff and the defendant agreed that Mr. Manning was an employee of Parkland College and "that the photographs at issue were prepared within the scope of the Plaintiff's employment." *Id.* at 979. Therefore, in this case, the determination of whether the photographs were works made for hire and consequently the ownership of the copyrights rested upon the effectiveness of the policy manual as an agreement between Mr. Manning and Parkland College to assign the copyrights to Mr. Manning. *Id.*

Mr. Manning argued that an employee handbook or policy manual can be interpreted as a binding contract between the employer and the employee. *Id.* at 980 (citing *Duldulao v. Saint Mary of Nazereth Hosp. Ctr.*, 505 N.E.2d 314, 318 (Ill. 1987)). Applying the concepts of *Duldulao v. Saint Mary of Nazereth Hosp. Ctr.*, the plaintiff argued that the policy manual provided a clear promise that copyrights would be retained by the staff member who produced the work, the policy manual was distributed to the staff members of Parkland College, and Mr. Manning accepted the provisions of the manual by continuing to work for Parkland College after he received the manual. *Id.* at 980. Furthermore, the plaintiff pointed to the provision in the policy manual that indicated that the copyright provision "should be a binding contract between the parties regarding the subject of copyright ownership." *Id.* at 980 (quoting the Parkland College Policy Manual). However, the court disagreed with the plaintiff and stated that in order to overcome the presumption that the copyright of a work made for hire vests in the employer, the agreement must be signed by both of the parties and must expressly indicate that the plaintiff had copyright to the photographs. *Id.* at 980–81.

Holding

The Court held that in order to meet the statutory requirements of 17 U.S.C. § 201(b) and overturn the presumption that the employer holds the copyright to works made for hire, the agreement between the employee and the employer needs to be signed and relate specifically to the materials. *Id.* at 981. Therefore, in this case, a policy manual does not suffice to overcome the presumption that the copyright of works made for hire vests in the employer.

UNIVERSITY OF COLORADO FOUNDATION, INC. V. AMERICAN CYANAMID, 880 F. SUPP. 1387 (D.COLO. 1995)

Parties

The plaintiffs in this case (The University of Colorado Foundation, Inc., The University of Colorado, The Board of Regents of the University of Colorado, Robert

H. Allen, and Paul A. Seligman) sued American Cyanamid for conversion, fraud, wrongful naming of inventor, copyright infringement, misappropriation, patent infringement, breach of confidentiality obligation, and unjust enrichment. The plaintiff claims that the defendant "wrongfully filed and obtained a patent on a reformulated prescription prenatal vitamin." *Id.* at 1389. Only the claim of copyright infringement is addressed here.

Facts

Stemming from a claim from a competitor that American Cyanamid's prenatal vitamin "Materna" was not providing sufficient iron to patients, Drs. Allen and Seligman of the University of Colorado Health Sciences Center were contracted by Dr. Ellenbogen of American Cyanamid to research these claims. *Id.* at 1390. The first series of studies conducted by Drs. Allen and Seligman determined that iron was absorbed at a reduced rate "from both Materna and the competitor's product." *Id.* Further study by the same scientists concluded that neither of the products would likely provide a pregnant patient with sufficient iron. *Id.*

At this point, Drs. Allen and Seligman alleged to have conducted independent research to determine "the reason for the poor iron absorption in from Materna and the competitive product." *Id.* After determining how to better formulate Materna to avoid the problem, Dr. Ellenbogen contracted "Drs. Allen and Seligman to conduct two further studies . . . to measure the iron absorption from several competing products and that from two new formulated versions of maternal, including" the reformulation suggested by Drs. Allen and Seligman. *Id.* The new formulation showed improved iron absorption. *Id.*

The plaintiffs and American Cyanamid dispute who "conceived of the revised Materna product." *Id.* at 1391. American Cyanamid points to a letter which Dr. Allen sent Dr. Ellenbogen which they claim confirms an earlier conversation between the two where Dr. Ellenbogen made the decision to change the formulation of Materna. *Id.*

American Cyanamid applied for and was issued a patent for the reformulated Materna in 1981. *Id.* At about the same time, Drs. Allen and Seligman attempted to publish an article in the *New England Journal of Medicine* describing their study results. *Id.* While the article acknowledged that American Cyanamid supported some of the research it "did not name Dr. Ellenbogen as a co-author." *Id.* Furthermore, American Cyanamid, in press releases, press conferences, correspondence with the U.S. Food and Drug Administration, and internal memoranda, cited Dr. Allen as the discoverer of the reformulation. *Id.*

Drs. Allen and Seligman, through an agreement with the University of Colorado, are required to assign their patent rights to the University in exchange for an interest in the royalties. *Id.*

Question Presented

Did American Cyanamid infringe the plaintiffs copyright of the article submitted for publication in the *New England Journal of Medicine* and, subsequently, *Obstetrics and Gynecology*, by copying portions of the text and figures for inclusion in its patent application?

Discussion

The plaintiffs assert that the basic "requirements for establishing a copyright infringement case" are: *Id.* at 1400.

> Reduced to most fundamental terms, there are only two elements necessary to the plaintiff's case in an infringement action: ownership of the copyright by plaintiff and copying by the defendant. *Id.* (citing 3 Melville B. Nimmer and David Nimmer, *Nimmer on Copyright* § 13.01 (1994)).

First, the ownership of the copyright must be determined. The defendant challenged the impact of a recently obtained copyright registration presented by the plaintiffs. *Id.* Additionally, the defendants noted that a certificate of registration of a copyright "is only prima facie evidence of the validity of the copyright if the registration is sought within the first five years of the first publication of the work." *Id.* at 1400 (citing 17 U.S.C. § 410(c)).

To underscore its claims to the copyright, the plaintiffs maintained that the Regents are the owners through the "work for hire" doctrine, an assertion that the defendants did not rebut. *Id.*

Second, the plaintiff must provide evidence that the item has been copied by the defendant. In the case at bar, the defendant provided no evidence to dispute that American Cyanamid copied portions of the articles written by Drs. Allen and Seligman. *Id.* at 1401. American Cyanamid argued that they had authorization to copy the material from the work granted by a letter from Dr. Allen to Dr. Ellenbogen which gave Dr. Ellenbogen and Lederle Laboratories (a subdivision of American Cyanamid) permission to "use and circulate the results of ours studies concerning the absorption of iron from prenatal multi-vitamin supplements prior to their publication." *Id.* However, the plaintiffs provided evidence that the reason for this letter was because many journals do not permit the display of the contents of a study prior to its actual publication and provide evidence that Dr. Ellenbogen was aware of this prohibition. *Id.* The Court determined that this evidence "contradict[ed] Cyanamid's contention that Dr. Allen authorized the copying of the figures and the table in the article." *Id.*

Third, the subject matter must be copyrightable. In this case, American Cyanamid argued that the bar graphs and data points which were used to illustrate the results of the studies performed by Drs. Allen and Seligman do not merit copyright protection. *Id.* The Court determined that this is an example of an original, coordinated and arranged compilation of facts and therefore copyrightable. *Id.* (citing *Feist Publ'ns, Inc. v. Rural Telephone Serv. Co.*, 499 U.S. 340, 344 (1991) ("facts are not copyrightable . . . compilations of facts generally are.")).

Holding

American Cyanamid infringed the copyright of the plaintiffs in copying sections of the article created by Drs. Allen and Seligman for incorporation in its patent application for the reformulation of Materna. *Id.* at 1403.

Chapter 3

APPENDIX C

AMERICAN GEOPHYSICAL UNION, ET AL. V. TEXACO, INC., 60 F.3D 913 (2D CIR. 1994)

Parties

The appellant, Texaco, Inc., appeals the decision of the district court that they infringed the appellee's, American Geophysical Union, et al., publishers of scientific journals, copyright by way of "unauthorized photocopying of articles from their journals." *Id.* at 914.

Facts

Texaco, Inc., employs between 400 to 500 research scientists who, in the course of their research, photocopy articles from scientific journals. *Id.* at 915. Texaco, Inc., circulates various scientific journals amongst its scientists to assist in their remaining current on the state of their respective sciences. *Id.* A study of one researcher, Dr. Donald H. Chickering, II, revealed that he photocopied eight copyrighted articles from the Journal of Catalysis, six of which he was made aware of through the circulation of the journal and the other two by virtue of citations within other articles. *Id.*

Question Presented

Does the fair use defense apply to copying articles in a scientific journal by a member of a corporation for research on behalf of the corporation?

Discussion

The court narrows the focus of this case to determine whether Texaco has engaged in or encouraged its employees to engage in a systematic copying of copyrighted articles. *Id.* at 916. Generally, examining the copyrights held by publishers over the journal article, it is noted that there are two different copyrights that are held. *Id.* at 918. The first is over each individual article, which the author has signed over to the publisher. *Id.* The second is over the entire volume of the journal which compiles the articles. *Id.* In this case, only the copyrights to the individual articles are in dispute. *Id.*

There are four nonexclusive factors that courts consider when determining if a use is a fair use. *Id.* Under the first factor "purpose and character of use" the Court discusses three different characters of use, commercial use, transformative use, and reasonable and customary practice. *Id.* at 918, 921–25. While the Court agreed with Texaco that the commercial nature of the appellant's business should not be the entire analysis of whether a use is commercial, the Court believed that this should be considered. *Id.* at 921–22. The Court further disagreed with Texaco that the copying transformed the article into a more suitable form for use in the laboratory. *Id.* at 923–24. Lastly, the Court disagreed with Texaco that the use was reasonable and customary practice because the circulation of the journals encouraged the creation of archival copies of the document that could be kept by each scientist in their own office. *Id.* at 924.

Second, the nature of the copyrighted work is considered in determining fair use. *Id.* at 925. Under this factor, the Court found for Texaco because the works were primarily scientific and factual in nature and therefore outside of "the core of the copyright's protective purpose." *Id.* at 925 (quoting *Campbell v. Acuff-Rose Music, Inc.*, 114 S. Ct. 1164, 1175 (1994)).

Third, the amount and substantiality of the portion copied is considered. *Id.* The Court found for the appellants noting that an entire article would be copied and therefore rejected Texaco's assertion that each article is only a small portion of the entire compendium of articles contained in the journal. *Id.* at 925–26.

Finally, the fourth factor requires that the Court examine the impact that the copying would have or had on the market value of the work. *Id.* at 926. The Court broke this determination into two parts, loss of subscriptions and loss of licensing revenues and fees. *Id.* at 927. While Texaco's actions had not lost the publisher any subscriptions, the actions did impinge on the copyright holder's right to license reproduction rights. *Id.* at 927–31. Additionally, Texaco had the opportunity to purchase reproduction licenses through the Copyright Clearance Center, Inc. *Id.* at 930.

Holding

Circulation of journals amongst scientific staff which results in the copying of documents by the scientists for future use does not qualify as a fair use and therefore violates the copyright of a scientific journal. *Id.* at 931–32.

PRINCIPLES FOR LICENSING ELECTRONIC RESOURCES

American Association of Law Libraries
American Library Association
Association of Academic Health Sciences Libraries
Association of Research Libraries
Medical Library Association
Special Libraries Association

Introduction

License agreements are a fact of life in conducting business in the electronic environment. Providers of electronic information resources are employing licenses as a legal means of controlling the use of their products. In the electronic environment where the traditional print practice of ownership through purchase is being replaced by access through license, libraries need to be aware that licensing arrangements may restrict their legal rights and those of their users. As responsible agents for an institution, librarians must negotiate licenses that address the institution's needs and recognize its obligations to the licensor.

To help provide guidance in this continuously evolving environment, the American Association of Law Libraries, American Library Association, Association of Academic Health Sciences Libraries, Association of Research Libraries, Medical Library Association, and Special Libraries Association have combined to develop a statement of principles. These six associations represent an international membership of libraries of all types and sizes. The intent of this document is twofold: to guide libraries in negotiating license agreements for access to electronic resources, and to provide licensors with a sense of the issues of importance to libraries and their user communities in such negotiations.

The Special Libraries Association provided funding to support the development and distribution of the principles. The Principles are available on the Web at: </scomm/licensing/principles.html>

Legal Background

A license agreement is a legal contract—"a promise or set of promises constituting an agreement between the parties that gives each a legal duty to the other and also the right to seek a remedy for the breach of those duties. Its essentials are competent parties, subject matter, a legal consideration, mutuality of agreement, and mutuality of obligations." [*Black's Law Dictionary*, 6th edition, 1990, p. 322.] Key to the concept of a contract is the fact that it is an agreement, a mutually acceptable set of understandings and commitments often arrived at through discussion and negotiation.

Most commercial contracts are intended to spell out the mutual understandings between buyer and seller for products or services.

Although the original contract document may be the work product of either the buyer or seller, in a licensing situation, it is generally the seller (or licensor) who has prepared the agreement. It is imperative that the buyer (or licensee) review the terms of the agreement and communicate concerns to the licensor before signing it. Discussion may continue until either agreement is reached or a decision is made not to contract for the particular product or service. In the area of licensing electronic resources, failure to read and understand the terms of the agreement may result in such unintended consequences as:

▶ the loss of certain rights to uses of the resource that would otherwise be allowed under the law (for example, in the United States, such uses as fair use, interlibrary loan, and other library and educational uses);

▶ obligations to implement restrictions that are unduly burdensome or create legal risk for the institution; or,

▶ sudden termination of the contract due to inappropriate use by a member of the user community.

Given the obligations that a contract creates for an institution and the possible liability associated with not meeting those obligations, most institutions will delegate the authority to sign contracts to a specific office or officer within the institution. In many institutions, this signatory authority will reside in the purchasing department, legal counsel's or vice president's office, or the library director's office, although in some institutions, a library staff member may be granted authority for signing license agreements. Nevertheless, library staff will often be responsible for initial review and negotiation of the material terms of the license because they have the most knowledge of the user community and of the resource being acquired. Library staff should be well informed of the uses critical to the library's user community (for example, printing, downloading, and copying).

An important category of license agreements is that including "shrink wrap" and "click" licenses. Such licenses are commonly found on the packaging of software, appear when software is loaded, or appear, sometimes buried, on Web sites. The terms of these licenses are made known to the user at the time the product is purchased, or just before or during use. The user has only two options: accept the license terms or do not use the software, electronic product, or Web site.

Traditional contract terminology defines these agreements as "contracts of adhesion," because there are no formal negotiations between licensor and licensee. Hence, the rules of use are imposed by one side, rather than evolved through a discussion leading to a mutual understanding or "meeting of the minds." While many courts reject these contracts or rewrite particular terms on the basis of equity, one cannot assume that the terms are unenforceable. In fact, some states are in the process of passing legislation that makes shrink wrap or click licenses enforceable. A purchasing library should consider contacting the licensor directly to determine if there are any license terms which can be modified to fit the special needs of libraries. Often, if there are competing products which can satisfy the user's needs equally well, exceptions to the form agreement may be negotiated. If negotiation is not possible, it is suggested that legal counsel be consulted for an opinion of enforceability prior to accepting or rejecting the product.

The following principles are meant to provide guidance to library staff in working with others in the institution and with licensors to create agreements that respect the rights and obligations of both parties.

Principles for Licensing Electronic Resources

1. A license agreement should state clearly what access rights are being acquired by the licensee—permanent use of the content or access rights only for a defined period of time.

2. A license agreement should recognize and not restrict or abrogate the rights of the licensee or its user community permitted under copyright law. The licensee should make clear to the licensor those uses critical to its particular users including, but not limited to, printing, downloading, and copying.

3. A license agreement should recognize the intellectual property rights of both the licensee and the licensor.

4. A license agreement should not hold the licensee liable for unauthorized uses of the licensed resource by its users, as long as the licensee has implemented reasonable and appropriate methods to notify its user community of use restrictions.

5. The licensee should be willing to undertake reasonable and appropriate methods to enforce the terms of access to a licensed resource.

6. A license agreement should fairly recognize those access enforcement obligations which the licensee is able to implement without unreasonable burden. Enforcement must not violate the privacy and confidentiality of authorized users.

7. The licensee should be responsible for establishing policies that create an environment in which authorized users make appropriate use of licensed resources and for carrying out due process when it appears that a use may violate the agreement.

8. A license agreement should require the licensor to give the licensee notice of any suspected or alleged license violations that come to the attention of the licensor and allow a reasonable time for the licensee to investigate and take corrective action, if appropriate.

9. A license agreement should not require the use of an authentication system that is a barrier to access by authorized users.

10. When permanent use of a resource has been licensed, a license agreement should allow the licensee to copy data for the purposes of preservation and/or the creation of a usable archival copy. If a license agreement does not permit the licensee to make a usable preservation copy, a license agreement should specify who has permanent archival responsibility for the resource and under what conditions the licensee may access or refer users to the archival copy.

11. The terms of a license should be considered fixed at the time the license is signed by both parties. If the terms are subject to change (for example, scope of coverage or method of access), the agreement should require the licensor or licensee to notify the other party in a timely and reasonable fashion of any such changes before they are implemented, and permit either party to terminate the agreement if the changes are not acceptable.

12. A license agreement should require the licensor to defend, indemnify, and hold the licensee harmless from any action based on a claim that use of the resource in accordance with the license infringes any patent, copyright, trademark, or trade secret of any third party.

13. The routine collection of use data by either party to a license agreement should be predicated upon disclosure of such collection activities to the other party and must respect laws and institutional policies regarding confidentiality and privacy.

14. A license agreement should not require the licensee to adhere to unspecified terms in a separate agreement between the licensor and a third party unless the terms are fully reiterated in the current license or fully disclosed and agreed to by the licensee.

15. A license agreement should provide termination rights that are appropriate to each party.

APPENDICES

A. Terms to be Defined by the Licensee Within a License Agreement

A license agreement should define clearly the terms used and should use those terms consistently throughout. The licensee should take responsibility for defining the following terms appropriate to its user community:

archive
authorized use
authorized user
concurrent use
institution
local access
local area network
remote access

simultaneous use

site

wide area network

B. Resources on Licensing

Brennan, Patricia, Karen Hersey, and Georgia Harper. *Licensing Electronic Resources: Strategic and Practical Considerations for Signing Electronic Information Delivery Agreements.* Washington: Association of Research Libraries, 1997. Also on the Web </scomm/licensing/licbooklet.html>.

"LibLicense: Licensing Electronic Resources." Web site and Discussion List. 1996. <http://www.library.yale.edu/~llicense/index.shtml>.

University of Texas System

Contains a range of resources related to copyright in the library. Includes an interactive Software and Database License Agreement Checklist. <http://www.utsystem.edu/ogc/intellectualproperty/cprtindx.htm> .

C. Sources Consulted

The Working Group would like to thank a number of individuals and organizations for sharing with us drafts, notes, and memos about licensing principles that are not publicly available: Trisha Davis and Brian Schottlaender, the Association of Academic Health Sciences Libraries, Massachusetts Institute of Technology, and the University of New Mexico. Other sources the Working Group consulted are listed below. We would also like to thank the many individuals—librarians, vendors, publishers, and lawyers—who reviewed earlier drafts and provided excellent feedback, and the Special Libraries Association for providing the funding for this effort.

American Library Association, Association for Library Collections & Technical Services, Publisher/Vendor Library Relations Committee, Electronic Publishing Licensing Agreements Subcommittee. "Guidelines Document, Draft 2.2." 20 June 1995.

Brennan, Patricia, Karen Hersey, and Georgia Harper. *Licensing Electronic Resources: Strategic and Practical Considerations for Signing Electronic Information Delivery Agreements.* Washington: Association of Research Libraries, 1997. Also on the Web </scomm/licensing/licbooklet.html>.

California State University Libraries. "CSU Principles for Acquisition of Electronic Information Resources (Draft)." <http://www.lib.calpoly.edu/csuecc/principles.html>, 9 Jan. 1997.

Coalition for Networked Information. "Draft Preliminary Findings of the Rights for Electronic Access to and Delivery of Information (READI) Project." Prepared by Robert Ubell Associates. <http://www.cni.org/projects/READI/draft-rpt/>, 3 Sept. 1996.

European Copyright User Platform. "Heads of Agreement for Site-Licenses for the Use of Electronic Publications." 25 Sept. 1996.

――――. "Position on User Rights in Electronic Publications." 25 Sept. 1996.

Ferguson, Tony. "I Am Beginning to Hate Commercial E-Journals." *Against the Grain.* Sept. 1996: 86.

Hersey, Karen. "Coping with Copyright and Beyond: New Challenges as the Library Goes Digital." *Copyright, Public Policy, and the Scholarly Community.* Washington: Association of Research Libraries, 1995. 23–32.

Jacobson, Robert L. "Colleges Urged to Protect Rights in Licensing Negotiations." *The Chronicle of Higher Education.* 5 July 1996: A15.

"LibLicense: Licensing Electronic Resources." Web site and Discussion List. 1996. <http://www.library.yale.edu/~Llicense/index.shtml>.

National Humanities Alliance. "Basic Principles for Managing Intellectual Property in the Digital Environment." 24 Mar. 1997. <http://www-ninch.cni.org/ISSUES/COPYRIGHT/PRINCIPLES/NHA_Complete.html>.

University of California Libraries, Collection Development Committee. "Principles for Acquiring and Licensing Information in Digital Formats." 22 May 1996. <http://sunsite.berkeley.edu/Info/principles.html>, 22 Oct. 1996.

Warro, Edward A. "What Have We Been Signing? A Look at Database Licensing Agreements." *Library Administration and Management* 8.3 (1994): 173–177.

Members of the Working Group

▶ American Association of Law Libraries, Robert Oakley

▶ American Library Association, Trisha Davis

▶ American Library Association, Association for Library Collections & Technical Services, Collection Management and Development Section, Chief Collection Development Officers of Large Research Libraries, Brian Schottlaender

▶ Association of Academic Health Sciences Libraries, Karen Butter

▶ Association of Research Libraries, Mary Case

▶ Medical Library Association, Karen Butter

▶ Special Libraries Association, John Latham

The members of the Working Group welcome your comments on this document.

---

* Association of Research Libraries, *Principles for Licensing Electronic Resources* (1997), http://www.arl.org/scomm/licensing/principles.html (last accessed October 28, 2005).

AGREEMENT ON GUIDELINES FOR CLASSROOM COPYING IN NOT-FOR-PROFIT EDUCATIONAL INSTITUTIONS WITH RESPECT TO BOOKS AND PERIODICALS†

The purpose of the following guidelines is to state the minimum and not the maximum standards of educational fair use under Section 107 of H.R. 2223. The parties agree that the conditions determining the extent of permissible copying for educational purposes may change in the future; that certain types of copying permitted under these guidelines may not be permissible in the future; and conversely that in the future other types of copying not permitted under these guidelines may be permissible under revised guidelines.

Moreover, the following statement of guidelines is not intended to limit the types of copying permitted under the standards of fair use under judicial decision and which are stated in Section 107 of the Copyright Revision Bill. There may be instances in which copying which does not fall within the guidelines stated below may nonetheless be permitted under the criteria of fair use.

Guidelines

I. *Single Copying for Teachers*

A single copy may be made of any of the following by or for a teacher at his or her individual request for his or her scholarly research or use in teaching or preparation to teach a class:

    A. A chapter from a book;

    B. An article from a periodical or newspaper;

    C. A short story, short essay or short poem, whether or not from a collective work;

    D. A chart, graph, diagram, drawing, cartoon or picture from a book, periodical, or newspaper;

---

† *United States Copyright Office, Library of Congress, Circular 21: Reproduction of Copyrighted Works by Educators and Librarians* 7-8 (1995), available at http://www.copyright.gov/circs/circ21.pdf (excerpting House Report on the New Copyright Law, H.R. Rep. No. 94-1476, pp. 65–74).

II. *Multiple Copies for Classroom Use*

Multiple copies (not to exceed in any event more than one copy per pupil in a course) may be made by or for the teacher giving the course for classroom use or discussion; provided that:

A. The copying meets the tests of brevity and spontaneity as defined below; and,

B. Meets the cumulative effect test as defined below; and,

C. Each copy includes a notice of copyright

Definitions

Brevity

(*i*) Poetry: (a) A complete poem if less than 250 words and if printed on not more than two pages or, (b) from a longer poem, an excerpt of not more than 250 words.

(*ii*) Prose: (a) Either a complete article, story or essay of less than 2,500 words, or (b) an excerpt from any prose work of not more than 1,000 words or 10% of the work, whichever is less, but in any event a minimum of 500 words.

[Each of the numerical limits stated in "i" and "ii" above may be expanded to permit the completion of an unfinished line of a poem or of an unfinished prose paragraph.]

(*iii*) Illustration: One chart, graph, diagram, drawing, cartoon or picture per book or per periodical issue.

(*iv*) "Special" works: Certain works in poetry, prose or in "poetic prose" which often combine language with illustrations and which are intended sometimes for children and at other times for a more general audience fall short of 2,500 words in their entirety. Paragraph "ii" above notwithstanding such "special works" may not be reproduced in their entirety; however, an excerpt comprising not more than two of the published pages of such special work and containing not more than 10% of the words found in the text thereof, may be reproduced.

Spontaneity

(*i*) The copying is at the instance and inspiration of the individual teacher, and

(*ii*) The inspiration and decision to use the work and the moment of its use for maximum teaching effectiveness are so close in time that it would be unreasonable to expect a timely reply to a request for permission.

Cumulative Effect

(*i*) The copying of the material is for only one course in the school in which the copies are made.

(*ii*) Not more than one short poem, article, story, essay or two excerpts may be copied from the same author, nor more than three from the same collective work or periodical volume during one class term.

(*iii*) There shall not be more than nine instances of such multiple copying for one course during one class term.

[The limitations stated in "ii" and "iii" above shall not apply to current news periodicals and newspapers and current news sections of other periodicals.]

III. *Prohibitions as to I and II Above*

Notwithstanding any of the above, the following shall be prohibited:

(A) Copying shall not be used to create or to replace or substitute for anthologies, compilations or collective works. Such replacement or substitution may occur whether copies of various works or excerpts therefrom are accumulated or reproduced and used separately.

(B) There shall be no copying of or from works intended to be "consumable" in the course of study or of teaching. These include workbooks, exercises, standardized tests and test booklets and answer sheets and like consumable material.

(C) Copying shall not:

(a) substitute for the purchase of books, publishers' reprints or periodicals;

(b) be directed by higher authority;

(c) be repeated with respect to the same item by the same teacher from term to term.

(D) No charge shall be made to the student beyond the actual cost of the photocopying.

> Agreed MARCH 19, 1976.
> Ad Hoc Committee on Copyright Law Revision:
> BY SHELDON ELLIOTT STEINBACH.
> Author-Publisher Group:
> Authors League of America:
> BY IRWIN KARP, Counsel.
> Association of American Publishers, Inc.:
> BY ALEXANDER C. HOFFMAN,
> Chairman, Copyright Committee.

APPLYING FAIR USE IN THE DEVELOPMENT OF ELECTRONIC RESERVES SYSTEMS

For decades libraries have provided access to materials selected by faculty that are required or recommended course readings in a designated area of the library, with materials available to students for a short loan period and perhaps with additional restrictions to ensure that all students have access to the material. Libraries have based these reserve reading room operations on the fair use provisions of the Copyright Law (Section 107).

Within the past decade many libraries have introduced electronic reserves (e-reserves) systems that permit material to be stored in electronic form rather than storing photocopies in filing cabinets. Depending on the particular electronic reserves system, student access may occur in the library or remotely. Students who wish to have a copy of the reading can print it from the e-reserves systems rather than having to take the original volume to a photocopy machine.

The number of electronic resources licensed by libraries has increased significantly over the past decade. The licenses to these resources often include the right to use them in e-reserves systems. In such cases, no permission is required and a fair use analysis is unnecessary.

To ensure, however, that electronic content is effectively incorporated into e-reserve systems, there must be cooperation among library staff acquiring the digital resources and those managing e-reserves operations. They must work together to be certain that the license agreements do not preclude rights to make materials available through e-reserves systems, and that no one pays additional permission fees for uses already covered by a license.

As a result of the increase in licensed electronic resources, the percentage of print materials requested and digitized for e-reserves is diminishing. E-reserves practices for these materials vary widely and are influenced by institutional organizational structures, the information and technology infrastructure, manpower, demand, and the copyright law. The factors described below demonstrate a range of considerations when implementing fair use for e-reserves. They also distinguish the approach librarians are entitled to take when determining whether a use is fair from the approach librarians must take when determining whether a use falls within another statutory exemption. For example, Sections 108 (the library reproduction exemption) and 110 (exemption for public displays and performances including the TEACH Act) mandate a "checklist" approach: if a proposed use fails to comply with any condition, prohibition, or exclusion, the exemption does not apply.

Section 107's four-factor fair use test takes a fundamentally different approach: it simply directs that libraries assess overall whether a use is fair by considering the character of the use, the nature of the work to be used, the amount used in proportion to the whole and the impact on the market for the work. There is no fair use checklist, and there is no need to import from other sections of the law the detailed checklists of conditions, prohibitions, and exclusions that characterize their approach. Librarians balance their own interests with the copyright owners' interests. This summary illustrates ways in which libraries can apply fair use criteria in the development of best practices for e-reserves.

First Factor: The Character of the Use

► Libraries implement e-reserves systems in support of nonprofit education.

Second Factor: The Nature of the Work to Be Used

► E-reserve systems include text materials, both factual and creative.
► They also serve the interests of faculty and students who study music, film, art, and images.
► Librarians take the character of the materials into consideration in the overall balancing of interests.

Third Factor: The Amount Used

▶ Librarians consider the relationship of the amount used to the whole of the copyright owner's work.

▶ Because the amount that a faculty member assigns depends on many factors, such as relevance to the teaching objective and the overall amount of material assigned, librarians may also consider whether the amount, even the entire work, is appropriate to support the lesson or make the point.

Fourth Factor: The Effect of the Use on the Market for or Value of the Work

▶ Many libraries limit e-reserves access to students within the institution or within a particular class or classes. Many use technology to restrict and/or block access to help ensure that only registered students access the content.

▶ Libraries generally terminate student access at the end of a relevant term (semester, quarter, or year) or after the student has completed the course.

▶ Many e-reserves systems include core and supplemental materials. Limiting e-reserves solely to supplemental readings is not necessary since potential harm to the market is considered regardless of the status of the material.

▶ Libraries may determine that if the first three factors show that a use is clearly fair, the fourth factor does not weigh as heavily.

Summary

While there is no guarantee that a practice or combination of practices is fair use, such certainty is not required to safely implement e-reserves. The law builds in tolerance for risk-taking. At one end of the continuum are combinations of practices with which individuals and institutions tolerant of some risk will be comfortable. On the other end are combinations of practices with which those who are averse to risk will be more comfortable. Each institution's combination of practices reflects its tolerance for risk against the background of prevailing beliefs about fair use. Understandably, "not knowing" makes many people uncomfortable, so Congress explicitly addressed this aspect of fair use. Section 504(c)(2) of the Copyright Act provides special protection to nonprofit libraries, educational institutions and their employees. When we act in good faith, reasonably believing that our actions are fair use, in the unlikely event we are actually sued over a use, we will not have to pay statutory damages even if a court finds that we were wrong. This demonstrates congressional acknowledgment of the importance of fair use and *the importance of our using it!*

The **American Association of Law Libraries** (AALL) is a nonprofit educational organization dedicated to providing leadership and advocacy in the field of legal information and information policy. Our more than 5,000 members respond to the legal information needs of legislators, judges and other public officials, corporations and small businesses, law professors and students, attorneys, and members of the general public. <www.aallnet.org>

The **American Library Association** (ALA), the oldest and largest library association in the world, is a nonprofit organization of over 64,000 librarians, library trustees, and other friends of libraries dedicated to the development, promotion, and improvement of library and information services to enhance learning and ensure access to information for all. <www.ala.org>

The **Association of College and Research Libraries** (ACRL), a division of the American Library Association, is a professional association of academic librarians and other interested individuals. ACRL currently has a membership of approximately 12,400, accounting for nearly 20% of the total ALA membership. ACRL provides a broad range of professional services and programs for a diverse membership. <www.ala.org/acrl>

The **Association of Research Libraries** (ARL) is a nonprofit organization of 124 research libraries in North America. ARL programs and services promote equitable access to and effective use of recorded knowledge in support of teaching, research, scholarship, and community service. <www.arl.org>

The **Medical Library Association** (MLA) is a nonprofit, educational organization of more than 900 institutions and 3,800 individual members in the health sciences information field, committed to educating health information professionals, supporting health information research, promoting access to the world's health sciences information, and working to ensure that the best health information is available to all. <www.mlanet.org>

The **Special Libraries Association** (SLA) is the international association representing the interests of thousands of information professionals in over seventy countries. Special librarians are information resource experts who collect, analyze, evaluate, package, and disseminate information to facilitate accurate decision-making in corporate, academic, and government settings. The Association offers a variety of programs and services designed to help its members serve their customers more effectively and succeed in an increasingly challenging environment of information management and technology. SLA is committed to the professional growth and success of its membership. <www.sla.org>

Chapter 6

APPENDIX E

ALS SCAN, INC. V. REMARQ COMMUNITIES, INC., 239 F.3D 619 (4TH CIR. 2001)

Parties

The appellant, ALS Scan, Inc., appealed the district court's opinion that the appellee, Remarq Communities, Inc., "could not be held liable for direct copyright infringement merely because it provided access to a newsgroup containing infringing material . . . [and] could not be held liable for contributory infringement because ALS Scan failed to comply with the notice requirements set forth in the DMCA." *Id.* at 621.

Facts

ALS Scan, Inc. ("ALS") produces and markets "adult" materials which are distributed to paying subscriber by way of the internet, CD-ROMs, and video tapes. *Id.* at 620. Remarq Communities, Inc. ("Remarq") "is an online Internet service provider that provides access to its subscribing members" to online newsgroups. *Id.*

ALS discovered that two of Remarq's newsgroups contained ALS copyrighted materials and subsequently requested that Remarq "cease carrying [the] newsgroups" that violated the ALS copyrights. *Id.* at 620–21. Remarq refused to comply with ALS' request and informed ALS that it would only remove individual infringing items and only after ALS had identified them "with sufficient specificity." *Id.* at 621.

Question Presented

To what extent must notice comply with the prescription provided in the DCMA to deny a service provider the safe harbor defense?

Discussion

In order to qualify for the "safe harbor" provision under the DMCA, a service provider must show that:

(1) it has neither actual knowledge that its system contains infringing materials nor an awareness of facts or circumstances from which infringement is apparent, or its has expeditiously removed or disabled access to infringing material upon obtaining actual knowledge or infringement; (2) it receives no financial benefit directly attributable to infringing activity; and (3) it responded expeditiously to remove or disable access to material claimed to be infringing after receiving from the copyright holder a notification conforming with [the] requirements of [the DMCA]. *Id.* at 623.

The DMCA strives to balance the burden of protecting copyrights between service providers and copyright holders. *Id.* at 625. So long as the service provider has no actual or constructive knowledge of infringement using its system, the service provider is immune from liability. *Id.* However, once a service provider is made aware that third parties are using the system to infringe copyrights, then the burden shifts from the copyright holder to the service provider to "disable the infringing matter." *Id.* In order to achieve this balance "the DMCA requires that a copyright owner put the service provider on notice in a detailed manner but allows notice by means that comport with the prescribed format only 'substantially,' rather than perfectly." *Id.*

In this case, ALS provided Remarq with a written communication that identified sufficiently two sites whose "sole purpose" was to publish ALS' copyrighted material, indicated that virtually all of the material at these two sites was ALS copyrighted material, and provided Remarq with the exact Web address of the infringing sites. *Id.*

Holding

In order to comply with the notification provisions of the DMCA, a copyright holder must only comply "substantially" to defeat a service provider's "safe harbor" defense.

DMCA TIME LINE

The DMCA time line encompasses the years 1993–1998. Here are the highlights at this tumultuous half-decade.

Year	Activities
1993	Clinton Administration develops Agenda for Action: National Information Infrastructure (NII)
1994	NII Green Paper Department of Commerce organizes Conference on Fair Use (CONFU)
1995	NII White Paper: "The Report of the Working Group on Intellectual Property Rights" Initial congressional hearings on legislative reform Copyright Term Legislation Advances

(cont'd.)

Year	Activities
1996	CONFU strives to develop fair use guidelines World Intellectual Property Organization (WIPO) Diplomatic Conference adopts Treaties on digital rights
1997	House hearings on WIPO Treaties and digital legislation Limitation on liability for Online Service Providers advances
1998	Senate hearings on WIPO Treaties legislation renamed DMCA CONFU ends without adoption of guidelines DMCA enacted into law Copyright Term Extension enacted into law

1993   When the Clinton administration took office, one of the top priorities was to bring a new order to what was developing as the National Information Infrastructure ("NII"). It established a task force within governmental agencies and prepared an agenda for action. The goal was to define U.S. priorities and action points for domestic and international legal reform. The Internet in those days was clearly growing into an international communications medium, but its full potential remained open to speculation.

1994   In 1994, the NII Task Force, spearheaded by the Department of Commerce ("DOC"), published a *Green Paper*, calling for public input on the need for expanded regulation of the digital environment. In fulfilling its responsibilities, the DOC, led by the Commissioner of the U.S. Patent and Trademark Office, held public hearings and initiated a Conference on Fair Use ("CONFU"), designed ultimately to develop guidelines for use of copyright works in numerous educational settings.

1995   Following many hours of hearings and receipt of reams of comments, the NII Task Force released *The Report of the Working Group on Intellectual Property Rights*. The Report, dubbed the *White Paper*, stressed that U.S. copyright law was substantially fit for handling most important issues in the digital context; however, like a well-worn suit, some tailoring was needed to keep it fitting just right. The core recommendations included—

(a) expanding the exclusive rights of copyright owners to include the right of transmission;

(b) updating the library exemption in section 108 to permit making three copies of a work and allowing digital as well as facsimile copies;

(c) creating new prohibitions on devices or services designed to circumvent mechanisms which protect the rights of copyright owners and which affect newly recognized copyright management information; and

(d) establishing a new limitation on reproduction to help the visually impaired.

While the *White Paper* received mixed reviews, congressional committees held hearings on the legislative proposals. Concurrently, an international diplomatic copyright conference was planned by the World Intellectual Property Organization ("WIPO") 1996. Some legislators strenuously urged the DOC not to get ahead of Congress; that is, Congress wanted to set U.S. Copyright policy, not follow DOC's lead.

At the same time the digital agenda was being discussed, copyright owners pressed Congress for another legal reform—a 20-year extension of the term of protection from life of the author plus 50 (75 years in the case of work for hire) to life plus 70 (95 years for work for hire). The impetus for this reform stemmed from the goal of the copyright owners to secure protection in the U.S. equal to that provided by European countries. Noting that U.S. authors could not benefit in Europe from the full protection of European law unless U.S. law protected works for the same duration, term extension advocates urged expanding the term in U.S. law. The rationale of looking to European law enhanced the impetus toward copyright reform based on the notion of *harmonization*, i.e., bringing the copyright laws of all nations into general equilibrium. This notion supported the principle that the Berne Copyright Treaty, the leading international agreement covering copyrights, needed to be updated to meet the challenges that new technology posed to copyright.

Regarding term extension, the library community raised the specter of significant loss of rights to use works in the public domain. Once the term of copyright protection expires, users are free to take and republish or distribute works without prior approval of the author. The longer the term of protection, the longer clearance to use is required. The Register of Copyrights was delegated by the congressional committees to supervise discussions aimed at allowing libraries a limited right to use works during the last twenty years of any extended term.

1996   There was much public discussion about the copyright issues raised in the *White Paper*. Continued hearings in Congress and meetings of CONFU focused on how U.S. copyright law should be reformed. At the conclusion of the year, a Diplomatic Conference was held in Geneva under the auspices of the WIPO to consider three treaties:

(a) one proposed amending Berne along the lines set forth in the NII Report in order to develop an international consensus on treatment of copyright in a digital world;

(b) another urged adding additional protections for performers and producers of phonograms (sound recordings); and

(c) a third set forth standards for protection of databases as developed in U.S. and European legislative initiatives.

The Diplomatic Conference was heavily lobbied by commercial and public interest parties and resulted in the adoption of amendments to Berne (WIPO Treaty) and the Phonograms Treaty, but in the tabling of the Sui Generis Database Treaty.

1997 Following the return of diplomats, Congress began in earnest to consider core issues, including proposals to prohibit circumvention of technological protection measures, to protect a copyright management information system, and to modify copyright law to comply with the adopted WIPO and Phonograms Treaties. Also, high on the list of key issues was creation of a limitation on liability for "online service providers," those entities that link users to the Internet. A serious legal question had developed as to their liability for infringements that subscribers placed online. Although the OSPs did not place the content online, they greatly facilitated widespread public access. Their exposure to copyright liability had emerged as one of the pivotal brakes on developing the Internet to the next level as the communication medium of the 21st century. Under the direction of the House Judiciary Subcommittee on Copyrights, representatives of content owners, service providers, libraries, and education met over a period of months to hammer out the elements of a legal structure for OSPs. Also, the legislative agenda contained an update of the library exemptions and a focused database initiative.

1998 By 1998, it became apparent that passing the WIPO Treaty and addressing database issues were at the top of the legislative agenda for the administration and the Congress. Sen. Hatch, chairman of the Senate Judiciary Committee, renamed the WIPO Treaty Implementing Legislation, as the Digital Millennium Copyright Act, thereby stressing its importance for U.S. copyright policy. The bill became the focal point of all legislative debate on copyright issues, and most particularly, OSP limitation on liability, anticircumvention, database, library exemptions, and term extension. Throughout the session, negotiations were ongoing to resolve disputes involving each of these issues. Database protection emerged as a pivotal issue for key copyright interests after DMCA passed the House of Representatives. Even though the Senate Judiciary Committee had not held any hearings on database, publishers and the Chairmen of the House Copyright Subcommittee and House Judiciary Committee insisted that a database bill be included in final settlement of the DMCA.

Updating laws relating to distance education also developed as an important part of the educational agenda. The concept of reforming the limitation on public performance and display of copyrighted works in educational settings to enable their use in distance learning courses gained interest among key senators. However, with the legislative clock ticking to the final hours, there simply was not enough time to work through all the complex issues. So, with the commitment of Senators Hatch and Leahy that the matter would be addressed in the future, a provision requiring the Register of Copyrights to study the problem was drafted. Her Report, released a few years later, led to passage of The TEACH Act in 2002.

Equally important, politics played a role in the final developments of the DMCA. Although copyright jurisdiction belongs to the House and Senate Judiciary Committees, the impact of the legislation on commerce resulted in joint referral of the DMCA to the House Commerce Committee. This second House deliberative body played a crucial role in formulating the final policy of the DMCA. In particular, the Commerce Committee's staff managed direct negotiations between content owners and libraries and educational interests over the relationship between fair use (as well as other statutory copyright limitations) and the anticircumvention rules. This part of the DMCA's ultimate structure was laid out in these negotiations.

The other important development throughout most of the period of legislative consideration of the WIPO bills was the emergence of coalitions of disparate groups with joint purposes. For the library community, participation in the Digital Future Coalition brought in regular planning with device manufacturers (who fought limits on equipment) and certain publishers (who depended on access to factual information to develop their own works). This coalition helped devise a compromise strategy on anticircumvention and develop an alternative to the House-passed database bill. Following weeks of Senate-supervised negotiations, the Database Title was dropped from the final legislation.

Also in 1998, the CONFU process ended without the emergence of formal adoption of fair use guidelines. As the details implementing fair use were assessed, no consensus on final parameters was devised. Moreover, the parties in negotiations, content owners on the one hand, and libraries, educators, and other users on the other, failed to reach agreement on the ultimate purpose of the guidelines; that is, whether they were "safe harbor" standards (minimum standards that by consensus all interested parties could agree constituted fair use) or whether they were the maximum standards for fair use.

As 1998 drew to a close, the DMCA was passed by Congress and signed into law by President Clinton. It included provisions calling for a prohibition on circumvention of technological measures limiting access to digital works, copyright management rules which form the basis of digital rights management systems, amendment of the library limitation, and creation of an online service provider limitation on liability. In separate legislation, a 20-year extension to the copyright term was approved.

ELEKTRA ENTERTAINMENT GROUP, INC. V. DOES 1-9,
US DIST. LEXIS 23560 (S.D.N.Y. 2004)

Parties

The plaintiffs "are major recording companies who own copyrights in sound recordings." *Id.* at *1–*2. The defendants are or were college students who actively used a peer-to-peer file sharing system to offer copyrighted music to other network users for download. *Id.* at *2.

Facts

The plaintiffs alleged that they found the defendants openly disseminating copyrighted material over peer-to-peer networks. *Id.* at *3. However, even though the plaintiffs were able to collect information about the actions of the defendants they were unable to determine the name, address, or other contact information beyond the Internet Protocol ("IP") address that each of the defendants used to access the Internet. *Id.* at *4. The plaintiffs ascertained that each of the defendants was accessing the Internet through NYU and obtained a subpoena to compel NYU to release the contact information of each of the defendants to the plaintiffs. *Id.* at *4. In accordance with its privacy policy, NYU has contacted each of the defendants prior to releasing the information and has informed them that the plaintiff is seeking their contact information. *Id.* at *4–*5. In response to this notification, Doe No. 7 has filed a motion to quash the subpoena. *Id.* at *3.

Question Presented

Does Doe No. 7 and those similarly situated have a First Amendment right to privacy on the Internet which would overcome the subpoena to determine his or her identity?

Discussion

The Court recognized that "the First Amendment protects anonymous speech" and that this protection extends to anonymous speech on the Internet. *Id.* at *6 (quoting *Sony Music Entertainment Inc. v. Does 1-40*, 326 F. Supp. 2d 556 (S.D.N.Y. 2004)). However, the Court continues to explain that the First Amendment "does not protect copyright infringement." *Id.* at *6 (internal citations omitted).

In this case, the use of a peer-to-peer network to disseminate copyrighted material qualified as speech, however, only in a limited fashion. *Id.* at *8. Since the speech was not political in nature and "not seeking to communicate a thought or convey an idea" it only qualifies for a lesser degree of protection under the First Amendment. *Id.* at *8–*9 (internal citations omitted).

The Court evaluated five factors in determining if the defendant's identities were protected by the First Amendment.

> (1) whether plaintiff's have made "a concrete showing of a prima facie claim of actionable harm"; (2) the "specificity of the discovery request"; (3) "the absence of alternative means to obtain the subpoenaed information"; (4) "a central need to obtain the subpoenaed information to advance the claim"; and (5) "the party's expectation of privacy." *Id.* at *9–*10 (internal citations omitted).

The Court found that each of the factors favored the disclosure of the identity of the defendants. *Id.* at *10–*13. In addition to the evidence presented through screen shots (electronic copies of the computer screen) indicating that the defendants intended to share the files with peer-to-peer subscribers and not solely back up their own music on their computers, the "plaintiff's discovery request is sufficiently specific" in seeking only to discover the identities of the defendants with specific dates and times. *Id.* at *12. Furthermore, the public information available about the defendant leads the plaintiff back to NYU and no closer to discovering the defendant's identities making disclosure the only means for obtaining this information. *Id.* Finally, without this information, the plaintiffs will not be able to serve process upon the defendants and commence the suit and the defendants are not entitled to more than a minimal expectation of privacy due to NYU's clear policy that they will comply with civil subpoenas. *Id.* at *12–*13.

Holding

The identities of users of an Internet service is not protected from disclosure by the First Amendment if the following five factors weigh in favor of disclosure:

> (1) whether plaintiff's have made "a concrete showing of a prima facie claim of actionable harm"; (2) the "specificity of the discovery request"; (3) "the absence of alternative means to obtain the subpoenaed information"; (4) "a central need to obtain the subpoenaed information to advance the claim"; and (5) "the party's expectation of privacy." *Id.* at *9–*10 (internal citations omitted).

ELLISON V. ROBERTSON, 357 F.3D 1072 (9TH CIR. 2004)

Parties

The appellant, Harlan Ellison, appealed "the district court's summary judgment dismissal of his copyright infringement action against" the appellees, Stephen Robertson and America Online, Inc. ("AOL"), arising from the distribution of copies of some of Ellison's short stories via a peer-to-peer network. *Id.* at 1074.

Facts

Mr. Robertson scanned copies of Mr. Ellison's stories and uploaded them into an online newsgroup where they became available to readers of the newsgroup world-wide. *Id.* at 1075. Once Mr. Ellison became aware of this infringement of his copy-rights he notified via e-mail both the local service provider where the materials were posted (Tehama County Online) and AOL of the infringing activity. *Id.* The notification sent by Mr. Ellison complied with the DMCA. *Id.*

AOL changed its e-mail address in 1999 but failed to register the change until April 2000. *Id.* at 1077.

Question Presented

Can a failure by the service provider to provide an effective e-mail address for no-tification of copyright violation raise a triable issue as to whether the service provider had reason to know of the copyright infringement?

Discussion

In order for a plaintiff to prevail on a claim of contributory copyright infringe-ment, the plaintiff must demonstrate that the service provider had actual or con-structive knowledge of the infringing activity and that the service provider "materially contributed to another's infringement." *Id.* at 1077–78.

In this case, the court determined that a triable issue of fact exists as to whether AOL had reason to know of the infringing occurring on its system due to the po-tentially unreasonable manner in which AOL changed its e-mail address devoted to copyright infringement notification. *Id.* at 1077.

Holding

A service provider which fails to provide a valid e-mail for notification of infring-ing activity occurring on its system may be held to have had reason to know of in-fringing activity. *Id.* at 1077–78.

METRO-GOLDWYN-MAYER STUDIOS INC. ET AL. V. GROKSTER, LTD., ET AL., 125 S. CT. 2764 (2005)

Parties

Metro-Goldwyn-Mayer Inc. ("MGM") and other copyright holders, the appellants, appealed the opinion of the United States Court of Appeals for the 9th Cir. which barred their claim of copyright infringement based upon secondary and vicarious liability against Grokster, Ltd., et al. ("Grokster and StreamCast"), the appellees.

Facts

Grokster, Ltd. and StreamCast Networks, Inc. provide software that permits peer-to-peer sharing of computer files. *Id.* at 2770. Peer-to-peer file sharing is defined by the Court as sharing between individual uses without a central server serving as an intermediary for the transaction. *Id.* One of the main uses of this software was the transmission of copyright-protected music and video files without the permission of the copyright holder. *Id.* at 2770–71. In light of this infringing use, "[a] group of copyright holders . . . sued Grokster and StreamCast alleging that they knowingly and intentionally distributed their software to enable users to reproduce and distribute the copyrighted works in violation of the Copyright Act . . ." *Id.* at 2771.

While there are differences in the mechanics of the software provided by Grokster (a central computer called a supernode indexes all of the files available and directs requesting computers to the proper provider) and StreamCast (there is no indexing supernode and computers communicate with each other directly) each of the company's networks provides access to a significant amount of copyright-protected material. *Id.* While Grokster and StreamCast were passive recipients of information, they each took affirmative action to encourage infringing behavior. *Id.* at 2773–74. Each of the companies have answered requests for information regarding playing copyrighted material on an individuals machine. *Id.* The companies presented themselves to users as an alternative to Napster. *Id.* Furthermore, each of the companies earned revenue through the sale of advertising space and therefore benefited from the increase in advertising space value lent by the access to free copyrighted material. *Id.* at 2774. Lastly, "there is no evidence that either company made an effort to filter copyrighted material from users' downloads or otherwise impede the sharing of copyrighted files." *Id.*

The District Court and the Court of Appeals both held that both Grokster and StreamCast were not liable for the infringement because they did not actively infringe MGM's copyright. *Id.* at 2774–75. Furthermore, the Court of Appeals, relying upon *Sony Corp. of America v. Universal City Studios, Inc.*, 464 U.S. 417 (1984), opined that neither of the companies was liable for contributory copyright infringement due to the substantial noninfringing uses of the software and the absence of actual knowledge of infringing activity. *Id.* at 2775.

Question Presented

"[U]nder what circumstances [is] the distributor of a product capable of both lawful and unlawful use is liable for act of copyright infringement by third parties using the product." *Id.* at 2770.

Discussion

The general principle behind assigning contributory liability for copyright infringement is cited from *Gershwin Pub. Corp. v. Columbia Artists Management, Inc.*, 443 F.2d 1159, 1162 (2d Cir. 1971) indicating that it is "intentionally inducing or encouraging direct infringement." *Id.* at 2776. The Court further provides that vicarious liability in copyright infringement is defined as "profiting directly from direct infringement while declining to exercise a right to stop or limit it" citing *Shapiro, Bernstein & Co. v. H.L. Green Co.*, 316 F.2d 304, 307 (2d Cir. 1963). *Id.* Beginning with these statements of liability, the Court proceeded to discuss the case in light of *Sony Corp. v. Universal City Studios*, 464 U.S. 417 (1984) which held that secondary liability is barred when based upon "presuming or imputing intent to cause infringement solely from the design or distribution of a product capable of substantial lawful use, which the distributor knows is in fact used for infringement." *Id.* at 2778. The Supreme Court read *Sony* more narrowly than the lower courts to protect only those distributors who not only distributed products possessing a substantial noninfringing uses but also did not have "specific knowledge of infringement." *Id.* Additionally, vicarious liability extends to encompass situations "where evidence goes beyond a product's characteristics or the knowledge that it may be put to infringing uses, and shows statements or actions directed to promoting infringement . . ." *Id.* at 2779. From this the Court adopts a standard for inducement that explains that "one who distributes a device with the object of promoting its use to infringe copyright, as shown by clear expression or other affirmative steps taken to foster infringement, is liable for the resulting acts of infringement by third parties." *Id.* at 2780.

In this case, both Grokster and StreamCast actively promoted the use of their products to infringe copyright. *Id.* at 2780–81. The companies "beamed" messages to potential users and distributed electronic newsletters encouraging potential users to their products. *Id.* Additionally, StreamCast, predicting the elimination of Napster marketed its product as an alternative to accomplish the same tasks. *Id.* Generally, the Court found that each company aimed its product to meet a "known source of demand for copyright infringement," failed "to develop filtering tools or other mechanisms to diminish the infringing activity using their software," and the revenue earned by the sales of advertising space are a contributing factor toward the establishment of an unlawful intent. *Id.* at 2781–82.

Holding

The Court held that "one who distributes a device with the object of promoting its use to infringe copyright, as shown by clear expression or other affirmative steps taken to foster infringement, is liable for the resulting acts of infringement by third parties." *Id.* at 2780.

Concurrence by Justice Ginsburg, Chief Justice Rheinquist, and Justice Kennedy

This notable concurrence evaluated the use of the *Sony* standard differently and while agreeing with the majority would have instead of basing the discussion on inducement would have based their assessment on the substantiality of the non-infringing uses of the products. *Id.* at 2785–86. Since the evidence indicated that it was known that the products were being used "overwhelmingly" for the infringement of copyright, this concurrence would have found that the District Court erred in awarding summary judgment to Grokster and StreamCast based upon the significant non-infringing uses of their products. *Id.* at 2785–86.

Concurrence by Justices Breyer, Stevens, and O'Connor

Reponding to Justice Ginsburg, Chief Justice Rehnquist, and Justice Kennedy's concurrence, Justices Breyer, Stevens, and O'Connor opine that the Court of Appeals was not incorrect in upholding the summary judgment issued by the District Court because *Sony* defined substantial non-infringing uses to be "capable of." *Id.* at 2789. Relying upon the potential market for Grokster and StreamCast's products for non-infringing uses, Justices Breyer, Stevens, and O'Connor cannot agree with the assertion that the product does not have significant noninfringing uses. *Id.* at 2790.

HENDRICKSON V. EBAY INC., 165 F. SUPP. 2D 1082 (C.D. CAL. 2001)

Parties

eBay, the defendant, is a popular internet service which provides users with a forum for auctioning and purchasing products. Hendrickson, the plaintiff, is the owner of the copyright to a documentary entitled "Manson." *Id.* at 1084.

Facts

eBay provides a forum for prospective sellers and buyers to negotiate and communicate and products and services. *Id.* Each user of the system registers with eBay and is issued a user name and a password that allows for individual identification. *Id.* Sellers post listings of the products or services that they are offering for sale and buyers may bid on these items or purchase for a fixed price if the seller permits this option. *Id.*

Mr. Hendrickson contacted eBay by letter dated December 14, 2000, and demanded that pirated copies of a documentary entitled "Manson" be removed from the auctioning service's Web site. *Id.* However, Mr. Hendrickson's letter failed to specifically indicate which copies of the documentary "Manson" infringed his copyright. *Id.* Accordingly, eBay responded to Mr. Hendrickson with a request for more information, a notice that he must comply with the provisions of the Digital Millennium Copyright Act ("DMCA"), and an invitation to join eBay's VeRO system. *Id.* at 1084–85.

Subsequently, Mr. Hendrickson filed two lawsuits claiming copyright infringement. *Id.* at 1085.

Question Presented

Do the safe harbor provisions of the Digital Millennium Copyright Act ("DMCA") protect an Internet service provider "when a copyright owner seeks to hold the [provider] secondarily liable for copyright infringement by its [users]." *Id.* at 1083–84.

Discussion

In order to qualify for immunity under the DMCA first the defendant must meet the definition of "service provider." A service provider is defined as "a provider of online services or network access, or the operator of facilities therefore." *Id.* at 1088 (quoting 17 U.S.C. § 512(k)(1)(B)). In this case, there is no dispute over whether eBay is a service provider. *Id.* at 1088.

Furthermore, to qualify for immunity under the DMCA, eBay must demonstrate that it falls into one of four categories set forth by statute. In this case the record demonstrated that eBay fell into the category established by 17 U.S.C. § 512(c). Under 17 U.S.C. § 512(c) an Internet service provider is immune from liability if it can demonstrate that it did not have actual knowledge of the storage of infringing material on its system or knowledge of "facts or circumstances from which infringing activity is apparent." *Id.* at 1088 (quoting 17 U.S.C. § 512(c)(1)(A)(i)–(ii)). In the alternative, the Internet service provider must be able to demonstrate that it removed or disabled access to the infringing material expeditiously upon obtaining knowledge or facts which make the infringing activity apparent. *Id.* (citing 17 U.S.C. § 512(c)(1)(A)(iii)). Next, the service provider must be able to demonstrate that it did "not receive any financial benefit directly attributable to the infringing activity." *Id.* (quoting 17 U.S.C. § 512(c)(1)(B)). Lastly, the provider must be able to show that once it has received notification which substantially complies with the notification requirements of the DMCA that the provider expeditiously removed the infringing material. *Id.* (citing 17 U.S.C. § 512(c)(1)(C)).

Under the third requirement of immunity, the service provider is obligated to remove infringing material upon proper notification. Proper notification requires that the copyright owner provide:

(1) a physical or electronic signature;

(2) "identification of the copyrighted work claimed to have been infringed";

(3) "identification of the material that is claimed to be infringing or to be the subject of infringing activity and that is to be removed or access to which is to be disabled, and information reasonably sufficient to permit the service provider to locate the material";

(4) information that would allow the service provider to contact the copyright owner;

(5) "a statement that the complaining party has a good faith belief that use of the material in the manner complained of is not authorized by the copyright owner, its agent, or the law"; and

(6) "a statement that the information in the notification is accurate, and under penalty of perjury, that the complaining party is authorized to act on behalf of the copyright owner." *Id.* at 1089.

In the court's analysis, the Court found that the notification sent by the plaintiff to eBay failed to substantially comply with the requirements. *Id.* at 1089–92. The Court indicated that the plaintiff failed to provide a statement attesting to good faith and accuracy of the claim. *Id.* at 1089. In addition, the Court found that the plaintiff failed to adequately identify the material that was claimed to be the subject of the infringing activity. *Id.* at 1089–92.

Under the first requirement of immunity, the Court determined that since the notification provided to eBay by the plaintiff was insufficient under the requirements of the DMCA, eBay did not have actual or constructive knowledge of the copyright infringement. *Id.* at 1092–93.

Finally, the second requirement of immunity requires eBay to demonstrate that it had no right or ability to control the infringing activity. *Id.* at 1093. The Court rests upon the nature of eBay as an auctioning service where no infringing materials are posted or distributed through the site, the actual sales are consummated off-line, and which does not actively participate in the listing, bidding, sale, or delivery of any of the products or services to evidence that eBay does not have any right or ability to control the infringing activity short of removing a listing from the site. *Id.* at 1094.

Holding

The safe harbor provisions of the DMCA will immunize an Internet service provider from liability when a copyright owner seeks to hold the provider secondarily liable for infringement so long as the provider complies with the requirements of the DMCA.

IN RE: AIMSTER COPYRIGHT LITIGATION, 252 F. SUPP. 2D 634 (N.D. ILL. 2002)

Parties

In this case, owners of copyrighted music, the plaintiffs, sued Mr. John Deep, defendant, on theories of contributory and vicarious liability claiming that use of his Internet services (Aimster and Madster) infringe their copyrights. *Id.* at 645.

Facts

Aimster and Madster are services that enable peer-to-peer sharing of music files via the Internet. *Id.* at 645–46. While individuals who swap files are directly infringing, the plaintiffs are seeking to hold Mr. Deep and his services liable for contributory infringement due to the impracticability of locating all of the individual users who may have infringed the plaintiffs' copyrights. *Id.*

Generally, someone who wishes to utilize Aimster must download the appropriate software from Aimster's Web site and then register a username. *Id.* at 642. Aimster, which piggybacks off of America On-Line Instant Messager ("AOL IM"), designates all other Aimster users as "buddies" and therefore allows Aimster users to search through each other's computer hard drives for wanted files amongst those selected for sharing. *Id.* An Aimster member who is looking for a specific file need only log on to Aimster and then search for the file desired. *Id.* Aimster will return up to 500 hits of other users who have the file and have designated it for sharing. *Id.* In addition to providing the software for the interconnectivity, including the status of the file during the download, Aimster's system encrypts all files that are swapped back and forth. *Id.* at 643.

Additional services that Aimster provided included a tutorial on its Web site that instructed users on how to circumvent copyright, a bulletin board for users that appeared to have been used to share information on where to find copyrighted materials, and a special fee-based system that collocated copyrighted music for download. *Id.* at 643–44.

Question Presented

May Aimster be held liable via contributory and/or vicarious liability as the distributor of a product used by a third party to infringe copyright?

Does Aimster qualify as a "service provider" under the definitions provided by the Digital Millennium Copyright Act?

Discussion

Generally, injunctive relief is available "where it is reasonable for the purposes of restraining or preventing infringement of copyright." *Id.* at 647 (citing 17 U.S.C. § 502(a)) In this case, the plaintiffs sought a preliminary injunction to bar the use of Aimster and thereby stop third party infringement of their copyrights. In order to prevail and be granted a preliminary injunction, the plaintiffs had to demonstrate that: "(1) its case has some likelihood of success on the merits; (2) that no adequate remedy at law exists; (3) it will suffer irreparable harm if the injunction is not granted." *Id.* at 647.

First examining the likelihood of success on the merits, the court examined the claims of direct infringement, contributory infringement, and vicarious liability. *Id.* at 648. The court concluded that there is a high likelihood of success on the claim of direct infringement based on showings by the plaintiffs that "(1) they own the applicable copyrights and (2) there was unauthorized copying of the elements of the work that are original." *Id.* at 648. In this case, the plaintiffs' "unequivocally" demonstrated that Aimster's users "are engaged in direct copyright infringement" and that they are the owners of the infringed copyrights. *Id.* at 648. The defendant did not challenge the unauthorized copying being accomplished through the Aimster system, rather the defendant challenged the claim based upon the Audio Home Recording Act of 1992 which precludes "actions based on the non-commercial use of a device to record digital or analog music recordings." *Id.* at 649 (citing 17. U.S.C. § 1008). However the court rejected this argument because the defense was designed to permit individuals to make copies of their music for their own personal, private, noncommercial use. *Id.* at 649. In this case, the copies being made were for distribution and, therefore, failed to fall within the defense. *Id.*

The Court next turned to the claim of contributory infringement. The evidence presented to the Court, including cease and desist letters from the defendants, indicated that the plaintiff had knowledge of the infringement. *Id.* at 650. Although the defendants argued that they did not have any specific knowledge of infringement, knowledge as to which users were actually infringing copyrights, due to the encryption software that they use to protect files sent between users, the Court determined that there is no precedential authority that this level of specificity is needed. *Id.* at 650–51. Additionally, the evidence presented to the Court was found to support the claim that the defendants "materially contributed to the underlying infringement" by way of advertising and the provision of services that made the infringement feasible. *Id.* at 651–52. While the defendants argue that this was an unintended result of the program and that the service possessed substantial noninfringing uses, the Court was not swayed. *Id.* at 652–54.

Under the claim of vicarious liability, the Court found that there was a likelihood of success due to the defendants' ability to supervise the activity taking place on their system and that they had a "direct financial interest" in the infringing activities. *Id.* at 654–55.

As a defense, the defendants raise the safe harbors provided by the Digital Millennium Copyright Act ("DMCA"). As an initial matter the Court applied the definition of "service provider" to Aimster and determines that "Aimster is a service provider under the DMCA's definition in that it provides the routing of digital communications between its users." *Id.* at 657–58. However, the Court disagreed with the defendants' assertions that it is protected by the safe harbor provisions because while the defendants had adopted a repeat infringer policy, they had not implemented this policy effectively. *Id.* at 658. Furthermore, under the transitory communications safe harbor the defendants failed to establish that they served solely as a conduit for information because they provided searching services as well as expedited access to popular works. *Id.* at 659–60. The Court further determined that the system caching safe harbor was not applicable because the plaintiffs were not attempting to hold the defendants liable for the materials cached on the Aimster system. *Id.* at 660–61. Lastly, the defendants failed to meet the burdens outlined by the information location tools safe harbor. *Id.* at 661. In this case, the defendants could not demonstrate that they had no knowledge of circumstances "from which the infringing activity is apparent" nor could they argue that they did not receive any financial benefit from the infringing activity. *Id.*

After balancing the hardships associated with a preliminary injunction with the public interests, the Court determined that the injunction was an appropriate action. *Id.* at 665–66.

Holding

A company may be held liable via contributory and or vicarious liability for copyright infringement as the distributor of a product that is used by third parties to infringe copyrights. *Id.* at 654.

The DMCA defines "service provider" for the transitory communications safe harbor as:

> . . . an entity offering the transmission, routing, or providing of connections for digital online communications, between or among parties specified by a user, of material of the user's choosing, without modification of the content of the material as sent or received. *Id.* at 657 (quoting 17 U.S.C. § 512(k)(1)(A)).

The DMCA further defines "service provider" for the remainder of the safe harbor provisions as "a provider of online services or network access, or the operator of facilities therefore." *Id.* (quoting 17 U.S.C. § 512(k)(1)(B)). These definitions are drafted so broadly as to encompass virtually all online services.

PERFECT 10, INC. V. CYBERNET VENTURES, INC. ET AL., 213 F. SUPP. 2D 1146 (C.D. CAL. 2002)

Parties

The plaintiff, Perfect 10, Inc., which produces and distributes photographs of nude women by way of the Internet and a magazine, brought suit against the defendant, Cybernet Ventures, Inc., the operator of an Internet age verification service, for contributory and vicarious infringement of the plaintiff's copyright to the images it distributes. *Id.* at 1152.

Facts

The plaintiff sought a preliminary injunction to compel the defendant to stop linking to the plaintiff's copyrighted images. *Id.* at 1193–95. At the time of this suit, the plaintiff had created approximately 3,000 copyrighted images which it made available through its Web site and its magazine. *Id.* at 1157.

The defendant operates an age verification system called "Adult Check" which provides subscribers with a password with which they can access participating adult Web sites. *Id.* at 1157–58. Adult Check utilizes the customer's credit card as a proxy for age. *Id.* at 1157. While Adult Check maintains the passwords that customers use to access adult sites, it is not responsible for the content or running of the Web sites themselves. *Id.* at 1158. However, Adult Check does review Web sites prior to accepting them into their system. *Id.* at 1163–64.

Adult Check maintains policies which include policies against violation of copyright. *Id.* at 1160–62. However, the plaintiff alleged that this policy was not being enforced and located a number of Web sites accessed via Adult Check which displayed the plaintiff's copyrighted material without authorization. *Id.* at 1162–63. While the plaintiff did not provide notice to the defendant of the copyright infringement prior to filing this suit, the problems were brought to the defendant's attention by other copyright holders. *Id.* at 1169.

Question Presented

Does the failure to reasonably implement a policy to terminate repeat offenders a basis for denying a service provider immunity under the Digital Millennium Copyright Act ("DMCA")?

Discussion

The Court discussed the direct, vicarious, and contributory liability of the defendant as well as the availability of the safe harbor provisions of the DCMA to the defendant. Here only the availability of the safe harbor provisions are discussed.

To qualify for protection from vicarious or contributory copyright infringement liability under any of the four safe harbor provisions, the service provider must first demonstrate that it has:

> (1) adopt[ed] a policy that provides for the termination in appropriate circumstances of subscribers and account holders of the service provider's system or network who are repeat infringers; (2) reasonably implement[ed] the policy; and 3) inform[ed] subscribers and account holders of the service provider's system or network about the policy. *Id.* at 1174 (citing 17 U.S.C. § 512(i)).

The Court defined a reasonable policy as one which would provide for the termination of infringing user's access "at a minimum, [in] instances where a service provider is given sufficient evidence to create actual knowledge of blatant, repeat infringement by particular users, particularly infringement of a willful and commercial nature." *Id.* at 1177.

In this case, the Court found that the defendant failed to reasonably implement a policy to combat repeat copyright infringement stating that

> . . . Cybernet disclaims any intent to impose "impossible affirmative duties upon itself." In the context of this litigation, the Court sees this as an implicit argument that rooting out repeat infringers imposes such "impossible" duties and finds it runs against Cybernet's argument that it is actually trying to cope with repeat infringers. *Id.* at 1178.

Finally, the Court indicates that due to deficiencies with the defendant's notice procedures, direct financial benefit from the infringing activity, and lack of evidence that the defendant has ever expeditiously removed any infringing material, the defendant would likely not qualify for protection under any of the safe harbor provisions of the DMCA even if it met the first test of an implemented policy. *Id.* at 1179–82.

Holding

Failure to adopt and reasonably implement a policy to eliminate repeat copyright infringement is fatal to a claim of safe harbor under the DMCA.

RECORDING INDUSTRY ASSOCIATION OF AMERICA V. VERIZON INTERNET SERVICES INC., 351 F.3D 1229 (D.C. CIR. 2003)

Parties

The appellant, Verizon Internet Services Inc., is appealed the district court's rejection of its challenges to subpoenas issued under 17 U.S.C. § 512(h) by the appellee, Recording Industry Association of America ("RIAA"). *Id.* at 1231.

Facts

The most current generation of peer-to-peer ("P2P") file sharing systems do not rely upon a centralized computer system to direct users to the location of files. *Id.* at 1232. Instead, this newer generation permits users to search other users directly for the desired files. *Id.* With this advancement, RIAA began "to direct its anti-infringement efforts against individual users of P2P file sharing programs." *Id.* In order to succeed in their suits RIAA invoked the subpoena authority of § 512(h) of the Digital Millennium Copyright Act ("DMCA") to obtain the identity of suspected infringers from Internet service providers. *Id.*

In this case, RIAA sought the identities of users of an Internet service provided by Verizon. *Id.* Verizon refused to comply with the two subpoenas that RIAA served on them and challenged the subpoenas basing its refusal on the inapplicability of the subpoena provisions of the DMCA on a service provider that acts only as a conduit for activity and that does not store any infringing material on its system. *Id.* at 1233.

Question Presented

May the § 512(h) subpoena power of the DMCA be used to obtain the identities of individuals, which a copyright holder has reason to believe are infringing their copyright, from an online service provider which acts only as a conduit for information?

Discussion

Under the provisions of the DMCA, a copyright holder may utilize a subpoena to determine the identity of an infringer from an Internet service provider ("ISP"). *Id.* at 1232. The application for the subpoena must include:

> (1) a "notification of claimed infringement" identifying the copyrighted work(s) claimed to have been infringed and the infringing material or activity and providing information reasonably sufficient for the ISP to locate the material, all as further specified in § 512(c)(3)(A); (2) the proposed subpoena directed to the ISP; and (3) a sworn declaration that the purpose of the subpoena is "to obtain the identity of an alleged infringer and that such information will only be used for the purpose of protecting" rights under the copyright laws of the United States. *Id.* at 1232 (citing and quoting 17 U.S.C. §§ 512(h)(2)(A)–(C).

This subpoena authority must be viewed in the context of the four safe harbors that § 512(a)–(d) provide ISP's. *Id.* at 1234. Each safe harbor is designed to answer a different ISP situation. § 512(a) is directed at "transitory network communications" which include "transmitting, routing, or providing connections" to individuals and information that infringes copyrights. *Id.* § 512(b) provides for "system caching" which grants immunity to ISPs for infringing material that is stored on the ISP's system in a temporary manner. Id. § 512(c) grants immunity to an ISP for infringing material that is stored on the ISP's system "at the direction of users" so long as the ISP meets certain conditions. *Id.* The ISP must lack knowledge, not benefit financially, and move quickly to remove the infringing material when the ISP obtains knowledge. *Id.* (citing 17 U.S.C. § 512(c)(1)(A)–(C)). Lastly, § 512(d) provides protection for ISPs who link to Web sites and other materials that contain copyrighted materials "subject to the same conditions as in §§ 512(c)(1)(A)–(C)." *Id.*

It is important to note that the subpoena provisions of § 512(h) require that a copy of a notification of claimed infringement be provided as part of the application for subpoena. *Id.* For this notification to be effective it must comply with 17 U.S.C. § 512(c)(3)(A) which provides, in part, that the "material that is claimed to be infringing or to be the subject of infringing activity and that is to be removed or access to which is to be disabled, and information reasonable sufficient to permit the service provider to locate the material" must be provided. *Id.* at 1234–35 (citing and quoting 17 U.S.C. § 512(c)(3)(A)). Verizon argued that since they are not storing the material on their system RIAA cannot identify materials on Verizon's system and therefore cannot meet the requirements of § 512(c)(3)(A). *Id.*

RIAA argued that they must only "substantially" comply with § 512(c)(3)(A) which they argue is accomplished by providing the Internet protocol ("IP") address of the infringing user on the system. *Id.* at 1235–36.

The Court found that information was not sufficient under the notification procedure of § 512(c)(3)(A) stating that Congress intended that the term "substantially" means only "technical errors . . . such as misspelling a name" or "supplying an outdated area code." *Id.* at 1236 (quoting S. Rep. No. 105-190, at 47 (1998); H.R. Rep. No. 105-551 (II), at 56 (1998)). Here RIAA did not identify any material that could be blocked or removed from Verizon's system and therefore failed to meet the notification standard. *Id.* at 1236. The Court further found that the subpoena provisions applied to all of the safe harbors save the transmission safe harbor provided in § 512(a) because, as explained explained above, effective notification cannot be given to a service provider who only acts as a conduit because there is nothing stored that can be identified as infringing. *Id.* at 1237.

Holding

The Court held that the subpoena provisions of the DMCA could not be used to obtain the identities of infringing users from an ISP that acts solely as a conduit because the notification element of the application for the subpoena cannot be met.

▶Chapter 8

APPENDIX F

SAMPLE COPYRIGHT ASSIGNMENTS

Linking to Protected Works

Reproduced with permission by:
  The Copyrightsite.org
  Dr. Vivian H. Wright, Ph.D.
  Assistant Professor of Instructional Technology
  The University of Alabama

Key Ideas

What are the copyright implications of linking to other Web sites, especially links that bypass those sites' homepages?

Materials

- ▶ A word document including a number of links, especially deep links within Web sites.
- ▶ Internet-accessible computers
- ▶ A link to the copyright law

Background

An online teacher sends students to a link deep into a Web site to complete a lesson provided there. The Web site is operated by a vendor, who markets online instruction. There are hosts of excellent Web links available to support online learning and teaching. This particular teacher had found that she could substitute a vendor's lessons for her own. The link she provided bypassed the original vendor Web site with advertisements and instructions. Of course, she had no permission to do so. Is this violating copyright?

It would seem that the use of a link to a Web site would be harmless. In fact, one could argue that the links would increase the flow of traffic on the Web site. While this may be the case, the flow is counted, and advertisers are parked, on external sites. Bypassing those outer links has the potential to reduce the value of all associated links. The fair use measurement of value bring the infringement into question.

Then, there are cases that determine that while the link is not a copy, the selection of the link causes a copy to be made onto the RAM. And, the teacher does have ample time to obtain permission. Most likely, the case would not be in favor of the teacher.

The following cases make for interesting reading on deep linking:

▶ Ticketmaster Corp v. Tickets.com

▶ Washington Post v. Total News, Inc

▶ SNC Havas Numerique v. SA Kelijob

▶ Intellectual Reserve Inc. v. Utah Lighthouse Ministries, Inc.

Procedure

▶ Put students into groups.

▶ Provide each group with a list of Web sites, including deep links. Ask them to go to each site, and determine the following:

▶ How many links (or levels) are there between the given link and the homepage?

▶ How many advertisements are missed by using the deep link?

▶ Is there critical information on the skipped links?

▶ Which sites are likely protected under copyright law?

▶ Which are not likely protected?

Discussion

Discuss links and levels of links with the students. Then discuss the content changes as deeper links are made, especially in regard to marketing strategy. After the activity, have them share their findings as a group and discuss them.

Assessment

Have each student choose one of the sites explored and write a detailed analysis of the significance of skipping homepage information from both the linker's and the site owner's perspectives.

Copyright Lesson Plan

Reproduced with permission by:
   Laura Kaemming
   Christ the King School
   Toledo, OH

Topic

Copyright Laws

Suggested Grade Level

Eighth Grade

Objectives

1. Students will be introduced to and develop a basic understanding of copyright laws.
2. Students will identify examples of copyright infringement.

Materials

▶ *Music Alive* magazine (December 2000 issue);
▶ Musical excerpts from
  ▶ "Ice, Ice Baby" as performed by Vanilla Ice,
  ▶ "Under Pressure" as performed by Queen,
  ▶ "My Sweet Lord" as performed by George Harrison,
  ▶ "He's So Fine" as performed by The Chiffons,
  ▶ "I Want a New Drug" as performed by Huey Lewis and the News,
  ▶ "Ghostbusters" as performed by Pay Parker, Jr.;
▶ IUPI Checklist for Fair Use;
▶ Overheads;
▶ "Copyright" worksheet;
▶ "You Be the Judge" worksheets; and
▶ Written test

Procedure

Day One
  ▶ Students should answer pre-reading questions on "Copyright" worksheet, then discuss answers with classmates
  ▶ Students will read aloud the article entitled "Music as Intellectual Property— What's at Stake?" from the December 2000 issue of *Music Alive* magazine.
  (Students should answer remaining questions on "Copyright" worksheet.)

Day Two
  ▶ Students should share and discuss answers from "Copyright" worksheet,
  ▶ Discuss copyright rules/regulations, and fair use with students
  (Students should take notes based on presentation and overhead transparencies.)

Day Three
  ▶ Review copyright rules and regulations
  ▶ As a group, listen to/compare/discuss excerpts from the songs "Ice, Ice Baby" and "Under Pressure"
  ▶ Read/answer "You Be the Judge" worksheet while listening to musical excerpts (replay examples as needed)

Day Four
  ▶ Review fair use policy

▶ Discuss answers for "You Be the Judge" worksheet

▶ Oral Discussion: "Do you know of any other copyright cases in the field of music? What about in the movie industry? Elsewhere?"

Evaluation

Students will achieve both objectives through discussions and written assessments. Students must correctly answer at least 70% of items on graded worksheets and tests to receive a passing grade.

© 2001, Laura Kaemming, permission for reproduction nonprofit use only

COPYRIGHT

Copyright happens automatically as soon as a copy of the work is created. Just because you don't see the copyright symbol doesn't mean the work is "public domain" (you have the right to use it freely). In fact, the opposite is usually true. The symbol itself can provide the reader with important information including who owns the copyright and the first year of publication. A person does not have to register their work with the Copyright Office for action to be taken against a person infringing on that work; however it will help. Copyright registration is a public record and puts other people on notice.

The copyright "owner" has the exclusive rights to:

▶ reproduce the work

▶ prepare "spinoff" created from the work

▶ distribute copies or phonorecords (cassette tapes, CDs LPs, 45 RPMs as well as other formats) by sale or transfer of ownership, rental, lease, or lending

▶ perform the work publicly (for plays, musicals, poetry, choreography, pantomimes, movies, and other audiovisuals)

▶ display the work publicly (poems, musicals, plays, choreography, pantomimes, pictorial, graphics, sculptures, individual images from movies, and other audiovisual works)

▶ perform publicly (by digital audio transmission) sound recordings

They can also give permission for others to do the same.

Copyrights can be obtained for the following types of works:

▶ Literary (including computer programs)

▶ Musical (including accompanying lyrics)

▶ Dramatic (including accompanying music)

▶ Pantomimes and choreographic

▶ Pictorial, graphic, and sculpted (including maps)

▶ Motion picture and other audiovisual

▶ Sound recordings

▶ Architectural

Registration

Registering a work is a simple process. Send the following three items together in the same envelope.

1. A completed application form. (This can be found on the Copyright Office Web site at www.loc.gov/copyright.)
2. A $30 nonrefundable filing fee (effective through 6-30-02) for each application.
3. A nonreturnable copy of the work to be registered.

All three items MUST be sent in the same package! Just because your work is copyrighted in the U.S. does not mean it is throughout the world. Most countries offer some protection to foreign works under certain conditions. If you would like to see which countries maintain copyright relations with the U.S. visit the Copyright Office Web site mentioned above.

Length

Once you have obtained copyright protection, how long will it be safe? Currently once a work is created it is protected until 70 years after the author has died. If there are coauthors, the copyright lasts until 70 years after the last surviving author passes away. For works that were commissioned and those written under pseudonyms or whose authors are unknown, the copyright is effective 95 years from first publication or 120 years from creation—whichever is shortest. The author can sell their copyrights to another party (as was the case of Michael Jackson purchasing a large number of Beatles songs) and can even leave them to someone in their will.

© 2001, Laura Kaemming, permission for reproduction nonprofit use only

FAIR USE

If a person wishes to use part of someone else's work they have to obtain written permission from the author of that original work. Only in "fair use" cases do you not have to obtain this. The courts created fair use guidelines for teachers and students. This "policy" permits those of us working in the school setting to "borrow" parts of an original work without obtaining written permission from the author. There are four basic guidelines used for the fair use policy—purpose, nature, amount, and effect. The Copyright Management Center at Indiana University has a great checklist for fair use. You can view this whole document by going to their Web site at http://www.iupui.edu/%7Ecopyinfo/fuchecklist.html. Below are some of the acceptable and unacceptable uses mentioned on this site.

Purpose	Nature	Amount	Effect
Acceptable Teaching, research, news reporting	Acceptable Factual, important to education	Acceptable Small quantity, portion is not crucial to entire work	Acceptable No major effect on the market, user legally owns a copy of original work
Illegal Making money from sale of work, don't give credit to author of original work	Illegal Very creative work (art, music, literary, films, plays), fiction	Illegal Large or entire work used, the part of the original used is crucial to new work's success	Illegal Could replace selling of original, many copies made, used for a long time, made it available on the Web

* United States Government works are considered public domain and may be used freely.

Generally speaking up to 10 percent of a work can be used. See the chart below for more clarification.

Motion Media	Text Material	Music, Lyrics and Music Video	Illustrations and Photographs
Up to 10% or 3 minutes, whichever is less	Up to 10% or 1000 whichever is less; an entire poem of less than 250 words may be used but no more than 3 excerpts from a poet	Up to 10% but no more than 30 seconds of the music and lyrics, alterations to a musical work can't change the basic melody or character of work	An entire photo or drawing may be used but no more than 5 images from the same artist, or when from a published collective work not more than 10% or 15 images, whichever is less

© 2001, Laura Kaemming, permission for reproduction nonprofit use only

COPYRIGHT WORKSHEET ﹅

Name _____ Class _____ Date _____

DIRECTIONS: Answer the following questions.

Pre-Reading:

1. Have you ever visited a Web site such as Napster? _____
2. Have you ever downloaded a song from one of these sites? _____
3. If you did, did you ever buy the CD that particular song was on? _____
4. Do you think people should be allowed to copy items such as songs and movies without paying for them? Why? Explain your answer.

_____

_____

5. Do you own a CD burner? _____

6. Have you ever copied a song onto a CD or cassette? _____

7. What does the symbol © mean ? _____

Read the magazine article (pages 10–11) from the December 2000 issue of *Music Alive*. Then answer the following questions.

8. According to the article, why should the "record industry share some of the blame for the Napster/MP3 revolution?"

    _____

    _____

9. How much money did MP3 have to pay in damages to Universal Music Group?

    _____

10. Do you think this was a fair estimate? Explain.

    _____

    _____

11. Who does Metallica say "free downloads" will hurt the most? Why?

    _____

    _____

12. When you purchase a CD, who are all the people/groups that receive money from it being sold?_____

    _____

© 2001, Laura Kaemming, permission for reproduction nonprofit use only

YOU BE THE JUDGE!

Name _____Class _____ Date _____

CASE 1:

In 1976, ex-Beatle, George Harrison, was found guilty of copyright infringement for his hit single, "My Sweet Lord." Bright Tunes Music Corporation had obtained the copyright for the 1963 hit, "He's So Fine" which was written by Ronald Mack and originally performed by The Chiffons. Did George Harrison borrow his musical ideas from Mack's hit song? Judge for yourself. Look at the motifs on the overhead and listen to parts of the two songs.

RATING SYSTEM:

5=Exactly the same 4=Very similar 3=Somewhat alike 2=Barely the same 1=Not alike in any way

Melody: _____

Harmony/Chordal Structure: _____

Rhythm: _____

Tempo: _____

Lyrics: _____

Instruments: _____

1. How else are the two songs similar? _____

_____

2. How are the two songs different?

_____

_____

CASE 2:

In 1981, Huey Lewis (Hugh Cregg) accused Ray Parker, Jr., of copyright infringement after Parker released his single, "Ghostbusters." After more than 10 years of arguing, the two artists settled their case in private. Parker never publicly admitted his guilt but he did agree to pay an undisclosed amount to Lewis for "damages." The issue was brought up again during the spring of 2001. Lewis had taped a VH-1 *Behind the Music* segment and disclosed details of the 1995 settlement. Parker filed a lawsuit against Lewis in March 2001. Parker claims Lewis broke the "confidentiality agreement." Apparently part of the original settlement banned them both from revealing any information that was not in a press release they jointly issued at that time. Parker is asking for an unspecified amount of money to compensate him for "punitive" damages and to cover his lawyer's fees. No matter the outcome. . . . "who ya gonna call?" You be the judge!

RATING SYSTEM:

5=Exactly the same 4=Very Similar 3=Somewhat alike 2=Barely the same 1=Not alike in any way

Melody: _____

Harmony/Chordal Structure: _____

Rhythm: _____

Tempo: _____

Lyrics: _____

Instruments: _____

3. How else are the two songs similar?_____

_____

4. How are the two songs different?

_____

_____

5. Based on what you have learned, how have Ray Parker, Jr., and Vanilla Ice broken the copyright laws? Be specific. _____

_____

© 2001, Laura Kaemming, permission for reproduction nonprofit use only

COPYRIGHT RELATED LEARNING OBJECTS AND FILMS: A COLLECTED LIST

Authorship, 2002

Written, Directed, and Produced by Nicky Loi, 4:43 seconds
Hamster Wheel Productions
(http://hamsterwheel1.tripod.com/authorship.html)
In this short film the characters "Ben and Suzie are juvenile delinquents caught in a discussion that stems from a graffiti tag that Suzie draws which Ben claims to have been inspired from his own design."

The Case of Don Johnson . . . a Freshman

Center for Intellectual Property, University of Maryland University College
(http://marconi.umuc.edu/ramgen/cip/plagarism.rm)
In this short Real media video clip, a professor questions student Don Johnson about a possible occurrence of plagiarism after checking the student's submission in TurnItIn.com. This is an outstanding resource to initiate dialog about academic dishonesty with students and instructors alike. The latest free version of the RealPlayer plug-in is necessary to display this educational clip. For use in workshops and online or face-to-face classroom discussions.

The Case of Don Johnson . . . the Senior

Center for Intellectual Property, University of Maryland University College
(http://polaris.umuc.edu/cvu/mmedia/cip/vignettes_8_04/vignette_03.ram)
In this short Real media video clip, our previous character Don Johnson resurfaces. However the instructor is unable to verify a suspicion of plagiarism after checking the student's submission against the TurnItIn.com database. For use in workshops and online or face-to-face classroom discussions with faculty or students. The latest free version of the RealPlayer plug-in is necessary to display this educational clip.

The Case of Dr. Addison & Roland

Center for Intellectual Property, University of Maryland University College
(http://polaris.umuc.edu/cvu/mmedia/cip/vignettes_8_04/vignette_02.ram)
In this short Real media video clip, a professor and student begins to discuss inconsistencies in the student's writing assignment. This clip can serve as a helpful introduction to a discussion on identifying possible plagiarism in student writing

and the possible causes. For use in workshops and online or face-to-face classroom discussions. The latest free version of the RealPlayer plug-in is necessary to display this clip.

The Case of Dr. Grey

Center for Intellectual Property, University of Maryland University College (http://polaris.umuc.edu/cvu/mmedia/cip/vignettes_8_04/vignette_01.ram) In this introductory Real media video clip, a professor discusses a suspected case of plagiarism with a seemingly earnest but overloaded student. For use in workshops and online or face-to-face classroom discussions. While this clip is beneficial in discussions with students it has proven to be successful in developing a dialog among faculty. The latest free version of the RealPlayer plug-in is necessary to display this educational clip.

The Case of Dr. No

Center for Intellectual Property, University of Maryland University College (http://marconi.umuc.edu/ramgen/cip/educause_dr_no/case_of_no.rm) In this short Real media video clip, an instructor would like to create a CD-ROM to be distributed to their students of lecture notes, Internet resources, journal articles, and other resources. A workshop developer or department chair can use this clip to present to faculty the challenges faced when distributing copyrighted material from various sources. For use in workshops and online or face-to-face discussions. The latest free version of the RealPlayer plug-in is necessary to display this educational clip.

Copy Photography Computator

The Visual Resources Association (http://www.vraweb.org/computator/welcome.html) A very plain hyperlinked tutorial that can assist in determining the educational use of images. It is rare to find a tutorial specializing on one format other than text; a welcome addition.

The Copyright Court, 2004

Produced by University of Washington ResearchChannel, 13:39 seconds. (http://www.researchchannel.org/inside/participation/production.asp) Lighthearted dramatizations of a court cases on copyright law, with a focus on fair use, release forms, and copyright responsibility. Available on DVD for purchase.

Copyright Criminals: This is a Sampling Sport

Produced by Benjamin Franzen & Kembrew McLeod, 10 min Work in Progress
(http://kembrew.com/documentaries/)
This short film documentary illustrates the key arguments of the fair use in the
music debate.

Copyright Tutorial

University of Texas System's Office of General Council, Intellectual Property Section
(http://www.lib.utsystem.edu/copyright/)
The audience for this substantial tutorial is faculty and students. It explains fair use;
how to determine ownership of an item; copyright issues in libraries and other settings; guidelines for copyright management and marketing; and resources for licensing and permissions. It is accessible in multiple versions: (1) High bandwidth/Flash
& Audio, which requires flash 3.0 and a sound card and a browser capable of running
JavaScript; (2) Medium Bandwidth/No Flash-No Audio; and Text Only for which no
additional applications are needed. The first version is a pleasant learning experience with relatively high use of graphics and some JavaScript rollovers. It concludes
with a 12-question online quiz that displays the correct answers after submitting.

Copyright Lessons

By Jason Myers, Woodring College of Education,
Western Washington University
(http://it.wce.wwu.edu/344/copyright/)
This online tutorial consists of six lessons that each focus on a specific area of the
copyright law. Each lesson consists of two parts: (1) a presentation of important
concepts and (2) a series of scenarios designed to test your knowledge about the
section just completed. The scenarios include a different voice for each character.
It also includes quiz questions throughout the tutorial. It is reasonably interactive
and visually engaging. The latest free version of the RealPlayer plug-in is necessary
to display this tutorial.

©Primer

Center for Intellectual Property, University of Maryland University College
(http://www-apps.umuc.edu/primer/)
The ©Primer is an introduction to issues concerning copyright ownership and use
of information. The interactive tutorial overviews the underlying principles behind
copyright in the United States, outlines the requirements for copyright protection,

and discusses the parameters of use and access of copyrighted material. It opens with a short Flash animation and moves into a series of questions and answers. Resources for additional study of a particular issue are provided throughout. Upon completion, a user is e-mailed a transcript of their responses to the primer's illustrative scenarios. A Java-enabled Web browser and the free <u>Macromedia Flash Player</u> plug-in are necessary to view this tutorial.

Copyright Quiz

California State University
(<u>http://www.csus.edu/indiv/p/peachj/edte230/copyright/quiz.htm</u>)
Educators and students should appreciate these twenty questions on realistic scenarios of copyright issues in this online test. It gives immediate feedback when an answer is selected; however, the scoring can be unreliable. A Java-enabled Web browser is necessary to view and use this quiz.

Digital©Primer

Center for Intellectual Property, University of Maryland University College
(<u>http://www-apps.umuc.edu/dcprimer/enter.php</u>)
This primer focuses specifically on issues relating to copyright in digital works and the problems encountered by educational institutions in their use of digital materials for teaching, research, and service. It is presented in a question-and-answer format and provides links to additional resources throughout. Please see the FAQ for more information. A Java-enabled Web browser and the free <u>Macromedia Flash Player</u> plug-in are necessary to view this tutorial.

Don't Copy That Floppy, 1992

Software Publisher Association (Producer)
Although this source is stylistically dated, students will learn about software piracy via this educational video produced to outreach to children through rap music. Lesson plans are included with the video to lead classroom discussions on responsible software use. For more information on *Don't Copy that Floppy* or other titles available from SIIA please see: <u>http://www.siia.net/estore/</u>

Dr. No Returns!

Center for Intellectual Property, University of Maryland University College
(<u>http://marconi.umuc.edu/ramgen/cip/educause_dr_no/no_returns.rm</u>)
In this Real media video clip, an instructor would like to use the TEACH Act to

provide music from various sources to their "History of Music" course through a password-protected Web site. This can be used for discussions in workshops and online or face-to-face classes. Use to develop a faculty member's understanding of how different copyrighted resources can be used in designing course content. The latest free version of the RealPlayer plug-in is necessary to display this educational clip.

File Sharing @IU Copyright Tutorial

Indiana University, 2004
(http://filesharing.iu.edu/Tutorial/section_1b.php)
The online tutorial from provides a clear and direct description of the appropriate uses of peer-to-peer software. This tool is beneficial for students and faculty. The font size changes throughout. Although it is very text heavy, the organization of the context is well done and makes it quite readable.

Information Ethics Tutorial

UNC Libraries, University of North Carolina Chapel Hill
(http://www.lib.unc.edu/instruct/infoethics/introduction/index.html)
Although this tutorial was created to support students, it can benefit a broader audience. This brief tutorial consists of an introductory section, five main sections (on plagiarism, copyright, and fair use), and a quiz. A Java-enabled Web browser is necessary to view this tutorial and quiz.

Interactive Guide To Using Copyrighted Media in Your Courses

Baruch Computing and Technology Center (BCTC) and Kognito Solutions LLC
Baruch College, City University of New York
(http://www.baruch.cuny.edu/tutorials/copyright/)
This very creative and interactive "Copyright Metro" map works to assist faculty with deciding the appropriate copyright guidelines they must follow to use various types of copyright protected media in their classrooms. Set up like a game for big kids the graphics and audio keeps you tuned in long enough to learn something. Finally, it includes a set of practical scenarios and opinions arranged by material format (audio, video, etc.). It requires Flash Player 7 or above.

Licensing 101 International

International Licensing Industry Merchandisers' Association
(http://www.licensing.org/)
More of a guided educational site than a tutorial, this online resource is based on

a thesis written by Sabina Gockel at Johannes Gutenberg-Universitaet Mainz. The subjects covered are: (1) licensing basics, (2) history of licensing, (3) participants, (4) role of marketing, and (5) international licensing. Although this is a professional Web site, the information is also useful to a broader audience. The free Macromedia Flash Player plug-in is necessary to view this educational site.

Researching Ethically

Dalhousie University Libraries
(http://infolit.library.dal.ca/tutorials/Plagiarism/index.html)
This module provides for students the knowledge and tools necessary to define and avoid plagiarism. There is an audio component well integrated throughout the tutorial but it unfortunately makes the pages load very slowly—clunky.

Sonic Outlaws

Directed, and Produced by Craig Baldwin, 1:27:00 seconds
Other Cinema, 1995
(http:// www.othercinemaDVD.com)
This film chronicles the release of Negativland's parody of U2, Casey Kasem, and other intellectual property concerns with artistic flair. For more information on Sonic Outlaws or other works distributed by Other Cinema please see: http://www.othercinemadvd.com/

TEACH Act Toolkit

By Peggy E. Hoon, North Carolina State University
(http://www.lib.ncsu.edu/scc/legislative/teachkit/)
The most thorough online resource about the TEACH Act to date. This site includes a basic and expanded checklist for evaluating your use of copyrighted media in the online classroom; they are available as PDFs and online. In addition it includes: guidelines, PowerPoint presentations, best practices, articles, and additional resources.

Tutorial Series

Scholarly Communication Center of North Carolina State University
(http://www.lib.ncsu.edu/scc/tutorial/index.html)
This series includes four (4) tutorials: Copyright Ownership, Copyright Use, Plagiarism, or Licensing Guidelines. This source is relevant for faculty and students. There does not appear to be any special requirements to view; it consists of a short

click-through text screen, similar to a PowerPoint presentation. Very good content and well arranged though not visually engaging.

VAIL Tutorial

Center for Intellectual Property, University of Maryland University College (http://www-apps.umuc.edu/vailtutor/)
In four modules, the VAIL Tutor provides an overview of academic integrity concepts and practical tips for avoiding plagiarism. By assigning this tutorial, faculty will introduce their students to proper documentation practices and academic integrity policies. An electronic *Certificate of Successful Completion* is displayed on the screen and e-mailed to users after successful completion of the included online quiz. A Java-enabled Web browser and the free Macromedia Flash Player plug-in are necessary to view this tutorial.

A Visit to Copyright Bay

University of St. Francis
(http://www.stfrancis.edu/cid/copyrightbay/)
Some may argue that this tutorial is only for the nautical fans among us; however this playful Web site speaks directly to educators. The site intends to enable teachers to be able to apply fair use practices to the classroom or to nontraditional settings. Also, it should help teachers to identify copyright practices that are questionable so that infringements may be avoided in the future. This site is visual and "object-oriented"; which at times can be distracting. It has a wealth of information and includes a short quiz.

▶ Index

A

A&M Records, Inc. v. Napster, Inc., 98
Academic Senate of the California State
    University, 28
ACRL Standards Toolkit, 135
Adler, Allan, 62
Adult Check, 222
age verification services, 222–223
Agreement on Guidelines for Classroom Copying.
    See Classroom Guidelines
Aimster and Madster, 219–221
ALA Model Policy, 59–60, 61, 63. *See also*
    American Library Association
    ALA's disassociation from, 64
Allen, Robert H., 187–190
allocation of rights. *See* divisibility of rights
ALS Scan v. RemarQ Communities, Inc., 97,
    98, 205–206
American Association for Higher
    Education, 135
American Association of Law Libraries, 63,
    193, 203–204
American Bar Association (ABA), 49, 50
American Chemical Society, 169
American Council of Learned Societies, 63,
    157
American Geophysical Union v. Texaco, Inc.,
    43–44, 58, 191–192
American Library Association (ALA), 57,
    64, 141, 193, 204. *See also* ALA Model
    Policy
American Society of Journalists and
    Authors, 141
American Society of Media Photographers,
    141
Andrew W. Mellon Foundation, 119
AOL (America Online), 97, 212–213, 219

architectural works in copyright, 9
ASCAP (music publisher), 46
Association of Academic Health Sciences
    Libraries, 193
Association of American Publishers (AAP),
    62, 63
Association of American Universities, 164
Association of American University Presses,
    63, 64, 168
Association of College and Research
    Libraries (ACRL), 193, 204
    Information Literacy Standards,
        125–126, 133, 135
    Statement on Fair Use and Electronic
        Reserves, 44
Association of Research Libraries (ARL),
    46, 164, 166, 204
    Principles for Licensing Electronic Resources,
        47
Audio Home Recording Act, 220
authors, 3, 7

B

Barbour, Diane, 141
Bawden, David, 135
Bayh-Dole Act, 172
Berne Convention, 88, 178
Bits of Power, 157
Blackboard, 45, 65, 119
BMI (music publisher), 46
Bonner, Kimberly M., 1–12, 71–86, 107–121
Boyer Commission Report, 133
Boyle, James, 161
Breyer, Stephen (U.S. Supreme Court
    Justice), 180, 216
Brown University, 22, 24, 26, 184–185
browse-wraps, 46, 49–51, 194–195

bulletin board services, 89, 219
Bush, George W., 76

C

California State University, 28, 29, 141
Campbell v. Acuff-Rose Music, Inc., 192
Carnegie Foundation for the Advancement
of Teaching, 110
Caxton, William, 2
CCC. *See* Copyright Clearance Center
Center for Academic Integrity, 142
Center for Intellectual Property (CIP), 80,
110, 142, 145
Center for the Public Domain, 142
Central Missouri State University, 10
CETUS. *See* Consortium for Educational
Technology for University Systems
Chase, Mark E., 128, 129
Checklist for Fair Use, 10
Chickering, Donald H., II, 191
City University of New York, 28
Classroom Guidelines, 42–43, 59–60, 63
click-throughs, 46, 49–50, 194–195
Clinton, Bill (William), 88, 210
Cohen, Julie, 109
colleges. *See* educational institutions
Colorado Mountain College District, 21,
181–182
*Community for Creative Non-Violence et al. v.
Reid*, 182–184, 186
Conference on Fair Use (CONFU), 43,
62–63, 207, 210
Congress. *See* U.S. Congress
Consortium for Educational Technology for
University Systems (CETUS), 27–28
Constitution. *See* U.S. Constitution
contracts, 47–51
copyright
difficulty in obtaining permissions, 157,
160
divisibility of rights, 20, 23–25

copyright *(cont'd.)*
financial costs in securing permissions,
72, 157, 160
sharing of rights, 17, 23
transfer of, 20, 23, 29–30
types of works and, 3, 73
Copyright Act, 4, 7, 9, 11
1976 revision to, 22, 39, 42
amendments to, 11–12, 71
anti-circumvention provision, 44, 67
technical neutrality of, 45
works made for hire and, 22
Copyright Clause, 2, 3, 73
"limited times" prescription, 177, 178,
179
Copyright Clearance Center (CCC), 43, 65,
142, 192
Electronic Course Content Service, 64
copyright duration, 6–7, 177–180
educational class sessions and, 78, 79
Sonny Bono Term Extension Act, 11,
162–163
copyright education, 130, 136–137, 141
assessment in, 146–147
barriers to, 131
instructional requirements for, 142–143
instructional standards in, 136
outreach tools, 138–139
sample materials for, 144, 147
copyright guidelines. *See* copyright policies
copyright infringement, 4, 79, 190, 205, 215
contributory, 11, 89, 213, 219, 220, 222
"Good Samaritan" immunity, 94
higher education and, 11, 90, 181–182
in medicine, 21, 187–190
of films, 217–219
of photographs, 22, 24, 41, 184–185
Online Copyright Infringement Liability
Limitation, 90–91
right of public display, 61
scientific journals and, 192

copyright infringement *(cont'd.)*
vicarious, 11, 89, 219, 220–221, 222
copyright law
deliberate circumvention of, 44, 219
effects of technology on, 75
history of, 1–2, 5
legal framework for, 73–74
copyright licenses, 20, 26, 47
browse-wraps and click-throughs, 46,
49–51, 194–195
Creative Commons, 50–51
for online materials, 46
library reserves and, 62, 64
copyright literacy, 130, 131
copyright management, 133
*Copyright Office Report. See Report on Copyright
and Digital Distance Education*
copyright ownership, 4, 182–184
categories of, 7
exclusive rights of owner, 9, 73
limitations on, 74, 82
statutory limitations of, 8
transfer of, 19, 185
unbundling of rights, 20, 24, 25
copyright piracy, 108
copyright policies, 25–31, 131–133, 185,
186–187, 222
common types of guidelines, 134
in libraries, 64
suggestions for, 25–26, 31
copyright protection, 3–4, 5, 76, 79
Copyright Quiz, 145
copyright registration, 8
Copyright Revision Bill, 199
Copyright Site, 145
Copyright Term Extension Act (CTEA),
177–180
copyrightable works, 3, 18, 73
Council of Independent Colleges, 135
course management systems, 45, 65,
119

Creative Commons (nonprofit group),
50–51, 142, 166, 170
Crews, Kenneth, 15–31
Cybernet Ventures, 222–223

D
D-Lib Magazine, 171
Dames, K. Matthew, 82
data mining, 155
database legislation, 88, 158
database protection, 11
Davidson, Hall, 145
Davis, Cheryl L., 10, 39–52
Deep, John, 219
Defense Department. *See* U.S. Department
of Defense
derivative works, 5
digital content control systems (DCCS),
108–109, 114–120. *See also* digital rights
management
problems with, 110
surveys about, 111–115
types of, 112
*Digital Dilemma: Intellectual Property in the
Information Age*, 140, 157
Digital Future Coalition, 210
Digital Millennium Copyright Act (DMCA),
2, 44, 75, 158. *See also* Online Copyright
Infringement Liability Limitation
evolution of, 87–88, 206–210
liability limits in, 11
online service providers and, 89–103,
205–206, 213, 219–225
digital rights management, 113, 158. *See also*
digital content control systems (DCCS)
in higher education, 80
overview of, 108–109
distance education, 15, 24, 29
as addressed by Congress, 75
fair use in, 82–83
financial costs of, 72

digital rights management *(cont'd.)*
  TEACH Act and, 76–77, 78, 81, 88, 124
  written copyright agreements for, 30
distribution rights, 23
divisibility of rights, 20, 23–25
  CETUS recommendations for, 27–28
  suggested policies for, 26–27
  written agreements for, 30
DMCA. *See* Digital Millennium Copyright
  Act
Dreamland Ball Room, Inc. v. Shapiro,
  Bernstein & Co., 89
DRM. *See* digital rights management
Duldulao v. Saint Mary of Nazareth Hospital
  Center, 187

E
e-reserves. *See* electronic reserves
eBay, 97, 216–219
educational institutions, 4, 12, 41. *See also*
  faculty; instructional materials
  copyright policies at, 25–31
  court rulings and, 21–22
  divisibility of copyright and, 24, 25–27
  ineffectiveness of copyright policies at,
    22–23
  leaving copyright with authors, 17
educational materials. *See* instructional
  materials
EDUCAUSE, 141, 164
Eldred, et al. v. Ashcroft, 177–180
Eldred v. Reno, 177
Electronic Course Content Service, 64
Electronic Frontier Foundation (EFF), 142
electronic reserves, 44, 48, 78, 201–203. *See*
  also library reserves; photocopy reserves
  Electronic Course Content Service, 64
  Electronic Reserve Guidelines
    (CONFU), 63–64
  publishers' objections to, 60, 61–62
  sound recordings in, 66

electronic reserves *(cont'd.)*
  uniqueness of copyright problems with,
    61
  video portions in, 66–67
electronic serials, 46
Elektra Entertainment Group, Inc. v. Does 1-9,
  98–99, 211–212
Ellenbogen, Leon, 188–190
Ellison v. Robertson, 97, 212–213
ephemeral recordings, 9
exclusive rights of copyright owners, 4, 7–9,
  178

F
faculty. *See also* "teacher's exception"
  as copyright owners for instructional
    materials, 17, 18, 24, 26
  as online service providers, 94–95
  knowledge of copyright law, 127–129
  online instructional materials and, 46,
    48, 65
  photocopying by, 43, 59, 199–201
  works by, 166–167
  works made for hire, 18–19, 181–182
fair use, 9–10, 48, 199
  amount and substantiality of portion
    used, 42–43, 58, 192
  Checklist for Fair Use, 10
  Conference on Fair Use (CONFU), 43,
    62–63, 207, 210
  course management systems and, 44
  difficulties in determining, 58
  digital materials and, 44–45
  distance education and, 82–83
  importance to higher education, 41, 118,
    159
  in electronic reserves, 61, 64, 201–203
  in library reserves, 57, 62
  in licensed materials, 45–52, 58, 64
  in unpublished works, 42
  language in, 48

fair use *(cont'd.)*
   legal guidelines for, 40
   overview of, 39, 57, 158
   photocopying for educational purposes,
      43, 56
   photocopying for research purposes,
      191–192
   purpose and character of use, 41, 58, 192
   student familiarity with, 129
   transformative use, 41, 58, 192
   use for market effect, 43–44, 58, 203
Faulkner v. National Geographic Society, 41
*Feist Publications, Inc. v. Rural Telephone
   Service Co.*, 190
file sharing. *See* Internet file sharing
first sale doctrine, 9, 46, 56, 110
fixation requirement, 4
Forasté v. Brown University, 22, 24, 26, 184–185
François, Olga, 123–152
Freid, Laura, 184

G
Garon, Jon M., 126, 127
Gasaway, Laura N., 55–70
*Gershwin Publishing Corp. v. Columbia Artists
   Management, Inc.*, 89, 215
Getty Museum. *See* J. Paul Getty Museum
Gilmore, Elizabeth, 146
Ginsberg, Ruth Bader (U.S. Supreme Court
   Justice), 216
"Good Samaritan" immunity, 94
Google, 168
Graham v. John Deere Co., 179
Grenquist, Peter, 63
Guidelines for Off-Air Taping, 128
Guidelines on the Educational Use of
   Music, 66

H
Hamilton, Ian, 42
Hamma, Ken, 171

Harvard University, 57, 168
Hatch, Orrin (Sen.), 76
Hendrickson v. eBay, Inc., 97, 216–219
higher education institutions, 5, 45. *See also*
   faculty; instructional materials
   as online service providers, 90–92, 96, 124
   copyright infringement and, 11, 90,
      181–182, 185
   importance of scholarship in, 154–156
   Internet file sharing in, 98–99, 129, 132
   missions of, 164–165
Hoon, Peggy E., 10, 39–52
Hutchinson, Kristine H., 76

I
independent contractors, 18, 29
independent creation, 4
Indiana University, 10
   Digital Images Delivered Online, 44–45
Indiana University Purdue University
   Indianapolis (IUPUI), 28, 29
INDUCE Act, 101
infringement of copyright. *See* copyright
   infringement
Instant Messenger (AOL), 219
instructional materials, 16, 17, 21. *See also*
   educational institutions; faculty
   Classroom Guidelines and, 59–60
   copyright policies for, 131–133
   course packets, 43, 57, 63, 66
   online versions, 16, 24, 76
   written copyright agreements for, 30
interlibrary loan, 48
International Coalition of Library Consortia
   (ICOLC), 47
International Federation of Library
   Associations (IFLA), 47
Internet file sharing, 41, 100–102, 224–225
   music and recordings, 98–99, 211–212,
      214–215, 219–221
   students' attitudes toward, 129, 132

Internet service providers, 11, 205–206, 213, 224–225, 219–221. *See also* online service providers

Internet Use Education Program, 125

IP addresses, 95

iPods, 102

IPSOS Public Affairs/Business Software Alliance survey (2005), 129

J

J. Paul Getty Museum, 171

Joint Committee of the Higher Education and Entertainment Communities, 100

Journal of Catalysis, 191

K

Kaemming, Laura, 143

Kelley, Kimberly B., 1–12, 107–121, 144–145

Kennedy, Anthony M. (U.S. Supreme Court Justice), 216

L

Leaffer, Marshall, 110

Leahy, Patrick (Sen.), 76

learning management systems. *See* course management systems

Lederle Laboratories, 189

Lessig, Lawrence, 109, 155

Liblicense (Yale University), 47

libraries, 4, 12, 44, 140

    acquisitions in, 47

    adaptation of copyright guidelines in, 133

    as online service providers, 90–91

    license agreements in, 193–198

    licensed resources in, 46–52, 202

Library of Congress, 65

library reserves, 44, 56–57. *See also* electronic reserves; photocopy reserves

license agreements, 114, 117, 193–198, 202. *See also* copyright licenses

    at MIT, 28–29

license agreements *(cont'd.)*

    fair use and, 45–52, 58, 64

    faculty and student ignorance of, 118–119

    iTunes, 102

    technology transfer operations, 171–173

Licensing Principles (IFLA), 47

Litman, Jessica, 4

Liu, Joseph, 80–81

Ludlow, Barbara, 135

Lutzker, Arnold P., 87–106

Lynch, Clifford A., 107–121, 153–174

M

Makin, David Alan, 132

Manning v. Board of Trustees of Community College District No. 505 (Parkland College), 22, 24, 26, 186–187

market effect, 43–44, 58, 203

Massachusetts Institute of Technology, 164

    OpenCourseWare at, 28–29, 166

Materna (prenatal vitamin), 188–190

McCabe, Donald, 127

McDonald, Mary, 62

Medical Library Association, 193, 204

Metro-Goldwin-Mayer Studios, Inc. et al. v. Grokster, Ltd., et al., 98, 99–100, 101, 213–216

Model Policy Concerning College and University Photocopying for Classroom, Research and Library Reserve Use. See ALA Model Policy

Moodle (digital content control system), 113

Music Guidelines. *See* Guidelines on the Educational Use of Music

N

Napster, Inc., 98

National Academies, 157, 172

National Association of College and University Attorneys (NACUA), 141

National Digital Information Infrastructure and Preservation Program, 65

National Information Infrastructure (NII), 88, 207

National Institutes of Health, 169

National Research Council, 140–141

New England Journal of Medicine, 188, 189

New York Public Library, 168

New York University (NYU), 211, 212

newsgroups, 205, 213

NII. *See* National Information Infrastructure

North Carolina State University Libraries, 46

notice and takedown, 93–94

O

Objectives for Information Literacy Instruction, 135

Obstetrics and Gynecology, 189

O'Connor, Sandra Day (U.S. Supreme Court Justice), 216

Online Copyright Infringement Liability Limitation, 90–91

    case law for, 96–100

    qualifications for, 91–92, 95–96

online education. *See* distance education

online service providers (OSPs), 89–90, 95, 222–223. *See also* Internet service providers

definitions of, 91

notice and takedown, 93–94

open source software, 119–120

OpenCourseWare, 28–29, 166

Organisation for Economic Cooperation and Development (OECD), 172

originality requirement, 4

orphaned works, 163–164

OSP Limitation. *See* Online Copyright Infringement Liability Limitation

Oxford University, 168

P

Park, Jaehong, 107–121

Parkland College, 22, 24, 26, 186–187

Parliament (British legal system), 1

parodies, 9

patents, 158, 172, 178, 188

peer-to-peer networks, 99, 211, 212. *See also* Internet file sharing

Perfect 10, Inc. v. Cybernet Ventures, Inc., 97–98, 222–223

performance and display rights, 9, 45, 71, 74, 75, 77–78

permissions fees, 43

Perseus Project, 155

Peters, Marybeth, 163

Pew Internet and American Life Project, 129

Phonograms Treaty, 209

photocopy reserves, 55–56, 57–60. *See also* electronic reserves; library reserves

    cumulative effect, 59, 200

photographs, 8, 22, 24, 41, 184–185, 186–187

Piracy Deterrence and Education Act, 125

Pirates, Thieves, and Innocents (keynote address), 153

"Pirates with Attitude" (PWA), 41

plagiarism, 127

Pogue, Mary, 128, 129

Princeton University Press v. Michigan Document Services (MDS), 43

Principles for Licensing Electronic Resources (ARL guidelines), 47

printing press, 1, 2

privacy, 95

professional societies. *See* scholarly societies

PubChem (database), 169

public domain, 4–6, 61, 161–164

publishers, 3, 55, 58, 63, 64

    ALA Model Policy and, 60

    fear of lost sales by, 61, 62, 65

    university presses, 167–168

PWA. *See* "Pirates with Attitude"

R

re *Aimster Copyright Litigation*, 97, 219–221

Recording Industry Association of America (RIAA), 66, 100

Recording Industry Association of America v. Verizon Internet Services, Inc., 99, 223–225

Register of Copyrights, 59, 76, 163

Rehnquist, William H. (U.S. Supreme Court Justice), 216

Reid, James Earl, 182–184

Reinventing Undergraduate Education, 133

Religious Technology Center v. Netcom On-Line Communications Services, Inc., 89

"remix culture," 155

RemarQ Communities, 97, 98, 205–206

Report of the Working Group on Intellectual Property Rights, 207

Report on Copyright and Digital Distance Education, 72, 75–76

reproduction rights, 23

reserves. *See* electronic reserves; library reserves; photocopy reserves

Robertson, Stephen, 212

Rochester Institute of Technology, 141

royalties, 56, 63, 64

S

safe harbors, 11, 43, 97

    in Digital Millennium Copyright Act, 90, 205–206, 221, 222–223

SAKAI (digital content control system), 113, 119

Salinger, J.D., 42

Samuelson, Pamela, 5–6

satellite transmissions, 75

scholarly societies, 169–170

scientific journals, 191–192

"screen scrapping," 51

Segue (digital content control system), 113

Seligman, Paul A., 188–190

Shapiro, Bernstein & Co. v. H.L. Green Co., 215

sharing of rights. *See* divisibility of rights

Sonny Bono Copyright Term Extension Act, 11, 162–163

Sony Corporation of America v. Universal City Studios, 99–100, 214, 215

Sony Music Entertainment, Inc. v. Does 1-40, 211

Special Libraries Association (SLA), 63, 141, 193, 204

SPIRO (University of California at Berkeley), 45

Stanford University, 168

State University of New York, 28

Statement of Current Perspective and Preferred Practices for the Selection of Electronic Information, 47

"Statement on Fair Use and Electronic Reserves", 44

Statute of Anne, 1–2, 3, 73

statutory damages, 90

Stevens, Paul (U.S. Supreme Court Justice), 179, 216

StreamCast Networks, Inc., 214–216

subpoenas, 95, 98, 224–225

Sui Generis Database Treaty, 209

Swain, Colleen, 146

Sweeney, Phillis C., 128, 129

syllabi. *See* instructional materials

T

TEACH Act. *See* Technology, Education, and Copyright Harmonization (TEACH) Act

teachers. *See* faculty

"teacher's exception," 16, 21, 22, 25, 74

    questionable validity of, 29, 31

technology transfer operations, 171–173

Technology, Education, and Copyright Harmonization (TEACH) Act, 2, 11, 65, 88, 115

    conditions for performance or display, 77–78

Technology, Education, and Copyright
  Harmonization (TEACH) Act *(cont'd.)*
  distance education and, 76–77, 78, 81,
    88, 124
  goals of, 76–77
  lack of use in higher education, 80–82,
    115–116
  limitations of, 78–79, 83
Tehama County Online, 213
television, 74, 75
text mining, 155
theses, 169
"Third World America" (sculpture), 182,
  184
transformative use, 41, 58
Tufts University, 155

U

U.S. Congress, 19, 40, 44, 75, 82
U.S. Constitution, 2–3, 73
U.S. Copyright Office, 4, 65, 72, 75, 93,
  163
U.S. Department of Defense, 88
U.S. Food and Drug Administration, 188
"unbundling" of rights. *See* divisibility of
  rights
Understanding Copyright Law, 110
Uniform Commercial Code, 49
universities. *See* educational institutions
University of Alabama, 145
University of Baltimore, 129
University of California at Berkeley, 45
University of California at San Diego, 62
University of Colorado Foundation, Inc. v.
  American Cyanamid, 21, 187–190

University of Maryland University College,
  72, 143, 153
University of Michigan, 168
University of Texas System Office of
  General Counsel, 141
University of Wisconsin, 45
university presses, 167–168

V

Vanderhurst v. Colorado Mountain College
  District, 21, 181–182
Verizon Internet Services, 223–225

W

Walt Disney Corporation, 162
Washburn University, 137
Washington Post, The, 72
Web site agents, 93
Web-based instruction, 16–17, 71. *See also*
  distance education
Webcasts, 47
WebCT, 45, 65, 119
works made for hire, 7, 18, 21, 22, 29
  artwork and, 182–183
  in academic settings, 18–19, 25, 26, 185,
    186–187, 189–190
  transfers of copyright and, 20
World Intellectual Property Organization
  (WIPO), 88, 208

Y

Yale University, 47

Z

Zurkowski, Paul, 135

►About the Center for Intellectual Property

The Center for Intellectual Property in the Digital Environment educates, conducts research, and provides resources on the intellectual property issues that impact the delivery of digital resources for teaching, learning, and scholarship. The Center accomplishes its mission through the delivery of several on-site and online workshops, electronic and print publications, and continuous updates on state, national, and international legislative developments.

►About the Authors

Kimberly M. Bonner, J.D.

Kimberly M. Bonner is the Executive Director of the Center for Intellectual Property in the Digital Environment at the University of Maryland University College (UMUC). As Executive Director, Ms. Bonner coordinates the education, research, and resource initiatives of the Center. In addition to directing the Center's initiatives, Ms. Bonner has taught copyright and communications law courses at both the Undergraduate and Graduate School for UMUC. Her recent papers include "Intellectual Property, Ownership and Digital Course Materials: A Survey of Intellectual Property Policies at Two- and Four-Year Colleges and Universities" (*portal: Libraries and the Academy*, 2(2), 255–266) and "Academic Dishonesty: Faculty and Administrator Responses and Perceptions of the Impact of Digital Text and Distance Education." Over the past five years, Ms. Bonner has given presentations on copyright-related issues at several higher education policy conferences including Educause and the Higher Education Law and Policy Institute. Prior to joining UMUC, Ms. Bonner was a law clerk for Chief United States District Court Judge W. Louis Sands in the Middle District of Georgia. After her clerkship, Ms. Bonner joined the law firm of Howrey, Simon, Arnold & White, LLP in Washington, D.C. At Howrey, she specialized in trade secret, trademark, and insurance coverage litigation. Ms. Bonner received her B.A. degree from the University of Virginia in 1993 in Foreign Affairs and her J.D. from the University of Virginia Law School in 1996. While at the law school, she served on the editorial board and was a book review editor for the *Virginia Journal of International Law.*

Kenneth D. Crews, M.L.S., Ph.D.

Kenneth Crews is a professor at the Indiana University (IU) School of Law–Indianapolis and at the IU School of Library and Information Science. He is also Associate Dean of the Faculties for Copyright Management, and in that capacity he directs the Copyright Management Center based at Indiana University–Purdue University Indianapolis (IUPUI). His principal research interest has been the relationship of copyright law to the needs of higher education. His first book on copyright, *Copyright, Fair Use, and the Challenge for Universities: Promoting the Progress of Higher Education*, was published by The University of Chicago Press in October 1993, and it reevaluates understandings of copyright in the context of teaching and research at the university. A more recent book, *Copyright Essentials for Librarians and Educators*, published by the American Library Association in 2000, is an instructive overview of copyright law. Mr. Crews has been an invited speaker on college and university campuses and at conferences in 37 states, and five foreign countries. Mr. Crews is also serves as a faculty member for the Munich Intellectual Property Law Center. He practiced general business and corporate law in Los Angeles from 1980 to 1990, primarily for the entertainment industry. During those years, Crews returned to graduate school, and he earned his M.L.S. and Ph.D. degrees from UCLA's School of Library and Information Science.

Cheryl L. Davis, J.D., M.S.L.S.

Cheryl Davis currently serves as administrator of the North Carolina Guardian ad Litem Program (GAL), managing the statewide pro bono attorney project. She developed and currently manages the statewide GAL Web site that provides resources and training for staff, attorneys, and volunteers. Her responsibilities include grant writing and directing the organization and cataloging of the Guardian ad Litem library with a group of volunteer paralegals. Ms. Davis is a member of Raleigh Area Law Librarians and the American Library Association, and she has served as cochair of the Judicial Training Subcommittee of the Court Improvement Project Advisory Committee and as a board member of the Wake County Association of Volunteer Administrators. Ms. Davis was appointed Triangle Research Libraries Network (TRLN) Doctoral Fellow in the Scholarly Communication Center at the NCSU Libraries on September 1, 2004. She holds an M.S.L.S. from the University of North Carolina–Chapel Hill, a J.D. from Ohio Northern University, and a B.A. in English Language and Literature from Ohio Northern University.

Olga François, M.L.S.

Olga Francois is the Senior Research Librarian for the Center for Intellectual Property, where, collaboratively, she writes instructional tools and delivers professional development programming. In addition to her role at the Center, she teaches research methods courses for the School of Undergraduate Studies and the Graduate School of the University of Maryland University College. She received her B.A in Fine Arts from Smith College, and a Masters in Library and Information Science from the University of Pittsburgh. She has taught Information Competency curriculum, research methods, and course-related Library Instruction at John Jay College, Borough of Manhattan Community College (City University of New York), and Pierce College in Washington State. Ms. François has given conference presentations and has a forthcoming essay titled, "Standard 5: Information, social contexts, ethical and legal issues" in a book about assessment of information literacy in higher education.

Laura N. Gasaway, J.D., M.L.S.

Laura "Lolly" Gasaway is a Law Professor and Law Library Director at the University of North Carolina School of Law. She is the author of many publications dealing with the intersection of copyright law and librarianship. Her recent titles include: *Growing Pains: Adapting Copyright for Libraries, Education & Society* (Fred B. Rothman and Co., 1997); *Libraries & Copyright: A Guide to Copyright Law for the 1990s* (Special Libraries Association, 1994); "The New Right of Access and Its Impact on Libraries and Library Users" (*Journal of Intellectual Property Law 10*, 269 (2003); and "Libraries, Users, and the Problems of Authorship in the Digital Age" (*DePaul Law Review, 52*, 1193, 2003). She teaches courses on Copyright Law, Cyberspace Law, Intellectual Property, and Law Librarianship and Legal Resources. Professor Gasaway earned her B.A. in 1967 and M.L.S. in 1968 from Texas Women's University and her J.D. from the University of Houston in 1973.

Peggy E. Hoon, J.D.

Peggy E. Hoon currently serves as North Carolina State University Libraries' Scholarly Communication Librarian. She has managed their Scholarly Communication Center and its programs since its founding in 1998. Ms. Hoon provides guidance to the library staff on matters pertaining to scholarly communication, including electronic resource licensing, copyright and fair use, and user privacy issues. Additionally, she provides guidance to faculty and others in the N.C. State community on scholarly communication matters and copyright ownership or use issues and policies; she speaks frequently on these topics. Previously Ms. Hoon was the Copyright Specialist for Washington State University in Pullman, Washington, where she developed and implemented a copyright awareness program; wrote policies and guidelines; and provided workshops for Washington State University's branch campuses, learning centers, and cooperative extension offices. She has been an adjunct professor at the University of Idaho College of Law and associate attorney with two Seattle law firms specializing in health law and medical negligence. In addition to a J.D. Degree from the University of Washington, Ms. Hoon holds a B.S. in Nursing from the University of Colorado.

Kimberly B. Kelley, Ph.D.

Dr. Kelley is currently the Vice Provost and Dean for Academic Resources and Services for the University of Maryland University College. She oversees the university's worldwide library operation, the Office of Instructional Services and Support, the Office of Career Services, and the Center for Intellectual Property. Under her leadership, the Center for Intellectual Property has become a successful research and education operation that has achieved self-sufficiency through its noncredit educational offerings and has funded research projects, including those supported by the Mellon and Sloan Foundations. In addition, Dr. Kelley cochairs the decennial reaccreditation review process on behalf of the entire university. Recently, she received a national award from the University Continuing Education Association for her outstanding contribution to information resources management. Previously, Dr. Kelley was the Associate Provost for Information and Library Services at UMUC and the Executive Director of the Center for Intellectual Property at UMUC. Dr. Kelley is well known nationally for her presentations, research, and writing on the areas of distance education, digital libraries, and intellectual property. Her recent publications include "Trends in Distant Student Use of Electronic Resources: A Survey in College and Research Libraries" (*College and Research Libraries*, *64*(3), 176–191 and "Intellectual Property, Ownership and Digital Course Materials: A Survey of Intellectual Property Policies at Two- and Four-Year Colleges and Universities" (*portal: Libraries and the Academy*, *2*(2), 255–266). Prior to arriving at UMUC, Dr. Kelley was the Chief Librarian of the Museum Support Center at the Smithsonian Institution, and Head of the Engineering Library at Cornell University in New York City. She earned her doctorate in higher education policy, planning, and administration at the University of Maryland, College Park.

Arnold P. Luztker, Esq.

Arnold Lutzker practices copyright, trademark, Internet, art, and entertainment law. He counsels on issues of ownership and use of intellectual property. He assists clients in matters of selection and registration of trademarks, licensing and effective management of trademark and copyright portfolios, and taking action on infringement claims. He has special expertise in the trademark and copyright issues that surround new media, intellectual property policy, and education. He has represented a consortium of five national library associations on the Digital Millennium Copyright Act, Copyright Term Extension Act, and the TEACH Act. He also has represented the Directors Guild of America and the Film Foundation in connection with their effort to protect classic American movies. Mr. Lutzker also is the author of three books: *Content Rights for the Creative Professional: Copyrights and Trademarks in a Digital Age* (Focal Press, 2002); *Copyrights and Trademarks for Media Professionals* (Focal Press, 1997); and *Legal Problems in Broadcasting* (Great Plains University Press, 1974); plus a video, *Copyrights: The Internet, Multimedia and the Law* (Taylor Communications, 1997) and numerous articles on copyright and trademark issues. Prior to establishing Lutzker & Lutzker with his wife, he was a principal in the Washington law firm of Fish & Richardson, P.C. and a partner in Dow, Lohnes & Albertson. He graduated from City College of New York (1968, magna cum laude) and Harvard Law School (1971, cum laude).

Clifford A. Lynch, Ph.D.

Clifford Lynch has been the Director of the Coalition for Networked Information (CNI) since July 1997. CNI, jointly sponsored by the Association of Research Libraries and EDUCAUSE, includes about 200 member organizations concerned with the use of information technology and networked information to enhance scholarship and intellectual productivity. Prior to joining CNI, Dr. Lynch spent 18 years at the University of California Office of the President, the last ten as Director of Library Automation. Dr. Lynch, who holds a Ph.D. in Computer Science from the University of California, Berkeley, is an adjunct professor at Berkeley's School of Information Management and Systems. He is a past president of the American Society for Information Science and a fellow of the American Association for the Advancement of Science and the National Information Standards Organization. Dr. Lynch currently serves on the National Digital Preservation Strategy Advisory Board of the Library of Congress; he was a member of the National Research Council committee that published *The Digital Dilemma: Intellectual Property in the Information Infrastructure* and *Broadband: Bringing Home the Bits*, and now serves on the NRC's committee on digital archiving and the National Archives and Records Administration. His recent articles include: "The New Dimensions of Learning Communities" (*Threshold*, Winter 2004); "Life After Graduation Day: Beyond the Academy's Digital Walls" (*EDUCUASE Review 32*(5), 12–13); and "The Visible Classroom" (*EDUCAUSE Review 38*: 4, 68).

Jaehong Park, Ph.D.

Jaehong Park is currently an assistant professor at Eastern Michigan University. While with the CIP, Dr. Park was a Mellon postdoctoral research associate. Previously he was a research associate in the Laboratory for Information Security Technology (LIST) at George Mason University, Fairfax, Virginia. He has been involved in various research projects on information security. His current research interests include Access Control, Digital Rights Management (DRM), Usage Control (UCON), copyright protection, large-scale security architectures and models, trusted computing, secure B2B and B2C e-commerce, and network and distributed systems security. Mr. Park received his Ph.D. in Information Technology from George Mason University in 2003, his MS degree in Information Systems Technologies from George Washington University, Washington D.C., in 1998, and his BBA degree in Information Management from Dongguk University, Seoul, Korea, in 1995. He was formerly a software engineer at POSDATA Co. Ltd. Seoul.

7589 072